FAMILIES IN TRANSFORMATION

The EFPP Book Series

OTHER TITLES IN THE SERIES

Chief Editor: John Tsiantis

- *Countertransference in Psychoanalytic Psychotherapy with Children and Adolescents*

- *Supervision and its Vicissitudes*

- *Psychoanalytic Psychotherapy in Institutional Settings*

- *Psychoanalytic Psychotherapy of the Severely Disturbed Adolescent*

- *Work with Parents: Psychoanalytic Psychotherapy with Children and Adolescents*

- *Psychoanalysis and Psychotherapy: The Controversies and the Future*

- *Research on Psychoanalytic Psychotherapy with Adults*

Series Editors: Monica Lanyado and Didier Houzel

- *The Therapist at Work: Personal Factors Affecting the Analytic Process*

- *Invisible Boundaries. Psychosis and Autism in Children and Adolescents*

- *The Development of Consciousness: An Integrative Model of Child Development, Neuroscience, and Psychoanalysis*

- *The Analytic Field: A Clinical Concept*

- *Play and Power*

- *Crossing Borders—Integrating Differences: Psychoanalytic Psychotherapy in Transition*

- *Assessing Change in Psychoanalytic Psychotherapy of Children and Adolescents*

- *Bearing Witness: Psychoanalytic Work with People Traumatised by Torture and State Violence*

Series Editor: Anne-Marie Schloesser

- *Psychoanalytic Psychotherapy: A Handbook*

FAMILIES IN TRANSFORMATION
A Psychoanalytic Approach

Edited by

*Anna Maria Nicolò, Pierre Benghozi,
and Daniela Lucarelli*

KARNAC

First published in 2014 by
Karnac Books Ltd
118 Finchley Road
London NW3 5HT

British Library Cataloguing in Publication Data

A C.I.P. for this book is available from the British Library

ISBN-13: 978-1-78049-111-0

Typeset by V Publishing Solutions Pvt Ltd., Chennai, India

Printed in Great Britain

www.karnacbooks.com

CONTENTS

ABOUT THE EDITORS AND CONTRIBUTORS   ix

SERIES EDITOR'S PREFACE   xvii

PREFACE   xix
Otto F. Kernberg

PROLOGUE   xxi
Pierre Benghozi

INTRODUCTION   xxv
Anna Maria Nicolò and Daniela Lucarelli

PART I: COUPLES AND FAMILIES TODAY

CHAPTER ONE
The psychical reality of linking   3
René Kaës

CHAPTER TWO
Intersubjective links in the family: the function of identification   21
Alberto Eiguer

CHAPTER THREE
The mythic narrative neo-container in psychoanalytic family
    therapy: shame and treason as heritage   41
Pierre Benghozi

CHAPTER FOUR
Where is the unconscious located? Reflections on links
    in families and couples   65
Anna Maria Nicolò

CHAPTER FIVE
The frightened couple   85
Stanley Ruszczynski

CHAPTER SIX
Adoptive families: what pathways for subjectivisation?   97
Daniela Lucarelli and Gabriela Tavazza

CHAPTER SEVEN
Transformations through repetitions of female and male
    representations in reconstructed families   109
Diana Norsa

PART II: OEDIPUS IN THE NEW FAMILIES

CHAPTER EIGHT
The Oedipus complex and the new generations   129
Philippe Robert

CHAPTER NINE
When the fraternal prevails over the oedipal:
    a possible interpretative model for modern couples   139
Massimiliano Sommantico

PART III: CLINICAL WORK WITH FAMILIES
AND COUPLES

CHAPTER TEN
Couples and the perverse link   157
Anna Maria Nicolò

CHAPTER ELEVEN
Couple and family psychoanalytic psychotherapy's
  contribution to current psychoanalysis   171
Jean-George Lemaire

CHAPTER TWELVE
Fraternal incest: fraternal links   187
Rosa Jaitin

CHAPTER THIRTEEN
Anamorphosis, sloughing of containers, and family psychical
  transformations   199
Pierre Benghozi

CHAPTER FOURTEEN
Infidelity in the couple relationship: one form of
  relationship suffering   219
*Carles Pérez-Testor, Montse Davins, Inés Aramburu,
  Berta Aznar-Martínez, and Manel Salamero*

CHAPTER FIFTEEN
The other, the stranger, the unconscious: psychoanalysis
  and multi-ethnic therapeutic relationships   233
Ludovica Grassi

CHAPTER SIXTEEN
Old and new couple secrets: how to deal with them?   249
Giorgio Rigamonti and Simona Taccani

CHAPTER SEVENTEEN
Family myths and pathological links   279
Anna Maria Nicolò

INDEX   293

ABOUT THE EDITORS AND CONTRIBUTORS

Inés Aramburu has a bachelor in psychology. She earned a master in clinical psychopathology (2007–2009) and an additional master's degree in psychoanalytic psychotherapy (2009–2011) from the Fundació Vidal i Barraquer, whereshe is a child psychotherapist. She received a research grant (BRB) financed by the Blanquerna Faculty of Psychology, Education Science and Sport (2007–2009) and a grant to study international adoption financed by the Institut Universitari de Salut Mental, Fundació Vidal i Barraquer (IUSM) (2009–2010). She is currently a PhD candidate and a researcher in the Research Group of Couple and Family (GRPF) at the Universitat Ramon Llull (URL).

Berta Aznar-Martínez has a diploma in education and a bachelor in psychology. She is a professor at the Blanquerna Faculty of Psychology, Education Science and Sport and a researcher at the Institut Universitari de Salut Mental, Fundació Vidal i Barraquer (both institutions affiliated to the Universitat Ramon Llull). She earned her doctorate in psychology with a thesis on "The therapeutic alliance in psychoanalytical couple therapy: Analysis and differentiation of the alliance and other components of the therapeutic relationship" (summa cum laude, 2012). She is a member of the Research Group of Couple and Family at the URL. She has a postgraduate degree in couple and family psychology (2011) and a master in clinical psychopathology (2011) from the IUSM.

Pierre Benghozi is a psychiatrist, child psychiatrist, psychoanalyst, psychoanalytical therapist for group, couple, and family, as well as a training analyst and supervisor. He is president of the Research Institute for Psychoanalysis of the couple and the family (IRPcf), and doctor in charge of the psychiatric department for children, teenagers and families, responsible for the clinical Unit of the Link, for family psychotherapy, perinatal period and networks, at Hyères, France. He is professor of postgraduate studies, USP Laboratory of Psychoanalysis and Social Link, São Paulo University, Brazil. He is responsible for teaching, Paris XIII University, France. A board member of the European Federation for Psychoanalytic Psychotherapy in the Public Sector, he is coordinator and founder of its section, Psychoanalytic Couple and Family Psychotherapy. He is a member of the SFTFP, the French Society of Psychoanalytical Family Therapy, and of the International Association of Couple and Family Psychoanalysis, AIPCF. He is a former vice-president of SFPPG, the French Society of Psychoanalytical Group Therapy, and former president of the French Inter-ministerial national committee on violence. He is a committee member of the editorial review boards of the journals *Psychoanalytical Group Psychotherapy*, *Dialogue*, and *The Other One*, and a member of the editorial board of the French *Review of Psychoanalytic Group Psychotherapy*.

Montse Davins is a psychologist specialising in psychotherapy at the Fundació Vidal i Barraquer and has been the coordinator of the Specialised Care Unit for Battered Women since 2003. She earned her doctorate in psychology with a thesis on abuse in couple relations (summa cum laude and Extraordinary Prize, 2005). She has been a professor in the master's course in clinical psychopathology at the Fundació Vidal i Barraquer since 2008. She was a junior researcher at the Alta Scuola di Psicologia Agostino Gemelli at the Università Cattólica del Sacro Cuore in Milan (2008–2009). She has been a researcher in the Research Group of Couple and Family of the Universitat Ramon Llull.

Alberto Eiguer is a psychiatrist and psychoanalyst (SPP, APDEBA-IPA), president of the International Association of Couple and Family

Psychoanalysis, research director at the Laboratory PCPP, EA 4056, Institute of Psychology, University Paris 5 Sorbonne-City. He is the author of many works, including the recently published *Votre maison vous révèle* (*Your House Reveals You*) (Paris: Michel Lafon, 2013).

Ludovica Grassi is an MD, child psychiatrist, associate member of the Italian Society of Psychoanalysis (SPI) and of the International Psychoanalytical Association (IPA), qualified in child and adolescent psychoanalysis. Her main areas of work are in the Italian National Health Service, with a focus on severe family troubles, infant–parent psychotherapy, and migration related issues; and in private practice including psychoanalysis and psychotherapy with adults, children, adolescents, couples, and families.

Rosa Jaitin is a doctor of clinical psychology, with accreditation to supervise research. She is an associate member of the LPCP—Clinical Psychology and Psychopathology Laboratory at Paris Descartes University; scientific director of APSYLIEN-REC (Association of The Psychoanalysis of Bonds—Research); scientific-secretary, AIPCF (International Association of Couple and Family Psychoanalysis), and international affairs secretary at SFTFP (French Society of Psychoanalytical Family Therapy).

René Kaës is a psychoanalyst, emeritus professor of psychology and clinical psychopathology at the Lumière Lyon 2 University. He is a psychodramatist and group analyst (circle of French studies for training and research in psychoanalysis (groups, psychodrama, and institutions)). He has authored many psychoanalytical books on groups, dreams, the subject and intersubjectivity, unconscious alliances, and the intergenerational transmission of psychic life.

Jean-Georges Lemaire is honorary professor of clinical psychology at the Descartes Paris V University, psychoanalyst member of SPP and API, couple and family therapist member of Psyfa, former director of the journal *Dialogue, recherché sur couple et famille*, former paedopsychiatrist at the Versailles hospital, and founder of the French association of consultation for couples and of the Psyfa research group. After initial research on the psychology of mathematical thinking, he worked on unconscious processes in families and on the unconscious structuring of couples. He has authored about 100 articles and a dozen book chapters, among them: *Le couple, sa vie, sa mort*; *Amour, famille, folie* (Ed. Bayard-Centurion, Paris, 1989); *Les mots du couple* (Ed. Payot, Paris, 1998); *Comment faire avec la passion* (Ed. Payot, Paris, 2005); *L'inconscient dans la famille* (Ed. Dunod, Paris, 2007, in collaboration).

Daniela Lucarelli is a psychologist, psychoanalyst, full member of SPI, and expert in SPI and IPA psychoanalysis with children and adolescents. She is a member of the EFPP (European Federation for Psychoanalytic Psychotherapy in the Public Sector), board member and delegate of the Couple and Family Section, and member of IACFP (International Association of Couple and Family Psychoanalysis). She teaches in the ASNE-SIPSIA Specialisation Programme in Psychotherapy with Children, Adolescents and Couples in Rome. She is supervisor of clinical groups under the PCF (Società di Psiconalisi della Coppia e della Famiglia) post-specialisation course in "Clinical research in couple and family psychoanalytic psychotherapy". She is editor of the journal, *Interazioni: psychoanalytic clinic and research on individual, couple and family*. She is editor of the *International Review of Psychoanalysis of Couple and Family*.

Anna Maria Nicolò, MD, is a psychiatrist for children. A full member and training analyst, SPI-IPA, she is an IPA recognised expert on children and adolescents. Since 2011 she has been a member of the board of representatives of the International Psychoanalytical Association. Since 2005 she has been chair of the forum for adolescence of the European Psychoanalytical Federation (FEP). She is a founding member of the Society for Psychoanalytic Psychotherapy for Children, Adolescents and Couple (SIPsIA); scientific secretary of the Istituto Winnicott (ASNE-SIPsIA), member of the European Federation for Psychoanalytic Psychotherapy in the Public Sector (EFPP), member of Société Européenne pour la Psychanalyse de l'Enfant et de l'Adolescent (SEPEA), president of the Italian Society of Psychoanalysis of the Couple and Family (PCF), and co-founder of the AIPCF (International Association of Couple and Family Psychoanalysis). She is co-editor of the series "Contemporary Psychoanalysis" (Franco Angeli, Milan), director of the journal *Interazioni* (Franco Angeli), co-founder and former editor of the *International Review of Couple and Family Psychoanalysis* (AIPCF), supervisor at the therapeutic community for young psychotic patients, and author of many papers in Italian, English, French, Spanish, Portuguese, and German.

Diana Norsa, PhD, is a psychoanalyst member of SPI and IPA and a child analyst. She is a member of the Psychoanalytic Perspectives of Families and Couples Work Group of the IPA. She is an editorial board member of "Richard & Piggle" and "L'Annata Psicoanalitica Internazionale", the *International Journal of Psychoanalysis*'s yearbook in Italy. She is a teacher and supervisor for ASNE-SIPsIA (Infant and Adolescent Section of the EFPP) and PCF (Couple and Family Psychoanalytic Psychotherapy Section of the EFPP).

Carles Pérez-Testor is a doctor of medicine and surgery, specialising in psychiatry. He is the director of the Institut Universitari de Salut Mental, Fundació Vidal i Barraquer of the Universitat Ramon Llull (URL). He is a full professor in the Blanquerna Faculty of Psychology, Education Science and Sport. He is the lead investigator in the Research Group on Couples and the Family (GRPF) of the URL, which is recognised as a "consolidated research group". He is the coordinator of the Couple and Family Unit at the Fundació Vidal i Barraquer. He is a professor in the master's programme in clinical psychopathology and the postgraduate programme on couple and family psychology (URL, IUSM). He is the president of the European Network of Institutes of the Family (REDIF) and a member of professional organisations including the International Association of Couple and Family Psychoanalysis.

Giorgio Rigamonti is FMH in psychiatry and psychotherapy (Switzerland) and is a member of the Swiss Society of Psychiatry and Psychotherapy, and a psycho-oncology and couples psychoanalytical psychotherapy specialist. He works in a private studio in Mendrisio, Switzerland, with individual patients and couples. He is a teacher of CeRP (Centre for Psychotherapy Research), located in Trento and Milan, Italy.

Philippe Robert, a psychoanalyst member of IPA, is a member of the Laboratoire de Psychologie Clinique et Psychopathologie, master of conferences, Paris Descartes University, family therapist, president of Psyfa (2000–2010), full member of SFPPG (Société Française de Psychothérapie Psychanalytique de Groupe), and member of EFPP

(European Federation for Psychoanalytic Psychotherapy in the Public Sector).

Stanley Ruszczynski is consultant adult psychotherapist and clinical director of the Portman Clinic (Tavistock and Portman NHS Foundation Trust, London); he is a psychoanalytic psychotherapist with the British Association of Psychotherapists, a psychoanalyst with the British Psychoanalytic Association, and a member of the British Society of Couple Psychotherapists and Counsellors.

Manel Salamero is a doctor of medicine and surgery, a clinical psychiatrist, and an associate professor in the Department of Psychiatry at the University of Barcelona, Spain. He is also the director of the Research Department of Fundació Vidal i Barraquer in Barcelona. His research interests are primarily psychometry and research methodology in neuropsychology and clinical psychology. At the Fundació Vidal i Barraquer, he is involved in different projects related to interpersonal violence and international adoption. He is a member of the Research Group of Couple and Family (GRPF) at the URL.

Massimiliano Sommantico is a psychologist, psychotherapist, candidate of the Italian Psychoanalytical Society, and researcher in clinical psychology at the University of Naples "Federico II", where he teaches fundamentals of psychoanalysis. He is a founder member of the Department of Psychoanalysis Applied to Couple and Family, member of the board of the International Association of Couple and Family Psychoanalysis and of the Séminaire Inter-Universitaire Européen d'Enseignement et de Recherche en Psychopathologie et Psychanalyse; he is author of many papers published in different international journals and, recently of the book *Il fraterno. Teoria, clinica ed esplorazioni culturali* (Borla, Rome, 2012).

Simona Taccani is a psychoanalyst and psychotherapist, specialising in psychoanalytical and psychotherapeutic theoretical and clinical approaches to couples, families, and institutions. She trained in psychotherapeutics and psychoanalysis in Lausanne, Switzerland with P. C. Racamier, French psychoanalyst and psychotherapist, with whom she has edited numerous publications. She was a founding member and remains in charge of CeRP, the Centre for Psychotherapy Research, located both in Trento and in Milan. She is director of the CeRP School for Specialisation in Psychoanalytic Psychotherapy, in Trento. She is on the editorial board of the journals *Groupal* (once called "Gruppo"), edited by the Collège de Psychanalyse Groupale et Familiale, Paris, and *Interazioni: clinica e ricerca psicoanalitica su individuo—coppia—famiglia* (Franco Angeli, Milan). She is the author of many works in Italian and French.

Gabriela Tavazza is a clinical psychologist, psychoanalyst, SPI/IPA associate member, and member of IACFP, the International Association of Couple and Family Psychoanalysis. She is head of the task force for the prevention of mental disorders and education in mental health at the Mental Health Department ASL RMD in Rome. She is editor-in-chief of the journal *Interazioni: psychoanalytic clinic and research on individual, couple and family*. She is professor of clinical psychology at the Nursing Department of Tor Vergata University in Rome, and professor of social psychology in the master's degree programme in public health at the same university. She is supervisor of clinical groups under the PCF (Società di Psicoanalisi della Coppia e della Famiglia) post-specialisation course in clinical research in couple and family psychoanalytic psychotherapy.

SERIES EDITOR'S PREFACE

There is an ongoing structural change of the family as way of living. We see multiple forms like one-parent-families, singles, couples without children. The same is true if we focus on the couple which today no longer is restricted to the male-female constellation. These demographic and social changes in our every day life are a challenge to psychoanalytic theory, research and practice.

Family and couple as centre and basis of the family exist in mutual influence with each other. The relations to mother, father, siblings, grandparents etc. in their unconscious representations have great impact on the individual's concept of the couple. Both partners of a couple bring in a whole unconscious inner world of conflicts and conflict solving which will be reflected and materialised in the newly created family and passed on from generation to generation.

These and other aspects of the theme are dealt with in this book which presents a collection of the contributions given at a EFPP conference held in 2010 in Florence. Italy. It presents the state of the art of psychoanalytic understanding of the complexity of the family and the couple in our times as well as examples of clinical work.

Anne-Marie Schloesser

PREFACE

Otto F. Kernberg, M.D.

Identification is not simply the modification of the self by taking on aspects of a significant object (other). It is a process of simultaneous internalisation of the relationship between self and other, and the modification of the self under the influence of this internalisation. And projective identification is not only projection of an internal object onto another person, but the actualisation of the internalised object relationship in new interactions with alternating role activations of self and object representations. This is an internal and an interpersonal process: object relations theory deals with both.

At the same time, however, in this transportation of an internalised and projected relationship with unknown aspects of the other, identifications with culturally and familiarly internalised roles and values are also included. The reality aspects of what is new in any interchange carry with them new unconscious meanings, and this justifies the concept of the link as the unconscious new meaning in the interaction. It co-determines the actual relationship, and becomes more and more influential and dominant as the number of participants of closely related groups increases. Here object relations theory becomes enriched by the implications of the link.

The present volume represents a broad expansion of and wide perspectives on the application of psychoanalytic object relations theory to the unconscious structures and processes in the interpersonal field generated by couples, families, group processes, and in the cultural realm as signalled by shared myths and ideological commitments. This is a field already initiated by Freud's early contribution to the study of mass psychology, and powerfully fostered by the pioneering contributions on group regression by Bion, the dynamics of couples by Henry Dicks, and the unconscious dynamics of family structure by Anzieu and Lemaire.

The concept of the link as the unconscious transportation of internalised object relations into the intersubjective realm relates the activation of projective and introjective mechanisms reflecting intrapsychic dynamics with the encounter of a realistic aspect of the other, with similarity and difference. It provides new meaning for the processes of identification and alienation, and for the merging of individual dynamics with unconscious cultural value systems reflected in ideologies, myths, and cultural bias. Here the work by a group of Argentinian authors, Barranger, Berenstein, and others, opened up the concept of the "unconscious field" that was developed further by Ogden and Ferro, and the study of unconscious group, institutional and political processes by Kaës, Tom Main, and Serge Moscovici.

This volume presents a new generation of scholarly contributions to this exciting area of application of psychoanalytic inquiry. It explores further the relationship between the development of the self and the internal world of object relations, on the one hand, and the modulation of mutual projective identifications by the reality of an interaction pregnant with other unconscious and conscious meanings, on the other.

The analysis of unconscious family myths and power distributions as reflecting both oedipal and pre-oedipal dynamics and the influence of social and cultural structures and biases reported in this book constitutes a fascinating enrichment of the psychoanalytic study of social structures. The clinical application of these approaches in the treatment of couples and families illustrates their practical implications.

There are important problems remaining in this field: a plethora of complementary and contradictory formulations still needs to be sorted out and integrated as a synthesis of theoretical and technical formulations, but the present volume is an original, courageous, informative, and stimulating step in that direction.

PROLOGUE

Pierre Benghozi

The creation of the section for Psychoanalytic Couple and Family Therapy (PCFP) EFPP

Since 1991, the European Federation for Psychoanalytic Psychotherapy (EFPP), an umbrella organization for associations, has been comprised of three sections representing three clinical fields (adults, children and adolescents, and groups).

In 1997 I brought up the idea of creating a section for Psychoanalytic Couple and Family Psychotherapy to Serge Frisch, who was the president at that time, during a general assembly of delegates at which I represented the French Society for Group Psychoanalytic Psychotherapy. Ten years passed between this initiative and its implementation through the ratification of the EFPP's new statutes in 2009. This established, besides the already existing ones, a fourth section for couple and family psychoanalytic psychotherapy. These intervening years bear witness to a long process, symptomatic of the importance of what was at stake, and of the care taken to gain a large consensus.

For the specific object of psychoanalytic couple and family therapy to be perceived and understood exactly, and for specific training standards to be clearly defined, consistent with the standard of other sections of the EFPP, the board had to pay close attention at many meetings since 1997, bringing together section members and therapists already engaged in psychoanalytic couples and family therapy in Europe. This process was supported by the president Siv Boalt Boëthius and continued by her successors Luc Moyson and Anne-Marie Schloesser.

I carried out this work of connection in tandem with Rudolf Balmer, member-delegate to the executive committee. A working group was organised, which also included Daniela Lucarelli, Peter Möhring, and Gisela Zeller-Steinbrich. Many other therapists participated in the work meetings, among them Anna Maria Nicolò, Antonio Brignone, Jean Georges Lemaire, Philippe Robert, Rosa Jaitin, Claude Bigot, Gabriela Tavazza, Lucie Lucka, Manuela Porto, Marion Bower, Lynne Cudmore, Jeannie Milligan, Peter Dott, Gérard Mevel, Nastasia Nakov, Alberto Eiguer, Gérard Decherf, Elisabeth and Thomas von Salis, Rick Berke, Maia Eugenia Cid Rodriguez, Thames Cornette-Borges, Graca Galamba, Montserrat Garcia Milà, Montserrat Martinez del Pozo, and Jörgen Nässèn.

At the delegates' meeting of the EFPP in March 2005 in Stockholm, we gave a summary of our work. In this report, PCFP is defined as "a specific field of application and adaptation of psychoanalytic theory, theory of technique, and technique. PCFP has developed a framework of specific concepts which form the base for specialization". Corresponding to different psychoanalytic traditions in various countries, we observe different approaches in PCFP as well. In some countries, it has developed from child psychoanalysis; in others, the development is centred upon an interactive or a group analytic approach. The working party therefore redefined PCFP in order to establish a common ground:

Psychoanalytic Couple and Family Psychotherapy is applied psychoanalysis characterised by the analysis of family and couple relationships through the use of transference and countertransference, and by the work on unconscious conflicts, wishes and anxieties and defences in the family group or in the couple.

The process of family therapy became necessary because of experience in clinical practice, particularly with psychosis, addictive behaviour, and in trauma clinics. Psychoanalytic couple and family psychotherapy is still in development. Confrontations both in Europe and abroad have allowed us to get a closer look upon the creativity developed according to the context, the history, and the psychoanalytic culture of each country.

In 2005 the PCFP section was officially established. The delegates accepted the revised training standards and by-laws. Another working party, consisting of three members of the already existing sections (Frank Castrillon, Adult Section; Maria Gemma Rocco, Child/Adolescent Section; Rudolf Balmer, Group Section) and three members of the previous working party (Peter Möhring, Germany; Daniela Lucarelli, Italy; Pierre Benghozi, France), was commissioned. The board gave me the mandate to organise the new section in close contact with it which underlined the official status of the new section-to-be.

Two meetings of the PCFP working party took place in 2007 and 2009. After the Stockholm vote, the EFPP statutes were completely remoulded, so that the PCFP was fully included within it. At the Delegates Meeting 2009 in Kortenberg, the amendment of statutes making the section official was agreed unanimously. By this decision, the delegates from different sections expressed the importance of psychoanalytic couple and family psychotherapy as a specific field of the application of psychoanalytic psychotherapy.

The PCFP section today is made up of organisations from those European countries where psychoanalytic couple and family psychotherapy has principally been developed: Italy (Daniela Lucarelli, Gemma Trapanese), France (Pierre Benghozi, Philippe Robert), Germany (Michael Stasch, Bernd Böttger), Spain (Pere Llovet, Lea Forster), Portugal (Manuela Porto, Ana Marques Lito), Czech Republic (Lucie Lucka, Slavoj Titl), Romania (Cristina Calarasanu), Greece (Nikos Stathopoulos, Anastasia Tsamparli), Russia (Konstantin Yagniuk), and Serbia (Jasna Veljkovic). Several other countries have taken the first steps towards admission (the UK, Finland, Sweden, and Israel). As section chair, I currently represent, with Daniela Lucarelli, the PCFP section on the board.

Applications for membership are addressed to and evaluated by the PCFP section chair and evaluated and then approved by the board.

Several of us have since initiated the founding of the International Association of Psychoanalytic Couple and Family Therapy (ACFP). The EFPP enables psychoanalytic couple and family psychotherapists to belong to a space where they are accompanied by members from other psychoanalytic psychotherapy sections, and can discuss and develop their field on an European level.

The founding congress, organised under the aegis of the PCFP section, took place in May 2010 in Florence, Italy, with the theme "Families in Transformation: A Challenge for Psychoanalytic Psychotherapy". This book collects most of the principal papers presented there and fits naturally into the perspectives of the project.

In these times, when psychoanalysis is being attacked on many fronts, the creation of new sections displays the EFPP's commitment to promoting fully the different facets of psychoanalytic psychotherapy and its dynamic character in both theory and clinical practice.

INTRODUCTION

Anna Maria Nicolò and Daniela Lucarelli

The aim of this book is to testify to the state of the art of couple and family psychoanalysis in Europe. The work in such settings has been relegated to the margins of official psychoanalysis due to the diffidence any deviation from standard therapy has always caused in many psychoanalysts.

As a consequence theory and practice, often developed by the same analysts that are present in the institutions, have grown at the sidelines without finding a position at official levels or in training. Freud's warning that psychoanalysis is a method which does not tolerate witnesses served as a constraint on the development of this approach. Freud, in fact, was always wary—even at the clinical level—of the "intervention of relatives" in individual analysis and in the 28th lecture (1916–17) he defined it as "a positive danger and a danger one does not know how to meet" (p. 458). Despite the fact that he had seen a connection between the symptomatology of a family member and the emotive functioning of that individual's closest relatives, he considered them a threat for analytical work: "the healthy party will not hesitate long in choosing between his own interest and the sick party's recovery" (ibid., p. 458).

However, these types of studies developed progressively, beginning with clinical stimuli, such as the treatment of seriously ill patients and work on the developmental age.

We owe studies on parenthood and on the family to the work of child psychoanalysts, whereas other models in these settings developed from the findings of group analysis.

Eventually, with respect to psychotic and borderline pathologies, intervention on the environment in which the patient lives and on the family group which includes him became unavoidable. Contrary to those who viewed work with the family only as a useful tool for therapeutic alliance with the patient whose principal treatment remained, however, individual, family psychoanalysts have stressed how much the family setting is, above all at the beginning, the vibrant heart of the therapy. This is because in the characteristics typical of such serious pathologies where the boundaries of the self are fragile, the transgenerational mandates weigh on the organisation of the individual's identity and functioning in relationships is acted out and concrete.

Thus, all over the world many clinical and observatory studies on these topics have developed, such as those into the phantasmatic and relational functioning of the couple and the family as a unit, with a unitary identity and super-individual unit, and this functioning has been studied in several generations both at an intergenerational and a transgenerational level.

Depending on the orientation of the psychoanalyst, for some, work swept from sometimes concentrating on interpersonal dimensions, at other times on the group nature of the family, and for others on the relationship between the intrapsychic and interpersonal. However, work on interactions within the family or on relationships among family members was considered by all to be the basis for achieving change.

Always at the margins of the official psychoanalysis circles, an enormous volume of studies has consolidated over time, some of which have de facto transferred, to the couple and the family, models of understanding and the techniques of classical psychoanalysis whereas others have taken new roads, putting the accent on the intersubjective dynamics and links among the members.

For people like us who have worked for over thirty years in this field, it is curious to observe how much psychoanalysis has today rediscovered, with other words, experiences and observations which for us are a patrimony already acquired.

We are not going to investigate today the reasons for this enormous scotoma. Could it be political, accidental, influential, scientific, or geographic? It is often the case that psychoanalysts locked within their own schools of thought will not read the works of colleagues of other schools, but certainly in this case we are dealing with a case of disownment and rejection that has only partially been resolved.

Moreover, wrongly or rightly, psychoanalytic work on families and couples has often been confused with the systemic approach in its more behaviouristic versions; it has therefore confused the setting with the model: working in the family setting meant ipso facto working with a pragmatic model. Until a few years ago the idiosyncrasy of Freud's followers towards anything that seemed to be connected with acting out, interaction, and what was scornfully defined as behaviour, drove them to reject any kind of position on families which they associated solely with a behaviouristic approach.

There has been so much confusion that perhaps only now are we really trying to clarify the situation. Two important associations have been founded to unite psychotherapists with a psychoanalytic orientation in this field. One is the AIPCF (Association Internationale de Psychanalyse de Couple et de Famille), founded in 2006 in Montreal on the initiative of some European and American analysts—to name a few, Alberto Eiguer, Rosa Jaitin, Anne Loncan, Roberto Losso, Daniela Lucarelli, Anna Maria Nicolò, Gabriela Tavazza, David and Jill Scharff, and the new section of the EFPP (European Federation for Psychoanalytic Psychotherapy in the Public Sector). The other, the PCFP (Psychoanalytic Psychotherapy with Couples and Families) was created in 2009 after lengthy preparatory work and whose founding convention is mentioned in this book.

It could certainly, however, be useful to readers to survey past theories which have constituted the reference for psychoanalytic work with couples and families, to enable them to acquire a better understanding of the complex panorama of the works we will be reading about in this book and their cultural background.

A retrospective look at family psychoanalysis

We will briefly summarise the main psychoanalytic orientations in this field, aware that our choice and our rapid, overhead review cannot do justice to the richness and variety of contributions which, starting with Freud himself, have come down to us today. There are very many authors we have not mentioned and we hope readers will forgive us since our aim is to contextualise the reading of this book, to offer points of reference in this sometimes untidy galaxy and disclose the past roots which have characterised it. In the field of psychoanalysis, the first, embryonic references to family therapy already appear in the writings of Sigmund Freud (1856–1939). Even though the founder of psychoanalysis has always laid the emphasis on the individual and laid the foundations for its treatment by developing a theory in terms of intrapsychic structures, he does however draw attention to the "social instinct" whereby "it may be possible to discover the beginnings of its development in a narrower circle, such as that of the family" (Freud, 1921c, p. 69).

Already in his earlier writings such as "Elizabeth von R." (Freud, 1905e), family history and its underlying dynamics occupy a large space and lead us to relate a symptom to a particular family dynamic. "Little Hans" (Freud, 1909b), whose phobic problems were dealt with through Freud's work with his father, can be considered the first case of an intervention on the family. Hans's phobia represented not only an intrapsychic conflict, but also difficulty in family relationships: the solution to the problematics can be attributed, therefore, also to the change in the attitude of his father who, after his meetings with Freud, became much more attentive to and aware of his son's needs. This paved the way for the disappearance of the son's phobic symptom whose principal objective, among other causes for his phobia, was to attract his parents' attention and get his father to run to his aid.

His study on Leonardo da Vinci led Freud to become interested again in the family constellation, in his opinion a significant factor in generating Leonardo's homosexuality owing to the very close bond with his mother and the absence of a strong father in the early years of his life (Freud, 1910c). On a theoretical level, the theory of identifications and the Second Topography introduce the theme of intersubjectivity. With *Group Psychology and Analysis of the Ego* (Freud, 1921c), an epistemological leap takes place. Freud affirms that "In the individual's mental life someone is invariably involved, as a model, as an object, as a helper, as an opponent: and so from the very first individual psychology, in this extended but justifiable sense of the words, is at the same time social psychology as well" (p. 69).

Up until now we have mentioned some traces in the writings of the founder of psychoanalysis where we can find the origins of family psychoanalysis. But further references, even if not explicitly formulated, can also be more substantially perceived in contemporaries and in Freud's pupils.

Among these we find Paul Federn (1871–1950), who was part of the small and well-known group of analysts who met at Freud's house on Wednesday evenings. He was one of the pioneers in the treatment of psychosis, introducing the concept of illness not so much of the ego itself but rather of the ego boundary whose origin was to be found in the distortion of the mother–son relationship.

Sandor Ferenczi (1873–1933), Freud's favourite disciple was concerned with the adult-child relationship and trauma. In introducing, inter alia, the concept of a conflictual, pathogenic relationship between the adult abuser and the abused child, he went well beyond the primary intrapsychic processes described by Freud in regard to psychic trauma by including the object relationships in his studies on trauma. In this way, he enriched the theory by clarifying the distorted functioning of the child's sense of reality. The attention given to the importance of disavowal and deceit by the adult provided a new tool for understanding and working through.

The development of child psychoanalysis and the attention afforded the mother–child relationship in the Twenties and Thirties would become one of the cardinal points for family psychoanalysis.

At the Congress of The Hague in 1920, Hermine Hug-Hellmut (1871–1924), by arguing that an analysis conducted with parents could have prevented their children's psychological difficulties, introduced the intuition of a close connection between the psychic functioning of parental couples and the child.

Anna Freud (1895–1982) introduced into psychoanalytic theory concepts which lend themselves to explaining the interpsychic functioning established between individuals such as the "displacement mechanism" or "identification with the aggressor". In *The Psychoanalytic Treatment of Children* (1927) she wrote about the forces against which one must fight in order to cure infantile neuroses which are not only of an internal origin but derive in part also from the outside. She went on to say that one has the right to demand of the child analyst a proper assessment of the environment in which the child lives, just as we insist that the analyst be in a position to understand the child's own internal situation (p. 92).

We are however still far from imagining an individuated and specific work in these settings.

From then onwards, positions would progressively emerge which were to highlight more and more the importance of context and relationships.

In 1936 at the IX International Congress of Psychoanalysis in Nyon, Switzerland, one of the first to be held in a Romance language, the theme of the family appears for the first time: "Family Neurosis and Neurotic Family". René Laforgue (1936), one the principal speakers, spoke about his experience of "analysing different family members at the same time" and affirmed that treating the parents reflected on the recovery of their children. René Spitz also attended and was responsible for the publication of the congress proceedings. The importance of this theme and the interest shown for the contributions, however, were not immediately felt, perhaps because the time was not ripe yet. Probably the dominant positivist mindset of the time did not allow analysts to stray from a view centred on the individual, thus hindering the broadening of their horizons to include the interpersonal dimension.

And later?

Family and couple psychoanalysis too, like the psychoanalytic movement tout court, feeds of social, economic, and historical changes.

After the war a new sensitivity began to appear and during that period Michael and Enid Balint, a married couple, were running a marital consultancy centre. Enid Balint (1963) was the author of a pioneering case study in this field. She highlighted how the couple relationship is not only an area of sharing but it is also undifferentiated and confused. She described how the relationship is characterised by a level of intimacy which sets up an exclusive communication between the unconscious minds of the couple.

John Bowlby published a clinical study during those years entitled *The Study and Reduction of Group Tensions in the Family* (1949), in which he described the interviews with family members as auxiliary to the individual sessions. In this article, he related the case of a boy he had been analysing for two years without any result, which was why he now experimented with a family psychoanalytic session. Even though Bowlby considered this experience of family sessions experimental, he wrote that he rarely uses this method more than once or twice in the same case; however, he reached the point of using it almost routinely after the first interview and before beginning the therapy itself (ibid.).

The years 1950–1970 would come to be seen as an extremely interesting and vivacious period in this regard.

In 1959, Harold Searles, a psychoanalyst at Chestnut Lodge, perhaps in his most famous essay, "The Effort to Drive the Other Person Crazy: an Element in the Aetiology and Psychotherapy of Schizophrenia", examined in depth the concept of pathological interaction.

This work has been recognised as being of great significance for all family therapists: in it the author shows us how one person's madness can be externalised in the other and how there are ways to cause mental illness in one's partner.

In the United States, N. Ackerman, M. Bowen, I. Boszormeny-Nagy, T. Lidz, and J. Framo were among the first to affirm a continuity with psychoanalytic theory but nonetheless proposed a development which went beyond the individual while at the same time not overlooking the importance of the individual.[1]

The application of the object relations theory to family and couple functioning began to orient, as it still does today, many English-speaking psychoanalysts who, referring to the arguments of Ronald Fairbairn and Melanie Klein and using the concepts of projective identification and projection, studied and are still studying these settings. And thus collusion, a reciprocal interweaving of projective identifications according to Dicks's definition, came to be considered to be the basis of couple and family functioning.

Continuing along these lines, Stanley Ruszczynski (1993; Ruszczynski & Fisher, 1995) in England, Andreas Giannakoulas (1992) in Italy, and Jill and David Scharff (1991) in the United States, have further developed this orientation as we can observe in Ruszczynski's accurate contribution to this book. He deals with the theme of violence and perversion by presenting a couple's clinical situation. The author describes this interesting clinical case by referring to the theory of object relations. He notes how it is more and more frequent to encounter couples without internal space in which to contain their instincts, anxieties, and conflicts and who mainly use splitting mechanisms, projective identification, or who evacuate their emotions externally. Violence, argues the author, is used as a perverse answer to face those anxieties and emotions which are projected onto their partner.

Exploring the topic in an innovative and creative way, Otto Kernberg (1991, 1998) argues that the couple is where the conscious and unconscious activation of interiorised object relations take place and inside which the superego functions of both partners are activated. Kernberg argues that a joint ego ideal exists which has a certain weight in the future of the couple's relationship. He also considers the reciprocal influence of the couple in the social context and in particular with regard to their group of friends.

In English-speaking countries we can assume that at the basis of the studies on these issues was the need to open up to the social dimension, which had already begun with the traumatising effects of the war and from the necessity for coherent and competent work with parents of children being treated. London itself was a crucible of ideas, theories, and experimentation.

The Tavistock Institute for Human Relations in London is and has been for many years a centre of excellence for research on couple and family studies and intervention with parents. Innumerable members of this institute have produced works of great significance in this regard, such as H. V. Dicks, Tom Main, Michael and Enid Balint, and G. Teruel.

In his work, *Marital Tensions* (1967), Dicks was the first to set up systematic clinical work with couples, using the following as a reference basis: a setting with four people (the patient couple and the therapists), the unconscious choice of the partner, the concepts of collusion, and the dyadic membrane.

If the war had definitely drawn attention to the social dimension, at the end of the Sixties the development of an anti-psychiatry movement made it necessary to widen interest in the cultural context from which the mental disorder emerged. This led to a widespread interest in the family. There were some studies and important research conducted in this field by Ronald D. Laing (1927–1989), a disciple of Winnicott, and a representative of the anti-psychiatry movement. The volumes, *The Divided Self* (1960), *Self and Others* (1961), and *The Politics of the Family and Other Essays* (1971) exercised a great cultural influence in English-speaking, European, and Latin-American countries.

To Laing we owe, inter alia, the development of the concept of "transpersonal defence" (1967), which was for some to become one of the conceptual pivots of family psychoanalysis. Taken up by various authors, including Anna Maria Nicolò in this volume, it illustrates one of the fundamental mechanisms of family functioning: transpersonal defence is a collective product, mutable in time and which the family members organise to defend themselves from anxieties which have a common base. Laing offers an understanding of the schizophrenic symptom within the family context by showing in an innovative way how mental disorders can represent a particular kind of recovery with regard to family and intrapsychic conflicts.

Laing's interest in the social and political aspect of mental disorders gradually made him withdraw from psychoanalysis while in the rest of the world the relational aspect of psychoanalytic theory was developing through the theory of groups and the theory of object relations.

In francophone countries, work in these settings takes the application of group analysis very thoroughly into account.

The Collège de Psychanalyse Groupale et Familiale, connected to the journal *Groupal*, currently refers to the work of Didier Anzieu (1923–1999) on groups. The French psychoanalyst introduced the concepts of "skin-ego" (1997) and "psychic envelopes" (1996), observing how couples and families develop their envelopes starting from a primordial object and thus create a common "skin-ego". The other great school, connected to the Societé de Thérapie Familiale Psychoanalytique de l'Ile de France, counts among its members psychoanalysts like André Ruffiot, Alberto Eiguer, Evelyn Granjon, and Rosa Jaitin. Since 1998 they and others have published a journal with the evocative name of *Le Divan Familial*.

This group offers a more composite view sharing with the work done by René Kaës the concept of a family psychic apparatus. In Kaës's theorising (1976), the concept of group psychic apparatus makes reference to the group as an individuated somatopsychic unit which is structured on the pretext and illusion of constituting a group formation of the unconscious. Other authors, including Ruffiot, Caillot, Decherf, and Decobert have underlined and developed concepts related to primal phantasies and the process of interphantasmatisation. At the base of this transgenerational route and that of phantasies on the origins of the family itself, the authors hypothesise the existence of the primal phantasies, bearers of differentiation between generations and sexes. These phantasies are mobilisers of the family's capacity to establish links. They also produce individuation and changes, absorb traumatisms, and elaborate losses and mourning.

As can be seen in various ways, all researchers of couple and family psychoanalysis question themselves as to what happens in relationships among family members and the functioning of the family as a unit. If some psychoanalysts highlight the phantasmatic functioning of the group, others like Eiguer take the Freudian concept of identification as a mechanism for relationships among individuals.

In his contribution to this volume, Eiguer describes the role played by the identification within a theoretical-clinical intersubjective approach according to which the psyche of two or more individuals function in reciprocity in such a way that they both influence each other on different levels. Each individual is influenced by the psychic state of the other and any variation in the identifications plays an active part in these interchanges.

The theme of transgenerational transmission of shame and humiliation is also dealt with by Pierre Benghozi, who introduces the notions of "inheritance of shame legacy of shame" or "inheritance of treason legacy of betrayal". He refers to interesting clinical material on the intrafamiliar transmission in contexts where the whole community has undergone catastrophic trauma. In concluding, he reflects on the difficulties of elaborating traumas, because there are situations whereby unearthing memories of past events, particularly collective traumatic ones, challenges the denial of the community. Benghozi (2005) also describes the transformations in the individual and family life cycle, which he calls the genealogical psychical anamorphosis, and which he conceptualises using the notion of "Sloughing of Containers". He wonders also if these sloughings of genealogical containers concern new family configurations, and if they also entail the emergence of a new clinical practice.

Alongside these psychoanalysts we must however recall the pioneering work of Jean-George Lemaire, founder of Psyfa, one of the oldest associations of French Psychoanalytic Family Therapy as well as of the journal *Dialogue*. In the material presented in this volume, he observes how clinical work with couples can lead to the need to review some classical concepts of psychoanalysis. It thus follows that the emergence of particular manifestations defined as "appropriation", almost of capture and of splitting, which do not occur in other life environments of the patients individually, induced him to broaden the concept of identification to include the frequent emergence of images linked to very archaic identification phenomena of the group type. He describes a "non-conscious space" rather than unconscious in which non-conscious images or other sensorial non-conscious perceptions, but not repressed, non-real phantasies or organised scenarios, simply live alongside other phenomena of neuropsychological origin. We could say "primal" in as much as they, probably, find their origin in the initial phases of neuropsychic development when the different sensorial systems are still undifferentiated.

The narcissistic dimension and the primal, almost pre-individual stages of the construction of the sentiment of identity give rise, in amorous relationships, to a psychic agency: "We". This becomes very cathected and keeps the traces of each individual's initial "We" and, at the same time, is represented in the link of the couple.

Continuing our look at the European countries and in particular, the United Kingdom, we cannot neglect two extraordinary psychoanalysts who, even though not working explicitly with couples and families, have nevertheless made significant contributions.

The first is Donald W. Winnicott. In his opinion families grow independently of their individual members. Families—he argues—are created through the contribution of all their members, not only the parents but also the children, even the youngest child. Winnicott underlines the reciprocal interaction between the child, each of its parents, the relationship between them, and the family, what some today would call a shared construction. He urges us to take into account family resources and to stimulate them above all in cases of physically or psychically ill children and parents. The second is Donald Meltzer who in a brief publication examines the family functioning by distinguishing it according to its global functioning and in particular to the identification types used internally, namely the projective, introjective, and adhesive types.

In Italy, too, movements and working groups developed around these themes, facilitated and influenced moreover by the context characterising all Italian psychoanalysis, which had very early on shown itself to be open to, and interested in the plurality of models and in the relationship (analytic or not). Nino Ferro's theory serves as a model regarding the openness of Italian psychoanalysts towards relational dimensions.

Starting from Bion's and later from Baranger's contributions, Ferro developed the theory of the analytical field, exploring and describing new dimensions of the mental functioning between the analyst and the patient in an analytical situation, from a bi-personal viewpoint. The "field" is created by the interrelation between the functioning of the analyst and that of the patient: the analyst is not present just as an answer or a filter, but "co-generates" the field with his or her mind and presence.

Ferro is interested in the development of the capacity for symbolisation opened up by the dialogue between two minds in the "field". To the actual, horizontal field must be added, he says, the vertical field which comprehends also the personal history and the transgenerational.

Stefano Bolognini has also shown himself to be attentive to and interested in interpsychic functioning and the importance which such functioning has in families. In his recent work *Passaggi segreti* (Bolognini, 2008), he deals with those ways that allow communication between the minds (interpsychic) and inside the mind (intrapsychic) and which are the basis not only for the analytic relationship but also the human relationship.

In 2000, when he attended the 1st International Congress on the Psychoanalysis of Families and Couples, in his intervention on "The Analyst's Family", Bolognini (2005) drew attention to an implicit phantasmatic reality, the family reality, which continues to remain with the analyst, at times unmindfully, in subsequent work: a reality which the analyst draws upon without recognition of the different phantasmatic levels involved. Bolognini underlined the fact that there are two "families" existing in the analyst, the historical one, that of childhood, and the institutional one, that of professional training. These families interact and intervene in work with the patients (and with their internal families) on an internal phantasy plane. Bolognini points out, in the way the analytic work is conducted, there should be an encounter between the family micro-cultures and the environment micro-culture where we analysts were formed analytically (Bolognini, 2005).

This background has had a strong influence on Italian psychoanalysts dealing with parental couples, marital couples, and families. Starting from psychoanalytic training with children and adolescents, some turned naturally to the relational world where their patients live. Since 1992, the journal *Interazioni. Clinica e ricerca psicoanalitica su individuo-coppia-famiglia*, edited by Anna Maria Nicolò, has gathered together many analysts belonging to various groups. These include P. Boccara, L. Grassi, D. Lucarelli, G. Martini, A. Narracci, G. Saraò, S. Taccani, G. Tavazza, G. Trapanese, and others.

The series of exchanges stirred by the scientific debate promoted by the journal led to the first International Congress on the Psychoanalysis of Couples and Families, held in Naples in the year 2000, thus providing an occasion for psychoanalysts of various nations to meet. Further stimulus to interest in family research and clinics and encouraging the future establishment of a society to unite European analysts dealing with these themes ensued. Those Italian psychoanalysts who promoted these studies, some of whom are contributors to this book (Lucarelli, Nicolò, Norsa, Tavazza), believe in the link as a third, newly formed component, and that treating that link is of fundamental importance in work with the family and the couple. The family is viewed as an interiorised system of links and constitutes the matrix of individual identity; it is characterised by specific interactive qualities and also by an intergenerational structure. On a phantasmatic level, the unconscious phantasies and basic anxieties of the family group are dealt with by transpersonal defences, being a collective product of the family members; in addition, each family member can rely on individual defences that each one has at his or her disposal. The focal point of this approach is the study of the continuous, reciprocal interweaving between the intrapsychic world of each individual member and the interpersonal functioning of the family to which each individual belongs (Nicolò, 1988, 1990).

On a diagnostic and therapeutic level, this method observes, for example, the consonance or dissonance of the individual as regards common anxieties or collective phantasies of the group. Furthermore it brings to light each individual's defences when faced with common conflict or faced with shared phantasies, and confronts the defence of the single individual as regards the collective interpersonal defence (Nicolò, 2006; Nicolò & Borgia, 1995).

The multiplicity and contemporaneous presence of multiple levels of functioning in these structures account for the diversities of the reactions received from the family which oscillate continually between the most undifferentiated and primal levels, including the use of the body, and the most differentiated, representational, or symbolical levels. These contemporarily present levels impose a need for articulate, therapeutic answers, which are also to be found on different levels, thus obliging the analyst to measure himself not only in an asymmetrical relationship but also as a member of that newly formed system composed of the family in a link with him.

Some of the works of these Italian psychoanalysts can be found in this volume.

Trans-cultural clinical work and multi-ethnic, therapeutic relations represent the field proposed by Ludovica Grassi. She argues the need for constant individual and group work on the analysis of the countertransference, and in particular, the cultural countertransference, referring to the implicit, cultural factors often radically discordant, on which is based the discourse between the family and the therapist/s.

The complexity of clinical work with adoptive families is dealt with by Daniela Lucarelli and Gabriela Tavazza. The authors underline how adoptive families experience difficulties during the course of subjectivisation, the identification process, and mutual recognition, in other words, these difficulties lie in reciprocal recognition of the alterity and the different places assumed by the family members.

The process of adoption emphasises the need to generate a "family Us" which in turn can encourage the emergence of an ego, sustained by a subjectivising environment that takes shape through a mutual recognition. The authors demonstrate in a convincing exemplification how therapy with adoptive parents can facilitate the development of the adoptive relationship and lead to integration of the traumatic experiences.

As far as couples are concerned, Diana Norsa examines a question which emerges from her clinical work. She asks, what reasons induce partners to contract second or third marriages and to create new families after previous failures? The author indicates how, at times, these unions can represent a search for the solution to a problematic which has its origins in the failure to elaborate the oedipal complex. Both partners seek to repair traumas of the primal Self, confusing female and male roles on a bisexual primal level. The new unions can be representative of attempts at transformation, through repetition of female and male representations.

The theme of the secret for the functioning of couples and families is explored by Rigamonti and Taccani. As they point out to us, the notion of a secret is both intrasubjective and intersubjective. On an intrapsychic level it carries out a vital, protective, and evolutive function for the psyche. However, a family secret often organises itself and develops when a previous generation experiences psychic traumas and is incapable of symbolising them. This incapacity also to share these traumas in words and emotions, in images and mental representations, results in transmitting to future generations traces of secrets, and confusing, unexplainable emotions, which are disorienting. A family secret is, however, not exclusively related to family events to be ashamed of or to be lived with with feelings of guilt, as specified by Tisseron (1996).

Rigamonti and Taccani are working on the possibility of developing a typology of secrets, similar to Racamier's proposal in 1992, to be used as a factor in defining the different types of functioning in the couple.

Massimiliano Sommantico puts the accent instead on another important theme, the fraternal complex. He observes how the influence of the fraternal link can often be observed in the psychic dynamic of some couples who characterise the actual clinical scenarios. From his experience in clinical practice, he observes a functioning in which the specular and narcissistic dimension of the fraternal relationship appears to prevail, acting as a bond on the couple relationship and maintaining the married couple in a game of rivalry, just like brothers, the consequence of which is the incapacity to assume a solid parental function. Moreover, Sommantico points out, in particular, that he has observed the prevalence of a "fraternal pre-oedipal" as a partial aspect, almost like an appendix of the maternal body, signalling the failure of an Oedipus complex to guarantee overcoming a specular and narcissistic relationship and the advent of a sexed identity.

Which conceptual challenges?

Work with families and couples has proved to be very effective and has even become unavoidable in pathologies during the age of development and in serious cases. It is absolutely unthinkable to work with a psychotic patient without treating his past and his present family. The reasons are not only those of sustaining a therapeutic alliance in individual therapy, as many authors, including Martha Harris, maintain. Whoever offers this as a reason creates great confusion. The reasons for this approach are in the very nature of this pathology, where the boundaries of the self are fragile and the confusion between the self and the other is a norm of the functioning. Psychosis is an expression of pathological interactions both in their genesis and continuation, as shown to varying extents by some of the authors of this book (Nicolò, Rigamonti, Taccani).

The absolute necessity for work with the parents in the treatment of children and adolescents, or the usefulness of this type of intervention in sexual disorders, or in couple crises, or in situations of developmental crises in families, is not under discussion, because work with parents is today so widespread among child psychoanalysts that no one has doubts about it any more.

It does appear advisable, however, to discuss how this type of work enriches us and which challenges it represents.

Whether we wish it or not, it involves work on links, on relationships, on interactions which unite members of families or couples and not only on the contents or internal world. This approach considers families and couples therefore as super-individual units, endowed with their own functioning and identity, as we can easily perceive from the works adhering to a group conception of the family and analysing it in terms of functioning on basic assumptions (Box, Copley, Magagna & Moustaky, 1981) or as a family group psychic apparatus (Kaës, 1976; Ruffiot, 1981; Ruffiot et al., 1981).

More recently, as indicated in some chapters of this book, emphasis has been placed on the concept of "link", in regard to what unites family members.

While Freud underlines identification as the mechanism which unites one individual to another even over several generations, Bion was the first to highlight the relationship of the mother–child couple, and the analytic couple in terms of "container-contained". He stressed the concept of link, both in the dual mother–child, patient–analyst context, and within the mind. Commenting on what happens in a dual context, he affirmed that the patient's relationship is predominantly with the couple in the room: it could be any couple, but the most obvious couple is that formed by the analyst and the patient (Bion, 1992, p. 94).

In family psychoanalysis, according to many authors who deal with this theme, the term "link" is used in the sense of an unconscious structure linking two or more individuals. It is distinguished by other concepts such as that of the object relation which each one of us keeps within his unconscious fantasy and which has its origins in our childhood history.

Already in 1985, Pichon Rivière, in his work *Teoría del vínculo* accentuated the difference between link and object relation. He asked why do we use the term "link"? He went on to explain that in reality we are accustomed to using the notion of object relation in psychoanalytic theory, but the notion of link is much more concrete. The object relation is an internal structure of the link. It could be said that the notion of object relation has been inherited from atomistic psychology, whereas the link is a different thing which includes behaviour. The link could be defined as a particular type of relationship with the object; from this particular relation a more or less fixed conduct with the object entails forming a pattern, a behaviour model which tends to repeat itself automatically both in the internal relationship and in the external relationship with the object.

In our opinion, in a certain sense this conception tends to act as a bridge connecting the internal world of the person to the external reality. A repeated behaviour model, if we have understood properly what Pichon Rivière tells us, forms a pattern which includes the two individuals sharing a relationship. For this reason Berenstein (2001), one of Pichon Rivière's Argentinian pupils, explains that if we recognise the existence of the link (*vínculo*) this entails a reflection on the subject, on the place of the other and on the difference with the internal object and the notion of external object; it also entails reflection on the internal reality and its relation with the external reality, the similarity and alienation of the link between individuals.

As one of us has expressed in this book (Nicolò), the link that is created, for example, between members of a couple, even if triggered in the encounter from the unconscious reasons for choosing that partner, is however a new element generated in the here-and-now at the origin of the encounter. In this volume Kaës writes about the link that is the more or less stable movement of the cathexes, of the representations, and of the actions which unite two or more individuals for the realisation of some of their desires.

Kaës (1994) clearly distinguishes between the field of the object relation and that of the link in which the other is also the other in reality, and different from the internal object. In this case the object of the relation is not only the object of the projection but also the end of a process of psychic exchange and therefore it is, as the other subject, another subject that insists and resists inasmuch as it is the other (ibid., p. 27).

But there is certainly a lot left to do in this regard. In fact, how will we be able to tell the nature, the form, and the quality of the links? How will we be able to distinguish the reciprocal link which unites members of a couple from the reciprocal projective identifications which also link and characterise them?

On this certainly crucial aspect, many authors give different answers.

The links are, however, undoubtedly inter- and transsubjective structures, entailing the shared construction of two or more persons; they always have an acted-out side to them, and it is therefore possible to observe them more in the actions, behaviour, non-verbal language, or in the corporal manifestations of the members. Even if they can be passed down from one generation to another, the links are the fruit of a reciprocal accommodation among the members.

The atmosphere in the house, its furnishings, the photos that record the family over the passage of time are at times representations from which we can unearth information about the identity of that family and on the links among the family members. However, the element in which we can perhaps more easily read the quality and the forms of the links within the family are above all the myths that the family hands down from generation to generation, and where these traumatic aspects of its history tend to condense like a kind of elaboration in progress, as we read in Anna Maria Nicolò's work.

Naturally, conceiving things in these terms is, in our opinion, revolutionary, but can also cause dismay given that the object of the link is not to be found in the individual mind but in the interpersonal space.

Kaës also points out that we may find ourselves facing a psychic reality without subject. This psychic reality, in order to acquire autonomy develops unavoidably among the subjects (the psychic space of inter-subjectivity), and it also develops via the subjects (the psychic space of transsubjectivity).

This prospect also challenges us conceptually because it asks us where the unconscious is to be found in settings with the couple or the family, a question which many authors have already asked themselves and which is discussed in a chapter of this book (Nicolò).

A theoretical approach which takes account of the interpersonal and intergenerational dimension has encouraged interest in a particular aspect of the real and phantasmatic structure of the family, that of fraternal links and the way in which these are impressed in the inter- and transgenerational filiation links, in other words, in an imaginary, real, and symbolic whole.

Rosa Jaitin (2006), as far as these notions are concerned, proposes the distinction between "fraternal complex" and "fraternal link". If the complex is founded, on one hand, on interpersonal and intergenerational links created during childhood history, it must not be confused with these fraternal links: its existence is independent of fraternal links. In the work presented in this book, Jaitin shows that the incestuous phantasy is a component of the fraternal complex, but she reminds us that all human beings are permeated by the phantasy of fraternal incest, which is a universal phantasy over and beyond the reality of the fraternal link. The fraternal link refers us to another level: it puts the relationships between the different complexes of brothers and sisters into the foreground.

We can certainly note that the couple is the privileged laboratory where we can study these functionings for various reasons. First and foremost, the lower the number of persons interacting in regard to the family the easier it is to observe. Moreover, it is generally the couple who can explain much more easily both the interlocking of the reciprocal projective identifications and the newly formed link which the partners create. This allows us therefore to highlight the interpersonal defences involving the use of the other, the transportation of mental suffering to one's partner, and the implementation of states of the Self in relation to the needs of that particular link. This viewpoint becomes particularly important above all in couples with serious pathologies or with primitive levels of functioning where representational difficulties open up the possibility for acted-out communications.

In order to ensure that the couple conducts itself in a syntonic way according to the reciprocal needs that the link requires, psychoanalysis of the couple attempts to explore the gap which can occur between the projective identification as a phantasy and the other's answer in reality. The link between the partners, even if triggered by the meeting of unconscious motivations, is nevertheless a new element, produced at the origin of the encounter, although independent of them it is capable of conditioning them. In such situations, where it is impossible to recognise the alterity of the other as an independent person endowed with his or her own differentiated mental functioning, it may be easier to observe in the couple setting the various defensive methods with which such misrecognition is brought about.

Particular pathologies are useful for this purpose: the *folies à deux* or perversions are the extreme points which allow us to study such functioning and require an intervention to the defensive organisation shared by the partners. This organisation would not always be possible to recognise in an individual psychoanalysis, leaving intact, therefore, in such cases, the area of the personality involved in the link with the partner.

At present, in the prospects opened up by various authors, it seems that they all agree upon sustaining the importance of integrating two points of view: first, the phenomenon of the internal world, and second, that which we observe in the interpersonal world. This is especially important when working with couples where the other is the object of one's projection, but where the other also cannot be reduced to one's own "representation more or less coloured by the imaginary" (Berenstein, 2001).

The concept of context

We cannot fully gauge the consequence of the contributions to this volume if we neglect the value of context.

For some years now a debate has been going on as to whether or how to evaluate the context in which the members of the analytic couple are immersed with their reciprocal relationships and interactions.

For couples and families this is a particularly important topic given that these group organisms bring with them their group functioning, their links, their internal atmosphere, and the contexts which will be discussed during the session with the psychoanalyst.

In any case, to talk about context also means taking a precise position and that is to say choosing to overcome a vision, which conceives of the mind as isolated from its reference context, and we have to make our observations as analysts comparative.

For example, to give meaning to the words we hear or the actions we see, it is not sufficient to analyse the components of the content or the syntax of what is communicated to us. Instead, it is necessary to take account of both the relationship with the situational context and with that of the linguistic context. This is particularly true for whoever wishes to work in these settings, because in families, experiences occur even prior to being told or communicated and are characterised by gestures, movements, acts, as happens right from the beginning of a child's life, where the reciprocal experiences of the mother, father, or the child are communicated through the body and acting-out, and through certain atmospheres, such as during the care of the child.

Cleaning your teeth in a public square does not have the same meaning as cleaning your teeth in your own bathroom. It is difficult to contemplate arriving at certain levels of generalisation that are distinct from the specific situation in which the communication comes about. For example, when Bloomfield (quoted by Giacometti) speaks about a child whose time has come to go to bed, and the child says, "I'm hungry", the mother understands that this remark does not really mean

"I'm hungry" but rather "I don't want to go to bed, I want to stay up with the adults and take part in what's going on", and consequently she takes the appropriate action (1933).

The situational and relational context in this case allows us to interpret the meaning, recognising in the message its communication value (Giacometti, 1997).

Therefore, analysis in these settings is also an analysis of the context which the family brings with it and which becomes relevant in the here-and-now of the relationship with the analyst. Thus new links are created and a new context is co-created: the therapeutic context. This co-creation includes the analyst who contributes in creating this new context.

It is our opinion that the more the family or the couple has undifferentiated and primitive functioning, the more they express themselves through the context they create, and this is important on a diagnostic and therapeutic level, especially as prior to taking a verbalised intervention in these situations it is better to operate a kind of "management" which includes, in our opinion, the transformation of the contextual aspects.

Various patients, adults, children, psychotics, neurotics, individual groups, or families challenge us and often, without noticing it, we use different models. Perhaps we should also observe how exactly (and here we refer to Bollas), the co-created communicative context evokes the most pertinent model through which we can conceive the patient (Bollas, 1987).

Relativising diagnosis

One of the most important consequences of this perspective, in the end, is the change of view in the evaluation of the pathology. Whereas on the level of those psychoanalyses which observe the individual and his or her internal world, we assess its psychic structure as Freud taught us to do: thus we assess the internal conflicts, the pressure of instinctual agencies, the strength of the ego, the functioning of the preconscious, or even attacks on the breast, etc.; according to the orientations followed, in these settings our assessment changes radically. Suffering found within the matrimonial link can also be considered a pathology of that link, and the patient is the "spokesperson" of a pain which does not belong only to one partner.

We can affirm, for example, that the growth and transformation of an individual may allow that partner to separate from a malfunctioning matrimonial link, but also the contrary, in other words, that the separation from that link can lead to the transformation of that person and the rapid disappearance of his or her suffering. This is frequently observed in couple and family psychoanalysis, the potentiality of which in the assessment and cure of mental suffering has not yet been sufficiently highlighted and developed. This can be considered a promise as the complexity of these issues at times can be frightening, but at other times fascinating, on account of the new territory it allows us to explore.

Note

1. Nathan Ackerman (1908–1971), originally from Russia, worked in New York where he founded the Family Mental Health Clinic. After his death this was renamed the Ackerman Institute and is one of the most important centres for family therapy.

   In his essay, "Family Psychotherapy and Psychoanalysis: The Implications of Difference" (1962) he illustrated and diffused a new therapeutic approach, a third kind of technique which continued to be based on intrapsychic work while integrating it with family group therapy. Ackerman considered the unconscious family processes to be fundamental, drawing attention, in clinical work, to the defences and resistance to the therapeutic process.

   He was the first to express the concept of the "scapegoat" with which he shows that the pathology of one family member can be made to emerge in a functional way that relates to all the family processes.

   Murray Bowen (1913–1990), with an initial psychoanalytic training, worked at the National Institute for Mental Health in Washington, mainly dealing with schizophrenic patients and the whole families of psychotic patients. He studied in particular the functioning of families with a psychotic member, observing the scarce differentiation among family members which constituted an "undifferentiated family ego mass" (1974); he also began to observe how this type of pathology is often connected with the functioning of the previous generations and coined the aphorism that it requires three generations to create a psychotic.

   Ivan Boszormenyi-Nagy (1920–2007), Hungarian by birth, directed the Eastern Pennsylvania Psychiatric Institute, which later became the Family Institute of Philadelphia, one of the major centres for family therapy at that time. He also maintained a substantially psychoanalytic approach in his studies on schizophrenia in which he dealt with loyalty among generations and how it influences family coalitions and alliances (Zuk & Boszormenyi-Nagy, 1969).

Boszormeny-Nagy's studies placed particular attention on relationships of dependency and autonomy and on the relationship between the multipersonal system and the individual one.

Theodore Lidz (1910–2001), who worked at Yale University, is famous for his numerous works on the causes of schizophrenia and on psychotherapy with schizophrenic patients. For many years he studied a group of families with psychotic members as patients on a continuous basis and carried out a great deal of research on the interpersonal origins of schizophrenia.

In the book, *Schizophrenia and the Family* (1965) written together with Fleck and Cornelison, he brings to light the concept of "marital schism" or that of "oblique marriage", the situation in which unrecognised discord leads to distorted communications and to conditions of *folie a deux* extended to the family.

James Framo (1922–2001), founding member and second president of the American Family Therapy Academy, developed an approach linked to the theory of object relations for intergenerational and family therapy. One of Framo's most important articles which contains his best theoretical thought was "Symptoms from a Family Transactional Viewpoint" (1970) in which he described the development of his theory based on Fairbairn's study of object relations applied to family therapy. This relates the internal object world to the transactional exchanges between people who are linked intimately.

References

Ackerman, N. W. (1962). Family psychotherapy and psychoanalysis: the implications of difference. *Family Process, 1(1)*: 30–43.

Anzieu, D. (1997). *Le Moi Peau*. Paris: Dunod.

Anzieu, D., Doron, J., Anzieu, A., Houzel, D., Guillaumin, J., Missenard, A., Lecourt, É., Enriquez, E., & Nathan, T. (1996). *Les Enveloppes Psychiques*. Paris: Dunod.

Balint, E. (1963). On being empty of oneself. *International Journal of Psychoanalysis, 44*: 470–480.

Benghozi, P. (2005). *Maillage, Dé-maillage et Remaillage des Liens des Contenants Généalogique* (Meshing, De-meshing/Un-meshing, and Re-meshing the links of genealogical containers), March 2005 at the Delegates EFPP Meeting Stockholm.

Berenstein, I. (2001). The link and the other. *International Journal of Psychoanalysis, 82*: 141–149.

Bion, W. R. (1992). *Cogitations*. London: Karnac.

Bloomfield, L. (1933). *Language*. New York: Henry Holt.

Bollas, C. (1987). *The Shadow of the Object*. London: Free Association.

Bolognini, S. (2005). *La famiglia dell'analista*. In: A. M. Nicolò & G. Trapanese (Eds), *Quale psicoanalisi per la famiglia?* Milan, Italy: Angeli.

Bolognini, S. (2008). *Passaggi segreti: teoria e tecnica della relazione interpsichica*. Turin, Italy: Bollati Boringhieri.

Bowen, M. (1974). *Toward the Differentiation of Self in One's Family of Origin*. New York: Jason Aronson.

Bowlby, J. (1949). The study and reduction of group tensions in the family. *Human Relations, 2*(2): 123–128.

Box, S., Copley, B., Magagna, J., & Moustaky, E. (1981). *Psychotherapy with Families*. London: Routledge & Kegan Paul.

Dicks, H. V. (1967). *Marital Tensions*. London: Routledge & Kegan Paul.

Framo, J. L. (1970). Symptoms from a family transactional viewpoint. *International Psychiatry Clinics, 7*(4): 125–127.

Freud, S. (1905e). Fragment of an analysis of a case of hysteria. *S. E., 7*. London: Hogarth.

Freud, S. (1909b). Analysis of a phobia in a five-year-old boy. *S. E., 10*. London: Hogarth.

Freud, S. (1910c). *Leonardo da Vinci and a Memory of his Childhood. S. E., 11*. London: Hogarth.

Freud, S. (1916–17). *Introductory Lectures on Psycho-Analysis*. Part III, general theory of the neuroses. Lecture XXVIII, analytic therapy. *S. E., 16*. London: Hogarth.

Freud, S. (1921c). *Group Psychology and the Analysis of the Ego. S. E., 18*. London: Hogarth.

Freud, A. (1927). *The Psychoanalytic Treatment of Children*. London: Hogarth, 1959.

Giacometti, K. (1997). Contesto. *Interazioni, 2*(10): 165–170.

Giannakoulas, A. (1992). La membrana diadica. *Interazioni, 0*: 129–132.

Jaitin, R. (2006). *Clinique de l'Inceste Fraternel*. Paris: Dunod.

Kaës, R. (1976). *L'Appareil Psychique Groupal. Constructions du Groupe*. Paris: Dunod.

Kaës, R. (1994). A propos du groupe interne, du groupe, du sujet, du lien et du porte-voix dans l'œuvre de Pichon Rivière. *Revue de Psychothérapie Psychanalytique de Groupe, 23*: 181–200.

Kernberg, O. F. (1991). Aggression and love in the relationship of the couple. *Journal of the American Psychoanalytic Association, 39*(1): 45–70.

Kernberg, O. F. (1998). *Love Relations: Normality and Pathology*. New Haven, CT: Yale University Press.

Laforgue, R. (1936). IX Conférence des Psychanalystes de Langue Française, Nyon 10–11 avril, La nevrose familiale. *Revue Française de Psychanalyse, 9(3)*. Tables 1926–2006. Paris: PUF, 2006.

Laing, R. D. (1960). *The Divided Self*. London: Tavistock.

Laing, R. D. (1961). *The Self and Others*. London: Tavistock.

Laing, R. D. (1967). *The Politics of Experience and the Bird of Paradise*. London: Penguin.

Laing, R. D. (1971). *The Politics of the Family and Other Essays*. London: Tavistock.

Lidz, T., Fleck, S., & Cornelison, A. R. (1965). *Schizophrenia and the Family*. Madison, CT: International Universities Press.

Lucarelli, D., & Tavazza, G. (2005). Configurations familiales d'hier et aujourd'hui: dénouer et renouer les liens en psychothérapie psychanalytique du couple. *Le divan familial, 14*: 13–26.

Lucarelli, D., & Tavazza, G. (2007). Quand le "processus de subjectivation" rencontre l'échec: la complexité du travail de transmission psychique dans les familles à fonctionnement psychotique. *International Review of Psychoanalysis of Couple and Family* (www.iacfp.net), *1*: 125–141.

Nicolò, A. M. (1988). La famiglia come matrice del pensiero. *Terapia Familiare, 28*: 5–16.

Nicolò, A. M. (1990). Soigner à l'intérieur de l'autre: Notes sur la dynamique entre l'individu et la famille. *Cahiers critique de thérapie familiale et de pratique de réseaux, 12*: 29–51.

Nicolò, A. M. (2006). Folie à deux as a model for transpersonal disorders. In: J. S. Scharff & D. E. Scharff (Eds.), *New Paradigms for Treating Relationships* (pp. 77–85). Lanham, MD: Jason Aronson.

Nicolò, A. M., & Borgia, F. (1995). Tra intrapsichico e interpersonale. La *folie à deux*: come ipotesi-modello di un funzionamento interpersonale. *Interazioni, 5*: 40–51.

Pichon Rivière, E. (1985). *Teoria del Vinculo*. Buenos Aires, Argentina: Nueva Visiòn.

Racamier, P. C. (1992). *Le génie des origines*. Paris: Payot.

Ruffiot, A., Eiguer, A., Litovsky de Eiguer, D., Gear, M. C., Liendo, E. C., Perrot, J., & Morel, B. A. (1981). *La Thérapie Familiale Psychanalytique*. Paris: Dunod.

Ruszczynsky, S. (1993). *Psychotherapy with Couples: Theory and Practice at the Tavistock Institute of Marital Studies*. London: Karnac.

Ruszczynsky, S., & Fisher, J. (Eds.) (1995). *Intrusiveness and Intimacy in the Couple*. London: Karnac.

Scharff, D. E., & Scharff, J. S. (1991). *Object Relations Couple Therapy*. Northvale, NJ: Jason Aronson.

Searles, H. F. (1959). The effort to drive the other person crazy—an element in the aetiology and psychotherapy of schizophrenia. *British Journal of Medical Psychology, 32:* 1–18.

Tisseron, S. (1996). *Secrets de Famille*. Paris: Ramsay.

Zuk, G. H., & Boszormenyi-Nagy, I. (1969). *Family Therapy and Disturbed Families*. Palo Alto, CA: Science and Behavior Books.

PART I

COUPLES AND FAMILIES TODAY

CHAPTER ONE

The psychical reality of linking*

René Kaës

In this study, I propose to develop some aspects of the concept of linking by focusing on the psychical reality which is proper to it. This approach differentiates the psychoanalytical conception of linking from all other ways of conceptualising it, psychosocial, sociological, and anthropological. But it also distinguishes it from what the practice of individual treatment teaches us about the unconscious psychical reality of the subject.

The subject that usually receives the care and attention of psychoanalysts is a "singular" subject. They treat it and think of it "one at a time" or, as we also say, "individually". Within the "individual" treatment setting, what interests us is the unconscious psychical reality of the subject: how its inner world and inner conflicts are organised, how its history is played out in its transformations and impasses, and the process of its subjectivisation.

Analysands as well as their own thought-work have taught psychoanalysts about the structure and functioning of this inner world. But in order to put together this knowledge *about* the unconscious using what

*This chapter is a reworking of two articles previously published: "Pour inscrire la question du lien dans la psychanalyse" (2005) and "La réalité psychique du lien" (2009).

is known *by* the unconscious, they have had to isolate the space of inner psychical reality from its social and intersubjective "surroundings". By suspending the inner world's extrapsychical and metapsychical factors, the rigorous artifice of the psychoanalytical method as applied to individual treatment has enabled the effects of the unconscious to become knowable in themselves, and has made the treatment effective in acting on them as such.

The concept of psychical reality and its applications

The unconscious, or more specifically, the unconscious psychical reality is the founding hypothesis of psychoanalysis. I would sum up this proposition in the following way: psychical reality is first defined by its own substance, that is, unconscious psychical material, which cannot be reduced or opposed to any other order of reality. The precedence given to unconscious desires is specific to psychical reality: "When one is in the presence of unconscious desires brought to their ultimate and most genuine expression, one must admit that *psychical reality* is a particular form of existence which must not be confused with material reality" (Freud, 1900a, p. 625). So the substance of psychical reality is that of unconscious formations, processes, and instances. Dreams, unconscious fantasies, drives, symptoms, and similar formations that have a compromise structure—the symptom, for example, and the whole series of conflicts between desire and defence, pleasure and displeasure—are effects of psychical reality. This reality stands in opposition to material or external reality, but must deal with it.

By methodologically partitioning the object of their theory and using a method that is fitted to the aims of psychoanalysis when applied to the singular subject, "couch-oriented" psychoanalysts push to the margins of the psychoanalytical situation something that "remains to be known". However, the contours and area of this remainder can be sketched out through speculation. This is what Freud and a number of his contemporaries did long ago, in works of so-called "applied psychoanalysis": *Totem and Taboo* (1912–13), and *Group Psychology and the Analysis of the Ego* (1921c) bear witness to this effort, as do the works of Abraham (1909), Ferenczi (1918), and Reik (1957).

It is striking that, at the very heart of his works that were most devoted to intrapsychical formations, Freud had the genius to open the way towards another dimension of unconscious psychical reality: some psychical formations are common to several subjects, may be shared, or are shared, with other subjects. Freud introduces this notion with the concepts of identification, fantasy community, the dependence of ego drives on the maternal ego, and shared ideals. Even though Freud did not conceptualise this *transversal* dimension of psychical reality, the perspective he opened up resulted in the representation that in different ways intrapsychical reality is formed from—or in interrelation with— formations and processes belonging to the psychical reality of other subjects. The same would be true of the theory of the ego, the super-ego, and identifications in the Second Topic, in the theory of psychical transmission between and through generations and the hypothesis of a "group psyche".

A second seminal act of modern psychoanalysis occurred when new psychoanalytical processes started to be established with novel arrangements of the setting bringing several subjects together with one or more psychoanalysts: group treatments, psychoanalytic therapies for families or couples, and work on early parent-baby relations. Neither Freud nor his contemporaries used such arrangements in their psychoanalytical practice. Once processes and formations of psychical reality having a specific character appeared in these settings, it was necessary to think of them as objects proper to the field of psychoanalysis.

But what concepts should be used for this? Should we consider only the effects of links and groups within the space of each subject, without dealing with their unconscious psychical reality, or should we think of this reality as being composed only of the intrapsychical formations (object relations and identifications) of their subjects? Or should it be admitted that psychical reality within links is made up of formations and processes which are proper to them and which give them a specific substance? The first two points of view focus on the space of the singular subject.[1] But if we retain the last hypothesis, what theory and metapsychology should we bring to bear on it? This question overlaps with another, more radical one: how do the relations between knowledge of the unconscious and the settings which provide access to it work?[2]

In this exploration of the substance of psychical reality in spaces other than that of the inner world, I have adopted as a central concept the definition of psychoanalysis that Freud gave at a time when psychoanalytical practice was exclusively the practice of individual treatment. He wrote: "Psychoanalysis is: a *method of investigation* of psychical troubles that would otherwise be barely accessible; *a method of treatment* of psychical troubles founded upon this investigation; and a way of conceptualizing psychical life which has been acquired by these means and which gradually forms a *new scientific discipline"* (1924f, p. 235, emphasis in original). This definition, with all its methodological, clinical and epistemological implications, should be kept in mind whenever an extension of the field of the unconscious psychical reality occurs.

Concerning intersubjectivity

The notion that there is a common reality shared by more than one subject is a contribution to the psychoanalytical theory of intersubjectivity. Though there is no theory of intersubjectivity in Freud and the concept itself is not found in his work, we can discern its premises there. But it is only *after Freud* that the psychoanalytical concept of intersubjectivity was formed, borrowing it from phenomenological philosophy and discourse linguistics and benefiting from some Lacanian propositions. I would emphasise, however, that it was mainly new forms of psychoanalytical treatment settings that played a decisive role. These arrangements of the treatment setting related the unconscious (desires, fantasies, dreams, defence mechanisms …) of several subjects to each other, thus creating the methodological conditions for revealing intersubjective determinations of repression and unrepressed forms of the unconscious.

On these grounds, I consider intersubjectivity to mean not the interactions observable in behaviours between subjects assembled within a given setting, but essentially the process of formation and the mode of existence of subjects of the unconscious in their relations with other subjects of the unconscious. I include in this concept formations of the unconscious that result specifically from these relations, and especially the unconscious alliances, for they are the principal formations of the psychical reality proper to linking and to intersubjectivity.[3]

Proposition for a psychoanalytical theory of linking

My proposition for a psychoanalytical conception of intersubjective linking entails a certain number of hypotheses that I would like to clarify by describing the overall framework of my research.

The three pillars of the psyche

The basic postulate of my research is this: the human psyche is upheld by three principal pillars: infantile sexuality, the spoken word, and intersubjective links. These fundamental pillars are in close relation with one another: the newborn's long period of dependence, due to its premature state at birth, is the geometrical locus of this; it affects the child's sexuality, linking, and access to speech and language.

Speech and language come to the *infans* (who does not speak) marked by the repression of his infantile sexuality and the intersubjective conditions in which his earliest environment—the mother—brings them to him, passing on to him her own unconscious material and her own repression: these conditions are both subjective (the maternal psyche) and intersubjective (the *encounter* between her psyche and that of the *infans*). As a correlative to this, intersubjective linking is inscribed in sexuality and in speech and makes its mark on these. Sexuality, speech, and linking work together in a distinct and fundamental way in the formation of the unconscious of the subject and the construction of his I. But within the same movement, these three pillars work together in the formation of the unconscious psychical reality of intersubjective linking.

Three psychical spaces

I have devoted a large part of my research to describing, trying to understand and make intelligible the complex relations which are specific to, distinguish, oppose, and connect three psychical spaces: that of the singular subject, that of intersubjective links, and that of complex wholes, such as groups, families, and institutions.

I refer to these three spaces as spaces of psychical reality, meaning that the unconscious is at work there. But unconscious content and processes are different in each of these three spaces. I conceive of these spaces, or at the very least of parts of each one, as common, shared, and *different*. To admit that a part of psychical reality can be shared and is shared with other subjects, that it is common to them, is not to reject the differences between the spaces belonging to each subject and between these spaces and what they have in common. I would insist here on the heterogeneity of both these spaces and of what passes between them.

The corollary of this conception is that the spaces are interconnected, that psychical reality circulates among them, that the effects of the unconscious are passed on from one to another. The three spaces that I have taken into consideration are interfering spaces (not interlinking spaces, as I first envisioned them) because of the porosity of their envelopes and the permeability of their boundaries.[4] Their radical impenetrability and opposition constitute only one possible case scenario for their relations with each other. They correspond then to more or less serious troubles in each of them.

In the late 1960s I constructed a model for depicting the functioning of these three spaces in groups conducted according to the psychoanalytical method (Kaës, 1976). I cannot, within the scope of this study, fully explain the substance of this model, nor can I describe each of its spaces, as I must focus solely on the space of linking.

The psychical space of linking

Because we are born in a state of prematurity, we are swaddled in caregiving, which is physical and, necessarily, psychical: the clothes that wrap us, the arms that hold us, the skin that warms us and sticks to our own, odours and images, showers of words and speech. In short, there is a whole weave of linking, connecting us within ourselves and with others, forming skeins and knots that we are ceaselessly tying and unraveling throughout our lives. It is a "text" certainly, but a text made of flesh, of emotions and thoughts, of signs and meaning, a palimpsest whose meaning we can often decipher without difficulty and sometimes with joy.

We are necessarily connected by all sorts of links before we can partially unlink ourselves and enter into other linkings, before we can become autonomous enough to accept ourselves as I. We cannot live without linking, although certain links, when they are excessive or faulty, will shackle us or prevent us from living, from loving, from knowing, from playing. So we learn to distinguish between links and fetters, between the kind of linking that brings life, love, and growth, and the kind that brings hatred, destruction, and death. All these links are interwoven with each other like life and death and, complicating matters, they are interwoven with the others' linkings, which are intermixed in the same way. This is why, as Aragon (1956) said, "Our lovely youth is used up in separating what's yours from what's mine." Some of us can spend our lives doing this, until we give up. It is true that we are reluctant to imagine confronting what links us within ourselves and with others, that we often confuse the two spaces, and that we would prefer to ignore what links the linkings.

Linking: an attempt at a definition

In order to give a first outline of our object, I propose to start with the following notion: I have called "linking" the unconscious psychical reality constructed by the encounter between two or more subjects (Kaës, 1994). Defining linking by its *content* emphasises the unconscious psychical reality, an object to which psychoanalysis devotes itself. Its specificity lies in an approach in terms of *process*: linking is the more or less stable movement of investments, representations, and actions which bring together two or more subjects in order to fulfil some of their desires.

I will complete my definition with a qualification of its *logical dimension*. Distinct from the logic which organises the intrapsychical space of the singular subject, the logic of linking is that of reciprocal implications, and mutual inclusions and exclusions.

These definitions enable us to describe different types of linking: parental, filial, fraternal, intergenerational, transgenerational, romantic, hateful, etc. The criteria for the definitions come from the psychopathology of linking, although it can be useful to describe linking in narcissistic or objectal terms, or in terms of neurotic, perverse, or psychotic organisation.

Psychical work required in linking

The place we hold in linking requires us to accomplish a certain psychical work. I use the notion of requirement of psychical work in the sense that Freud gave it when he constructed the first theory of drives: the drive requires the psyche to perform psychical work because of its relation with biology. Another type of psychical work is required by the encounter with the other, or more than one other, in order for the psyches or parts of psyches to come together, so that they can experience each other in their differences and switch each other on, and so that they can regulate each other.

I have distinguished four principal kinds of psychical work required by intersubjective linking or conjunctions of subjectivity. The first is the obligation for the subject to invest the linking and other people with his narcissistic and object libido in order to receive in return the investments necessary to be recognised as a subject belonging to the linking. This work requirement is shaped according to the model of the narcisoiotic contract described by Piera Castoriadis-Aulagnier (1975).

The second requirement is that certain formations belonging to the subject be made latent, repressed, renounced, or abandoned. Freud indicated in 1921 that the ego must abandon a part of its identifications and its personal ideals in favour of common ideals, in exchange for benefits expected from the group or the leader. Any linking implies constraints on belief, representation, perceptive norms, adherence to common ideals, and feelings. Being in intersubjectivity does not imply merely that certain psychical functions are inhibited or reduced while others are electively mobilised and amplified.

The clinical treatment of groups and families led me to the idea that there is a psychical "non-work" requirement: this requirement manifests itself in abandonment of thought, erasures of ego boundaries or of parts of psychical reality that define and differentiate each subject. This happens in the case of cults and ideological groups. As is shown by clinical analysis of subjects and families caught up in cults[5] or controlled by ideology, the processes of self-alienation meet the pathological demands of the link.

The third requirement involves the necessity of activating the operations of repression, disavowal, or rejection, so that the conjunctions of subjectivity may be formed and the links maintained. These operations involve not only the metadefensive supports that group members may find in them, as E. Jaques (1955) has shown. They also involve any linking configuration that ensures and maintains the metadefensive arrangements needed for its self-preservation and the achievement of its goals. They are therefore necessary to both the linking and the personal interests that subjects find in their contract with it. Such is the status and function of unconscious defensive alliances as we will describe them.

The fourth requirement is connected with the fundamental prohibitions that relate to the work of civilisation and symbolisation. Here again, the unconscious structuring alliances are the basis for intersubjective and transgenerational linking.

These four requirements work together to create a common and shared psychical space. From the perspective of the subject on which they are imposed, these requirements are structuring and conflicting. The central conflictedness lies between the necessity of being one's own end in oneself and the necessity of being with others, a subject of and for linking. In exchange for carrying out this psychical work, the participants in a link or the members of a group take or receive benefits and obligations. An economical balance, positive or negative, is established between what is gained and what is lost as they try to meet these requirements.

In a way, we cannot choose to exempt ourselves from these requirements: we must submit to them in order to enter into a linking and exist as a subject. But we must also free ourselves from it, unlink ourselves whenever these requirements and the alliances which give rise to them cause us to become alienated from ourselves or to alienate others, usually unwittingly. I think that this is the perspective from which we can define the practical field of psychoanalytical work in group situations.

Unconscious alliances are the foundation of the psychical reality of linking and of the subject

To create linking, from the onset of psychical life until later when it is time to form a couple, live in a family, group, or community with other human beings, we elect to invest in each other, identify with each other unconsciously through shared objects and traits. These processes and the experiences which characterise them come with our first intersubjective experiences. They are the substance of the psychical reality of linking. But they are not the only ones: other specific formations make up the psychical reality of linking: elementary contracts and unconscious alliances, both structuring and defensive, prohibitions, and the references provided by identifications, common ideals, shared imaginary, and symbolic representations.

Unconscious alliances are the foundation for the psychical reality of linking and of the subject.[6] They carry out several functions: I will briefly indicate the functions of metapsychical framing and guarantor further on. Unconscious alliances have different statuses in relation to time: some are synchronic (they are formed between contemporaries) and others are diachronic, crossing and binding different generations.

Four kinds of unconscious alliance

In the course of my research I have come to distinguish four kinds of unconscious alliance. Basic or primary unconscious alliances are the first principles of all links. They figure among the earliest processes and formations of socialisation. The first alliances are the *alliances of primal attunement* between mother and baby; these are reciprocal and asymmetrical, and imply an environment in which mother and child are involved in different ways. On these alliances, alliances of shared pleasure and creative illusion are formed, along with alliances of love and hate.

An essential part of the primal structuring alliances is the narcissistic contract (Castoriadis-Aulagnier, 1975). Freud called our attention to this vital formation: in *On Narcissism: An Introduction* (1914c), he presented a subject confronted with the "necessity of being one's own end in oneself" and, at the same time, the other necessity imposed on him by the fact of being a link (*ein Glied*) in a "chain" (*einer Kette*). The subject is divided between the requirements of these two necessities. Freud also says that His Majesty the Baby is invested with dreams of his parents' unfulfilled desires, and that his own narcissism leans on (*er lehnt sich an*) this narcissistic investment by his progenitors. Castoriadis-Aulagnier develops this observation, suggesting that these investments are the object of a contract whose particular characteristic is that it links together, through narcissistic economy, the human whole that makes up the primary emotional fabric of every new subject (each newborn) and of the group (in its larger sense) in which the newborn is and will create its place.

This is a structuring alliance. This narcissistic contract provides a foundation, defines a filial contract: it serves the self-preserving investments of the group and the subject of the group by requiring the latter to recognise the group as something that he comes from and that he must continue.

These are original narcissistic contracts. We are dealing with *secondary narcissistic contracts* when the subject establishes extrafamilial linking, within the various formal and informal social groups he belongs to: school, peer groups, clubs, etc. Secondary narcissistic contracts are affiliate contracts which redistribute the investments of the original narcissistic contract and enter into conflict with it, especially during adolescence.

A second set of structuring alliances, which we will call secondary, since they presuppose the existence of most of the preceding ones, is made up of contracts and pacts based on the law and fundamental prohibitions. Freud demonstrated the necessity of these in 1912–1913, when he described the pact between the Brothers and the symbolic alliance with the Father. In *Civilization and Its Discontents* (1930a), he affirmed the necessity of a mutual renunciation of direct attainment of the drives' destructive goals in order to establish a "community of rights" guaranteeing stable and reliable linking.

These secondary structuring alliances provide the intersubjective framework or basis of subjectivity; they are the conditions and the guarantors of common and shared psychical space in which "the I can come to be". They guarantee the prohibitions against incest and murder, and thus ensure the transmission of psychical life between generations. They require of all subjects and the groups which link them psychical work resulting in the protection of the mutual narcissistic investments necessary for life, the shaping of meaning, the activity of symbolisation and interpretation, but also the capacity for loving, playing, thinking, and working.

Defensive alliances constitute a second set of alliances: these are meta-defences which mobilise different types of defensive operations: repression and denial, but also disavowal, rejection, encystment. The denial pact (Kaës, 1989, 2009a) is one of these alliances. It designates an unconscious agreement imposed and concluded mutually on the basis of these defensive operations so that linking can be organised and maintained in keeping with the complementary interests of each subject in the linking framework. Investments in the linking must remain unconscious between those linked by it. The denial pact is necessary for the formation of linking; it exists in every linking, but in this one it creates zones of silence and, in some cases, of the unsignifiable, the non-transformable, pockets of intoxication which ensure that the linked subjects remain strangers to their own and others' commitment to the linking. When a crisis occurs in a couple, a family, or a group, it is the return of compromise formations which, by means of this pact, were made so that linking could take shape, at the cost of repression and disavowal.

The slide of these defensive alliances into pathology makes up the third category of alliances, the alienating effects of which are manifested in communal disavowal, perverse contracts, and narcissistic pacts. Their prevalence attests to the regression of contractual forms of linking founded upon structuring alliances towards power relationships favouring subjects, couples, and groups who can violently and arbitrarily define the place of everyone and what each must do to stay in the linking.

A fourth category is that of *offensive* alliances: they seal a group's agreement to conduct an attack, carry out a plan, or hold supremacy. Some alliances combine several characteristics. For example, a football team must have two unconscious alliances if it is to win: a group narcissistic illusion, plus an offensive alliance.

Unconscious alliances: their functions as framework and as metapsychical guarantor

Linking and unconscious alliances are psychical formations belonging to the space of the psychical reality of linking and configurations of linking in a *meta*position with relation to other psychical formations. I suggest that these formations be called metapsychical, insofar as they frame and inform the psychical life of every subject. They stay *in the background* of the individual psyche.

The concept of metapsychical framework is not only relevant to the analysis of linking. It is also useful for thinking about the organisation and functioning of the subject's psyche considered in its singularity. In the treatment, we use it "negatively" when we suspend the space of intersubjective and social linkings, which is that of unconscious alliances. Of these we know only their effects in the inner space and in the realm of transference and countertransference.

But we can truly perceive the relevance and interest of this concept when we change the psychoanalytical setting, opting for a psychical work setting which brings together several subjects—a family, a couple, a group, inter- and transsubjective linkings. The unconscious alliances and all the metapsychical formations remain in the background, but their effects and the processes of their formation, here and now, move to the forefront. Then it is clearly apparent that the metapsychical framework has an organising, containing, enveloping, and managing effect on the intrapsychical processes and formations, or, on the contrary, a de-structuring and alienating effect on inner space, the space of the linking and the space of the whole group which contains them.

Certain metapsychical formations act as the guarantor of psychical life. Structuring unconscious alliances are an example of this: the contract of mutual renunciation of direct attainment of the drives' destructive goals ensures the protection of the community to which the subject belongs; thus it guarantees the security necessary to the formation of the subconscious, of thought-work, and the maintenance of linking. Likewise the narcissistic contract guarantees the subject a place in the whole.

Unconscious alliances comprise the central part of these frameworks and guarantees; moreover, they include in themselves processes that produce the present unconscious in linking and they make up its neurotic and psychotic knots; for all these reasons, they are the major parts of the formation of psychical reality proper to the configuration of a linking. What is more, they take part in the formation of the individual unconscious: what is repressed by one is guaranteed by the repression of the other. Linking occurs, joining subjects in co-repression or co-disavowal. Consequently, some drive organisations, some protective shields, instances of the superego and the ideals, and some ego functions are framed and informed by these metapsychical frameworks.

The metapsychical formations that frame psychical formations and act as the framework and guarantor of psychical life, are supported by other frameworks and guarantors that are social and metasocial, cultural and metacultural. Therefore they cannot be dealt with solely in their psychical reality. But there is a relationship between these two sorts of *meta*formations.

Towards a metapsychology of the third type

The epistemological issue

As I stated in the introduction to this study, the problematics of linking and unconscious alliances open up an epistemological question which is central to psychoanalysis: it concerns the area of psychical reality and its boundaries and has to do with intersubjective conditions of the formation of the unconscious and of the subject of the unconscious.

The answers to this question affect the extension of psychoanalytic practice, the definition of its theoretical objects, and, consequently, the constructions it develops to account for the unconscious and its effects on the organisation of the psychical life of a subject considered in the singularity of its structure and history.

There is much talk nowadays of a third topic; this was an important theme at the 66th Congress of Romance Language Psychoanalysts (2006). There was a debate about the terms of the relations between the configuration of a subject's inner world and the relations the subject had with earliest others, the parents, the family. The focus was on the individual, not on the psychical reality of intersubjective linking. This was to be expected, given that the standard practice is that of the individual treatment. But when one is working with a pluri-subjective setting, where the developing psychical space is that of a specific, communal, and shared psychical reality, this third topic also includes the *intersubjective* space between the subjects. What one should take into consideration is the substance of this space *between subjects*, and not just the effect of intersubjective space upon inner space. This is what in my early research I provided a model of, under the name "group psychical apparatus".

The third topic, as I presented it in *Linking, Alliances and Shared Spaces* (2007a), is organised around an interconnection between the psychical reality of linking and the reality of the singular subject.[7] I think that, in this way, it is possible—it has become necessary—to give an account of the way the subject takes shape within intersubjectivity as the subject of the unconscious, and of the part that the subject plays in the formation of intersubjectivity.

The task of a third "topic" is to describe and give an intelligible account of the complex relations which connect, distinguish, and, in certain cases, oppose intrapsychical space, both the space of the singular subject and plural spaces organised by specific psychical processes. This is the epistemological issue.

The clinical issue

There is also a clinical issue: we should think, in and with psychoanalysis, about the psychical substance of intersubjective linking. This issue is part of psychoanalysis' twofold goal: to know unconscious psychical reality in the linking and to achieve a transformation when linking is a source of pathological suffering. These are the two principal objectives of the psychoanalysis of linking.

The new clinical practice, which was first established with treatment settings used in psychoanalytical work with couples, parents, and groups, drew psychoanalysts' attention to early and present afflictions and pathologies of linking, to disorders in the formation of the psychical apparatus's inner and outer borders: disorders of "borderline states", disorders or lack of psychical envelopes and of boundary-marking signifiers, failures or absence of the formation of systems for binding— or unbinding—pathology affecting the transmission of psychical life between generations, deficiency in the processes of transformation. These are pathologies of narcissism, of origins, and of primary symbolism. But they are also pathologies of linking and its intersubjective and transsubjective correlations. Clinical practice teaches us that, because of linking, a particular psychopathology affects couples, families, groups, and institutions.

The question of linking enters into the field of psychoanalysis because contemporary substance and forms of linking are undergoing change. The clinical treatment of linking emerges when the metapsychical guarantors can no longer perform their functions as framework or background: catastrophic breaks or transformations—or non-transformations—threaten the whole insofar as this is the space of the links that have formed, unbeknown to the subjects who make up this space. Here we could speak of a suffering of the group as a whole and of a pathology of linking. They are so related that the pathology of one is necessary to the pathology of the other.

Taking into consideration the consequences of defects in metapsychical frameworks and guarantors, we can see how much interest psychoanalytical work on linking configurations holds for the treatment of these forms of psychical suffering and for psychopathologies that are "barely accessible otherwise". We understand better that deregulation, weaknesses, and defects of these metapsychical frames and guarantors directly affect the structuring and development of everyone's psychical life. I have come to think that three important kinds of weakness are at work.

A first group involves weaknesses and defects in the intersubjective arrangements of protective shields and of repression in the structuring and buttressing of drive life.

Instead of the formation of stable and reliable internal objects, formations develop which are split and non-subjectivated, not conducive to the processes of symbolisation and sublimation. Intense narcissistic pain is at the bottom of antisocial conducts that arise in these conditions. These weaknesses affect the conditions of the formation of the unconscious and subconscious.

A second set is composed of failings in the processes of forming basic structuring intersubjective *identifications* and *alliances*. These alliances consist in pacts that establish major prohibitions (against murdering a fellow human being, against cannibalism, against incest), in what Freud described as the communal renunciation of direct attainment of the drives' destructive aims, and within the narcissistic contract.

A third set are the failings in the processes of *transformation* and *mediation*. What is most fragile in all living organisations are intermediary formations and connecting processes. In psychical life, these are the conditions that enable the work of symbolisation and the formation of otherness, as well as of the ability to love, work, play, and dream. These formations and processes are in their greatest danger when there is a crisis affecting the metapsychical guarantors. The biggest consequence of their failure is that the subconscious is cast out of the circuit, the capacity for thought is crushed by the collapse of verbal representations. The work of the subconscious is always closely associated with the activity of symbolisation and the construction of meaning in intersubjective linking.

By offering these thoughts on the psychical reality of linking, I have merely helped to open up a vast and complex site for further work.

Notes

1. This point of view was adopted by the 66th Congrès des psychanalystes de langue française in Lisbon in 2006. Linking is considered in light of its effects within intrapsychical space.
2. This epistemological question is at the centre of the crisis of the objects and "boundaries" of psychoanalysis. The theme of the Congress of the International Psychoanalytical Association, New Orleans, 2004, was: "Psychoanalysis and its Frontiers". At this congress I presented an exploration of the consequences of group psychoanalytical intervention on psychoanalytical theory and practice. This presentation was developed and published in an English translation (2007a).
3. The reader can find an outline of this problematic in my 1998 study on "L'intersubjectivité: un fondement de la vie psychique. Repères dans la

pensée de Piera Aulagnier". See also R. Kaës, 2002, 2007a, and 2009a, 2009b, 2009c.

4. J. Puget suggested another conception of the three psychical spaces (1989). Her proposition is in part similar to mine, in that it distinguishes three psychical spaces; but it differs from mine in several respects. Basing her conception on the research of the philosopher R. Esposito, Puget considers these three spaces to be superimposed upon and impenetrable to each other; they are antagonistic in form and function.

5. Concerning cult-induced alienation, compare the work of Diet, 2007; concerning ideological control and the tyrannical linking, Kaës, 1980 and 2003.

6. Concerning unconscious alliances, compare Kaës, 1989, 2007a, 2007b, and especially 2009a.

7. For a more precise development of the notion of the third topic, the reader can refer to my 2008 study, "A hypothesis for a third topic regarding intersubjectivity and the subject in a common, shared psychic space", in *Funzione Gamma*, 21. http://www.funzionegamma.edu.

References

Abraham, K. (1909). Dreams and myths: A study in race psychology. In: D. Bryan & A. Strachey (Eds.), *Selected Papers of Karl Abraham, M.D.* London: Hogarth and the Institute of Psycho-Analysis, 1949.

Aragon, L. (1956). L'étrangère. In: *Le roman inachevé*. Paris: Gallimard.

Castoriadis-Aulagnier, P. (1975). *The Violence of Interpretation. From Pictogram to Statement*. Hove, UK: Brunner-Routledge, 2001.

Diet, E. (2007). L'aliénation sectaire, syndrome ethnique dans la mondialisation libérale. *Le Coq-héron, 190*: 103–117.

Ferenczi, S. (1918). A mese lélektanáról. *Bausteine zur Psychoanalyse, 4*. Vienna: Internationaler Psychoanalytischer Verlag.

Freud, S. (1900a). *The Interpretation of Dreams. S. E., 4–5*: ix–627. London: Hogarth.

Freud, S. (1912–1913). *Totem and Taboo. S. E., 13*: vii–162. London: Hogarth.

Freud, S. (1914c). On narcissism: An introduction. *S. E., 14*: 67–102. London: Hogarth.

Freud, S. (1921c). *Group Psychology and the Analysis of the Ego. S. E., 18*: 65–144. London: Hogarth.

Freud, S. (1924f). A short account of psycho-analysis. *S. E., 19*: 189–210. London: Hogarth.

Freud, S. (1930a). *Civilization and Its Discontents. S. E., 21*: 57–146. London: Hogarth.

Jaques, E. (1955). Social system as a defence against persecutory and depressive anxiety. In: M. Klein, P. Heimann, & R. E. Money-Kyrle (Eds.), *New Directions in Psychoanalysis* (pp. 478–498). London: Tavistock.

Kaës, R. (1976). *L'appareil psychique groupal: constructions du groupe* (3rd edition). Paris: Dunod, 2010.

Kaës, R. (1980). *L'idéologie. Étude psychanalytique.* Paris: Dunod.

Kaës, R. (1989). Le pacte dénégatif dans les ensembles intersubjectifs. In: A. Missenard (Ed.), *Le négatif. Figures et modalités* (pp. 101–136). Paris: Dunod.

Kaës, R. (1993). *Le Groupe et le Sujet du Groupe. Éléments pour une Théorie Psychanalytique du Groupe.* Paris: Dunod.

Kaës, R. (1994). *La Parole et le Lien. Les Processus Associatifs dans les Groupes.* Paris: Dunod.

Kaës, R. (1996). Souffrance et psychopathologie des liens institués. Une introduction. In: R. Kaës (Ed.), *Souffrance et Psychopathologie des Liens Institutionnels* (pp. 1–47). Paris: Dunod.

Kaës, R. (1998). L'intersubjectivité: un fondement de la vie psychique. Repères dans la pensée de PieraAulagnier. *Topique, 64*: 45–73.

Kaës, R. (2002). *La Polyphonie du Rêve.* Paris: Dunod.

Kaës, R. (2003). Tyrannie de l'idée, de l'idéal et de l'idole. La position idéologique. In: A. Ciccone (Ed.), *Psychanalyse du lien tyrannique* (pp. 69–104). Paris: Dunod.

Kaës, R. (2005). Pour inscrire la question du lien dans la psychanalyse. *Le divan familial, 15*: 73–94.

Kaës, R. (2007a). *Linking, Alliances and Shared Spaces. Groups and the Psychoanalyst.* London: International Psychoanalysis Library.

Kaës, R. (2007b). The question of the unconscious in common and shared psychic spaces. In: J. Carlos Calich & H. Hinz (Eds.), *The Unconscious: Further Reflections* (pp. 93–119). London: International Psychoanalytical Association.

Kaës, R. (2008). A hypothesis for a third topic regarding intersubjectivity and the subject in a common, shared psychic space. *Funzione Gamma, 21.* http://www.funzionegamma.edu.

Kaës, R. (2009a). *Les alliances inconscientes.* Paris: Dunod.

Kaës, R. (2009b). Lógicas collectivas del inconsciente e intersubjectividad. Trazado de una problemática. *Psicoanálisis de las configuraciones vinculares, 32*(2): 81–115.

Kaës, R. (2009c). La réalité psychique du lien. *Le divan familial, 22*: 109–125.

Puget, J. (1989). Groupe analytique et formation. *Revue de psychothérapie psychanalytique de groupe, 13*: 137–153.

Reik, T. (1957). *Myth and Guilt: The Crime and Punishment of Mankind.* New York: Braziller.

CHAPTER TWO

Intersubjective links in the family: the function of identification

Alberto Eiguer

The word *identification* is polysemous; it is not quite the same thing to identify with your neighbour's enthusiasm when his favourite football team scores a goal as to identify with your parent's ethics and principles. And yet, in both cases, we are talking about identification.

Its psychoanalytical applications are marked by these complications while at the same time giving us a feeling of seriousness and solemnity because on identification depends what the child will do with the inheritance left to him by his ancestors. It marks his future. I have chosen to address the challenge of this complexity, by describing identification and intersubjectivity together.

The theory and practice of *intersubjectivity* demonstrates that the psyches of two or more subjects function in reciprocity, in such a way that they influence each other on several levels: affects, desires, and the other's fate. The subjects are affected by each other's psychic state, feel affected by and responsible for the other. A variant of identification plays an active part in these interplays; echoing with someone else, we put ourselves in their shoes, and identify with what they have lived; to understand someone we experience that person within ourselves. But at the same time, both subjects involved think of themselves

21

as being different people and as being in a dissimilar emotional state. Otherwise they would not be able to understand each other.

The concept of identification is broader than that of empathy, even though the two have points in common. In a child, identification is not just an immediate process which comes from nowhere; it implies a long development of impregnation of the ego, modifying it in order to include within himself aspects of the other's functioning or personality. We cannot identify with someone else, without being shaken by the link with this person, by what he expresses or shows. The child will identify with the parent in the same way the parent does with the child. This means that the parent unconsciously offers a personal model, but he or she will come out of this process profoundly touched and even changed. We can say that this is *introjective identification*.

In any case, projective identification precedes introjective identification. To be able to introject an aspect of the other and include it in one's own personality, the subject will bond with the other, consider him close, include him in his world, and eventually think that he shares similar principles, giving him a certain amount of his own elements. Without this preliminary, it will be difficult to introject and then identify with any of his personal characteristics. The primary mechanism in question is the projective identification of communication. Orality is omnipresent in this dialectic process. To identify with another is like eating him; the cannibalistic instinct is active. The digestion of this substance which is another even shows itself to be like the biological model which metaphorically emphasises that to introject implies the integration of the other in oneself, assimilating him into one's own substance. It is moreover well known that people who partake in ritual cannibalism think that by doing so they will assume the qualities of the person being eaten.

However, orality does not mean just "guzzling down" another. It must be done with pleasure. And really, introjective (mutative) identification is the only one that can provide satisfaction. This digestive metaphor lets us understand that this process requires time and comfortable conditions. If the introjections of another are done hurriedly, voraciously, which is what happens when ambivalence and envy are strongly felt towards the other, when we want to assimilate and behave like the other to calm this envy, then these conditions do not allow identification; this is what we call *incorporation*. In this case, the introject becomes a foreign object inside oneself, where it wreaks havoc. When merely imitating the other, because imitation is what can take place, the subject does not really have the other under his skin when talking and acting like him; it all seems false. I will come back to this.

Three syntactic forms

I think it might be useful to remind ourselves that the word identification has three forms depending on the grammatical variation of the verb *to identify: attributive, reflexive, and passive.*

Attributive: "to identify somebody or something". The movement is centrifugal. "I identify you with myself", "I identify you with somebody who is not me but is part of me". The subject is active; the other is passive. I would call it "identification of the first kind".

Reflexive: "to identify with". The movement here is centripetal. "I identify with you". It is "identification of the second kind".

Passive: "to identify you with a third party". This form refers to three people, one active one -the other; one passive one, the second one—the subject who is the object of this identification; and a third one who is not present, but fairly central after all, as in the examples: "My friend identifies me with his godfather", "My friend treats me or loves me as if I was his godfather", "I am identified with by another who sees a third party in me", or more lightly, "… who thinks I look like his godfather". This is "identification of the third kind".

Multiple combinations are possible, for example, "You treat me like your child [or like a dog]". The subject *attributes* to another a behaviour which refers back to the link with the subject. He attributes intentions to another (*projective identification*).

A large majority of analysts confine themselves to talking about reflexive identification ("I identify with …"). Others mention the breadth and importance of projective identification, which refers back to the attributive form. But those who are sensitive to the fact that one can be identified with by a third party, and among them those who underline the effect of the transgenerational are rare. Regularly, three or more generations and three persons are involved. In this case, the parent identifies his child with one of his internal objects, and this confirms the representation of the grandparent or the ancestor. In this kind of identification, what often comes into play are the affects and the link towards this ancestral object that the parent tries to find in the child who, for his part, remains passive. To start with, it is just moving the grandparent's representation onto the child ("I think you're like …"). And later, through induction and suggestion, the parent tries his best to make the child just like the third person.

What comes out of this is the power of this designation, which causes a reflexive identification from the child, who ends up "being like" the grandparent or the ancestor. Still, this is not a conscious process.

In the identification with the ancestral object, a new form of identification has been reported, an *alienating* one. The child identifies with the shameful and secret object of the parent that has been involved in an unelaborated trauma. This opens up a new chapter: the identification with a negative, with something unimaginable that creates voids and splits and vacuoles in the ego and that is responsible for thought disorders (unthinkables). In this case, another gives the subject an order, forbidding him to want to know more than what is being said or to call into question that which the subject hears. "That's the way it is!"

Threats in general are very persuasive, but so is seduction, as for example used by conmen. For example, the conman has to use all the means at his disposal to inspire confidence in an old woman who will trust him with all her savings so that he can invest her money in highly profitable operations, so he says. She imagines herself becoming rich, identifies with somebody who makes easy money, and thus integrates into herself a way of thinking which is after all not natural to her. She carries out an alienating identification without imagining the underlying violence of deception and theft. This happens without pressure, softly, softly. A temporary conclusion would be that the three forms of identification, attributive, reflexive, and passive move together in the same process, the attributive form often setting in motion the passive form, then the reflexive.

Designating before identifying

In the family, there is a first movement: the child must give to the parent his place as a parent before investing in him and afterwards identifying with him. Here we have identification of the third kind. For this, the mother has to designate the father as being the one who created the child with her. "This is your father." Before this, the father appears to the child as being undifferentiated from the others. This designation gives him a face, an identity. But this is not enough for the father to be recognised in his function. He will have to prove himself. Sooner or later, the child will need to know that the father is serene, solid, protecting, and able to renounce his own counter-oedipal or infanticidal desires, in other words, that he has himself introjected the law.

In practice, we can clearly observe that a father who has been disavowed by the mother in his function (or vice versa) can be rejected by his children when they are young or adolescent; this situation makes taking him as a role model rather difficult. Family violence can take roots in this situation, and contempt and humiliation, too, as well as lack of respect, although I think that if respect towards the parent is something the child has to be literally reminded of, chaos has already arrived. Links of filiations are then already in jeopardy. Because respect is something that is shown, it cannot be asked for or proclaimed. A variation on violence deserves our attention: hyper-excitation in the links and their impregnation with sensuality.

Sometimes, if the child thinks he is being rejected or if his feelings are too timid, the child will look for the parent and his love. It is not rare that a parent, fearing the loss of influence on the child, tries to re-conquer him by offering a large dose of eroticism, bordering sometimes on incest or even falling into it.

At other times, the opposite happens. Seeing the parent depreciated, the child might feel close to him and show consideration and respect, which in turn helps with identifying with the parent. The child can feel pain for the state the parent is in, can fathom that in the parent there are qualities of tolerance, patience, and strong will and the child wishes to repair "the injustice done" by offering his love. Worrying about somebody would be enough to try to help; identification is not necessarily indispensable, it might even be embarrassing. By being tempted to identify with the devalued parent, he can eroticise his marginalisation and his downfall. The result will be a predisposition towards masochism. Did we skid from empathy to a feeling of fascination? From building oneself up to self-deprecation? Did the desire for justice leave the door open to letting oneself be an instrument?

We understand that parental idealisation reinforces reflexive identification, even though it is the love-hate ambivalence which is decisive, or more particularly, the hostility towards the object, and this in turn triggers guilt. But this struggle would be immensely more violent if the constructive narcissism had not already suffused the filial link and formed the belonging to the family. The offspring cannot want to sleep with a parent who is like himself. He refuses to kill another being that is so similar. It would be like sleeping with yourself and killing yourself. The child has established strong alliances with his parents: he received an ideal; he cannot risk to thoughtlessly give up the mission that was bequeathed to him, which flatters him and calls upon his sense of responsibility. The alliances enslave him and deprive him of all movement. There is only one thing left for him … fantasies.

But thinking of intersubjectivity, it underlines the fact that this positioning is determined and overdetermined by the intersubjectivity between the parents and, on a broader scale, between the various members of the family. Their fantasies, defences, collective affects, and narratives strongly participate in this positioning. The mother identifies the father (names him) as the child's progenitor, and the father in turn names the mother. Their act of welcoming makes the child able to modify, metabolise, and transform the initial data it receives. Before this background of mutual acknowledgement, each parent then identifies the other as being capable of being a proper role model for the child. The parents use attributive identification, especially to hand down a legacy which they can use as a model to help with the child's progress. At the same time, they identify with the way the child sees them in order to better adapt their attributive identification, and modify it as they proceed. Thus they will find the most fitting answers for their child's needs and desires.

Just as acknowledgement is mutual, identification is always reciprocal. We understand that what we usually call the expectation of functioning regarding a subject is reinforced by the identifications put upon it, which correspond to unconscious object representations. A father, as well as a child or a mother must have concrete answers to the other's expectancies and conform to them. To ignore this means to leave oneself vulnerable and to be totally paralysed by disappointment when reality does not correspond to expectations, which are too often idealised.

This multiplex way of looking at identification, classifying it into three types that are, respectively, attributive, reflexive, and passive, and at the same time taking into account the fantastic interplays involved, is rather complicated, but it also is more pertinent and especially more likely to help with the analysis of family as well as individual cases. Increasingly we see family violence or the disavowal of a parent in clinics and this means we should try to assess and define functioning using other methods than those used in the past.

Thinking, intersubjectivity, and link

Until now we have looked at intersubjectivity by focusing on inter-functioning in the process of naming and identifying. We should mention that intersubjectivity concerns a vast area of work to the point that, for several analysts it represents the mode of psychic functioning par excellence. Our approach applies to the link of filiation and other family links. Its specificity is at stake here: talking of father, mother, and child goes beyond the concept of subject, however: for those studying links it is clear that as soon as we put two subjects at the same level, without favouring the one or the other, we do this already with a different mindset than that of solipsist psychology. Provocatively, Lebovici (1983) said that "It is not the mother who makes the child, but the child who makes the mother": the baby's attachment and its need for care stimulate or create the maternal instinct in the mother. The concept of instinct seems outdated. Intersubjectivity between mother and baby activates the internal model operating in the mother, which is itself inspired by her own link to her own mother and other maternal figures.

This way of thinking distinguishes itself from some other approaches. The introduction of the concept of subject in psychoanalysis reinforces the solipsist perspective, even more so given that it can with complete legitimacy conjure up an idealistic position in which it is the subject that will form the object and reality, even create them. But this concept finds an irrefutable answer: to have a subject, you need other subjects that have formed it. It is true that once the process of identification reaches maturity, the subject gains sufficient autonomy to break away from the original subjects who formed it, but it remains profoundly and forever touched by the links to them. The subject is from then on orientated towards them because in his psyche he has formed operating internal models (OIM), according to Bowlby (1969), or the distinct representations needed to be, talk and interact with another (Stern, 1985).

Unlike the concept of subject, subjectivity is totally compatible with our concept of intersubjectivity. Mostly unconscious, subjectivity is the movement which allows us to find ourselves in a dialogue with ourselves and with the objects of our internal group and those objects to be in dialogue with each other. This gives us satisfaction, a pleasure which is certainly autoerotic. It may happen that we imagine we are somebody else, a somebody who would talk with us, help us to understand what is going on, criticising us if necessary, suggesting ways forward or solutions if we happen to be stuck.

Reflexivity and the reversal of self and other here have a predominant function, as highlighted by Freud in his masterpiece *Instincts and Their Vicissitudes* (1915c). It is in reality a double reversal: from the other to oneself and from sadism to masochism, for example. When one can feel deep down inside the suffering that one's sadism caused in the other, then subjectivity appears inside that one.

Winnicott (1960, 1971) laid great stress on the idea of getting in touch with our true and authentic self to the extent of imagining putting it into perspective as a major objective of the healing process, after the false self has been deconstructed, its mirages are unmasked, and the faithful submission to our encroaching parents is highlighted. It is a unique and even foundational experience for the patient. Getting in touch with his intimate self estranges him temporarily from the outside world, yet without ignoring it altogether. Thus it contributes to setting up a differentiation between oneself and the other. Moreover, Winnicott (1960) thinks that each person is singular and unique and that recognising one's real self is a conquest of oneself by oneself. This self finds its origin in each person's sensory-motory behaviour and a good enough mother can just make it appear whereas a mother who is not skilled that way cannot make it happen.

In another work, Winnicott (1971) delighted us with this programmatic phrase: *being alone in the presence of another*.

This is one of the reasons why we would rather talk of intersubjective links: the link is in fact more than the interaction between two subjects intertwining their projective communication identifications. It is a structure which frames the movement of their inter-functioning, the analytical third (Ogden, 1994).

Inter-fantasy tightens the link; it unfurls as soon as the two subjects are in relation. The link is shot through with myths like the family myth and also with a series of representations that put to work each psychic agency: the family self, common ideals, and the superego which in itself has a relation with the social fabric, habits, beliefs, and family traditions. When talking about the third analytical element of the link, I would like to use the following metaphor: the *cupola of the link*. It is a mobile set of unconscious productions that also arise when participating in any of our relations, whether they be with friends or professionals.

Let us take the example of the company where we work. It is easy to see that each of our unconscious representations shows itself there: we see our boss as if he was our father, our secretary like our mother, our employee like our child, and the founder of the company, whose portrait above the boss's desk looks upon us in a paternalistic and severe manner, just like our ancestor. The concept of intersubjective links calls upon the idea of groups; in the case of the company, the unconscious alliances, loyalties, and ideals make our integration possible. Those who understand this really well are those managers who ask the employee to get really involved in the company, so that it becomes a second skin. The employees are asked to show their loyalty and devotion sometimes at the expense of their personal needs; they have to take on the objectives of productivity and achieving good results set by the management as if the company had become their family. This is one of the reasons why the story of a company is told to those beginning a job there and why it is told and retold again and again. The famous storytelling proves very useful in this case.

The belonging to a group, including to the family, may be formed through a weaving of stories, which, like the legends, refer to … family myths. It is also for this reason that every time there is a family gathering, the same story is told: it reminds us of our belonging, and our place in the family tree, and also of our often heavy duties and obligations towards the others.

From the link to reflexive identification

We are now in a position to suggest new thoughts on the family and reflexive identification that transforms the self when it takes on somebody else's traits, often just one trait, in fact. To identify with our father and/or mother, we need to believe and feel that they are our parents. Also, the analytical third, which represents the group and intersubjective family whole, creates the right conditions for identification to take place. Why? Family spirit, its values, its sense of honour, and its ethics, they all reassure us and inspire enough respect for us to believe in the family, and to feel together and proud of it to the point that it seems enriching for us to identify with this spirit and these values, as well as with our parents who uphold these values and are their guarantors.

I must say that this way of interpreting reflexive and introjective identification is not encountered frequently. Usually, we talk about identification with somebody and we highlight the fact that it follows a conflict of rivalry and hatred of the child against the parent. I am not just alluding to predisposition towards others, but also to a group, and then to another notion: direct identification without conflict, virtually through contact with another.

It is time now to introduce a new distinction: identification *through continuity and contiguity* (Eiguer, 2002). The first one sets itself up through skin to skin *osmosis* of the primary link: the child identifies with his mother's devotion, her ability to receive, the strength of her alpha elaborations, and thus founds the basis of his own subjectivity. The functions of feelings and senses, sight and hearing first of all, are undeniable. Freud has called this the *primary identification* (1921c). Melanie Klein (Klein, Isaacs, Heimann, & Riviere, 1952) insisted on the kindness of the mother, which contributes to the maturation of the child's internal object. "Continuity" puts the focus on managing and supporting.

A deep anxiety is felt by the mother, even a fear of disappearing through a cataclysmic collapse. The ability to welcome another in an active passivity depends on the success of this identification through continuity: identification with the mother's femininity, in league with the link's fundamental femininity and with the girl's femininity. The girl will develop and amplify it. The boy will use it in his own way.

It is tempting to connect this with Freud's considerations (1912d), when he highlighted that sucking represents the model for any sensuality, for boys as well as for girls: it consists of a penetration in an acme of pleasure.

The second form, identification through contiguity, highlights the proximity between the link's subjects, but they stay differentiated. Without this, the negative or positive Oedipus cannot take place. And it is the oedipal rivalry which finds its conclusion in identification. However, two remarks are of vital importance:

1. There can be malevolent affects, rejection, contempt, and underhand actions like betrayal, to be justified between the subjects in the grip of their rivalry. The parent might be tempted to put an end to these unpleasant games and force the child's identification through frustration, constraints, and threats, or by staying cold, and calling upon collective interests. But this is often a factor which complicates things, because identification is a natural process and cannot be dictated. In this way, forced by fear, the child could imitate at a

pinch, but still not make a trait of the parental personality become his own. Generally, these excesses turn against those who initiate them. Indeed, the process of identification through contiguity is unpleasant, even traumatic for the child. Another way, just as uncertain, to voluntarily calm the rivalry, is to use an excess of compliments and material gratifications. In general, it seems that the best way to ensure a failure of identification is to do too much: offering too much, explaining too much. This might be the cause of the current strong increase in the number of megalomaniac children who have very little feelings for others.

2. Finally, it is important to mention *seduction* by a parent, a seduction which must be seen as different from toadying. A kind of *attraction* towards oneself seems to occur so as to create the conditions for a successful identification. For the parent, it is interesting to find a balance between his distinct positions, to be able to renounce his drives and identifications with his own parents and ancestors: they will inspire the child. He may be happy to rejoin his lineage and to fit in with it. The parent feels protected by the analytical third and by the link's cupola which contains and regulates the oedipal passions. All in all, the cupola is something the parent should really mention and bring into play.

Mobilisation of identification in psychoanalytic family therapy

The following illustration will enable us to highlight the evolution of identifications in a child having reached puberty whose parents admitted that they did not have a proper role model to offer. It does not often happen that parents can put that into words in this way. Both parents have serious neurological illnesses, but their twelve-year-old child, René, is in good health. The father, Nestor, has a benign tumour of the brain which is spreading; it was diagnosed about ten years ago, and partially operated upon; he has been suffering from leg paresis for a long time. Recently, after the umpteenth stroke, he has been showing difficulties in his speech and thought processes. The mother, Lydie, also has a benign tumour situated in the cerebellum which cannot be operated upon. She has had a metal plate inserted on her cervical vertebrae to immobilise them, because the tumour leaned on her blood vessels, causing her to faint and making the paralysis in one of her arms worse. Her illness was diagnosed during pregnancy. We can imagine the anxiety and suffering she went through. Helped by the fact that these tumours have a slow evolution rate, the family was able to adapt to each of these crises with amazing versatility. The father changed his job to set up a shop with his wife, but he can go there only when his health allows it. In spite of his illness, he managed to make the shop work well and to give his family a life that is financially comfortable.

They asked for family therapy because the parents are worried about their child's future. He is a very good boy who appears to be a hyper-responsible small adult, never complaining, criticising, or asking for anything for himself, at least during the first few months of the treatment. His parents are aware that they impose a hard life upon him and that they offer an image not terribly conducive to his development.

René does not play much during the session, despite the toys on offer. He only draws. The drawings are very complex and do not leave any empty space on the paper. He draws countryside scenes, with fields clearly divided and hedged in, each one cultivated differently. There are few paths on the drawing. On one side, at the end of a narrow path, we can glimpse a very small house with a chimney from which escapes a very thin line of smoke.

Usually we, that is, both therapists (Danielle Quemenaire and myself), try to interpret the drawings according to the group's inter-subjective psychology, even if they are created by just one member of the family. In this case, we think that the boy represented himself as he sees himself and at the same time as his family sees him: like this house in the middle of the countryside, he seems to live an isolated life in his complex family which is marked by the tight weft of the links between its members, rendering it impenetrable. The family too is in the middle of a faraway, not easily accessible world. The fields are ploughed without leaving any free space: work *compensates* for the failings of the parental models.

Transgenerational links

The links between the members of this family are very affectionate; all three help each other in a very caring way. They appear to have completely integrated the idea of duty, but there are no gaps in the order they have established which would allow them to think their situation over.

Several times, Lydie seems cheerful and chatty but not overexcited; she then exudes an optimism and vitality which mean that the harsh situation is temporarily forgotten. This is not conflicting. The only thing which might make her fall would be being away, even briefly, from René or Nestor, she says. We often talk about other relatives. They are never criticised. On the contrary, they say idealising words to express their sense of solidarity. Periodically, Lydie's mother stays with them, to deal with everyday housework. Relieved of those duties, Lydie then focuses on the shop. She seems to come back to life, all perked up, and so do father and son. And then parents and son become the children of the house, carefree and spoilt. This may be the expected regressive state, which gives us some clues to understanding the origin of this family whose promising future has been broken. I wonder what having a child meant for this couple. Because having a child implies renouncing one's own childhood for good. Could they handle it?

Nestor, himself so ill, is more worried by his own father's (aged ninety) heart problems than by his own difficulties. He adds that he could not cope with his father's death. These many signs of family loyalty appear unusual these days; at the same time, the links remain superficial, responding to traditional values of respect for your elders and fairly well encrypted codes of conduct, dominated by gifts and the obligation to give because of gratitude, even for simple visits and invitations. The space for autonomous thinking is limited. However, this organisation does not cause any doubts, and no trouble is ever mentioned by the parents; however, when entering adolescence the young boy will start demanding a bit more independence.

When the parents talk about the way they see the intergenerational relationships in their own families, they seem to say to René that he has to be devoted to them. They strengthen the cupola of the family link. In reality, René's withdrawal proves to be a reaction necessary to diminish the weight of the constraints laid upon him.

All in all, the functioning in partitioned cells has enabled the family to gain energy to deal with the worsening health problems of the parents and to help each other in difficult moments. Their strategy of adaptation is totally remarkable. Even though Nestor and Lydie used to be intellectuals, they turned into shopkeepers when the neurological symptoms appeared, and managed to cope with a fairly demanding activity in spite of their partial incapability. They were certainly borne by the history of their lineage in which several ancestors had been able to deal with difficulties very well and had changed countries or jobs, with a state of mind where family comes first and nostalgia for the past gets glossed over.

The recovery of this family was helped by finding many memories linked to the *initial crisis* again during the sessions. These memories took the shape of tales which grew as time went by through adding elements which had been forgotten, through the emotional impact during the retelling, through a different interpretation, even a contradictory one. In the version mentioned during the first meeting, the medical aspects were prominent, set out in a slightly mechanical manner and with a great deal of anxiety. We, the therapists, at the time felt a staggering emotion as well as an enormous sadness. But through the telling of the next version, a few months later, we learnt that Lydie was the first one to fall ill, during pregnancy. As the tumour on her cerebellum was progressively paralysing her, she wondered how she would cope with the birth and care for a newborn. Nestor's reaction, however, was a relief for her; he took care of the child in a very practical way. We could feel how this actually contributed to their closeness. When his tumour was diagnosed, two years later, the father had to stop looking after the child. The shock was even greater. With both parents ill, what would happen to the child? Well, he grew up and has become the one we now know, the one who regularly gives up his own desires.

But where did the mother find the strength to help her husband? On reaching the depths of despair, the family members calmed their guilt at leaving the grandparents, and it also made them want to go forward. The legend of the father as an "exceptional clinical case" has been driving their spirit for a long while. Lydie then talked several times about when she had turned against the medical profession, claiming negligence on their part because she thought they were responsible for the persistence of some of his symptoms and that the doctors had let her husband down because they thought he did not have a chance, unlike her who still believed he did. The account of the past echoes the present. She suspects the doctors today to be still harbouring the same scepticism, while, fantasmatically, we therapists appear as if we shared the family conviction about the father's health improvement. When Lydie tells us this, the father and the son agree. Members of the family and therapists together become followers of the same cult of *believers*. Narratives feed this surge and are fed by it.

The projective movement was strengthening at the very moment that reality was hard to accept: the reality of a body that did not allow itself to be brought under control. The identification model seemed overdetermined because of a reinforced solidarity of illusion as well as split in a fusional context, but then there came a moment when René regressed as well. When he reached the age of fourteen, he was diagnosed with a malformation of the spine (kyphoscoliosis), which forces him to use furniture and walls to help him sit down or stand up. He "grew too much too fast", and this made him fragile. This illness suddenly gives him the appearance of somebody worn out, almost elderly. We made associations with his family life. Now he has his own physical suffering. He is not the only one to be healthy any more. The spine calls to mind standing straight, being able to look far ahead, to feel sure of oneself; it is a symbol of self-esteem.

Even though his symptomatology was basically anatomical, we can wonder if there was not some identification with his handicapped parents: did he feel guilty at being healthy? Guilty at having been born when his mother was diagnosed with her tumour? Guilty at having contributed to the estrangement of his parents from his grandparents?

Mirages

A session which took place three and a half years after the start of therapy, at a time when Nestor could not participate due to being yet again in hospital, further clarified the functioning of this family. In contrast to their attitudes during other times when the father was in hospital, mother and son this time express serious fears about his fate. Fear of death is directly mentioned. He has shown many complications after his latest and rather severe stroke.

The mother tells us of a "horrible" dream she has had: the doctors were showing her the body of her husband and gave her a bit of it, the thigh, for her to take home. She puts it in a pan to cook. When it is cooked, she eats a bit of it. When she wakes up, she feels disgusted and distraught.

I interpret it in this way: in spite of the terrible aspects of the dream, to eat a bit of him may represent her wish to keep him near her and inside her.

She says, after a short silence, that my words bring her relief. She is so afraid for him, she is so affected by his suffering! She finds it painful to imagine that he might be dead soon and that his body won't be recognisable. The thought of the decomposition of the body of a being we have loved, touched, and cuddled is horrible; it is oblivion.

She confirms that the dream reflects somewhat her wishes: to make her husband inseparable from her and her son, and ensure he will never ever leave her. This stay in hospital has turned out to be longer than the others, she adds. Then, Lydie explains that she has set up a security camera in the shop linked to the house so that Nestor, once back home, can see what happens in the shop and "be entertained".

René's social life is now the subject of discussion. He is now an adolescent, he is not a loner, but he would rather stay at home, even during the school holidays. He has made friends with those of his own age, children of his parents' friends. According to his mother, they adore him. And actually, a little while before, she organised a party for her son and these young people, boys and girls. They wanted to stay up all night and stayed in René's bedroom. His mother, who stayed up as well, would come and see them from time to time and take the opportunity to film them.

The son does not seem bothered at all by his mother's behaviour. He adds that they watched the film several times together. It's fun.

After this session, my co-therapist tells me about something that has just happened to her. At the very moment the mother was talking about the father, she thought she saw him sitting on the seat in the therapy room. It was like a hallucination, she says, fleeting, of course, but disturbing nevertheless. We discuss it together; we raise the question of "seeing, seeing oneself, and being seen". We had been struck by the importance given to intra-family control to the point of thinking how privacy here seems suspect; freedom, subversive; independence, heartrending. Think about the shop's security camera; the intrusion into the son's bedroom to film the young people having fun.

The son seems to have incorporated the mother's anxiety and modelled his mind to prevent her from feeling she was alone. René's feelings of obligation are nevertheless excessive. He lives as if responsible towards his parents, of course, but he is also ill at ease with the oppression exerted upon him, and which is a gentle terror.

There has been incorporation, but no real identification. This is the cause of the appearance of irrepresentable contents. René's psyche is troubled by motions of unlinked and therefore explosive affects, which may have produced micro-attacks on his body. Is it possible to imagine this might be the cause of his somatisation?

My co-therapist is quite relieved in the end to understand that what she experienced is an echoing identification with the idea of the security camera, and the strength of the family wish to stay together, glued to each other to avoid separation. Thanks to her ability to empathise, she felt within herself these wishes, in a burst of companionship towards mother and son during their time of distress.

A comment. Where a thought process cannot find articulation with the affect of a loss, meaning if it is overwhelmed by the beta elements that invade intersubjectivity, then hallucinations can appear. This calls to mind the process of *foreclosure*: what has disappeared inside, creating a vacuole, reappears outside (Freud, 1912d).

With this knowledge, we can put forward the thought that this fusional set-up marked by a tight grip contributed to the evolution of this family. What would have been a handicap elsewhere contributed to create resilience after the family trauma of the appearance and development of both tumours. This case is not one to be interpreted with the usual criteria, those of the ideal family encouraging independence for all its members. The therapeutic process certainly played a role in this. We were extremely careful to respect their style and we sincerely told them we appreciated the affectionate attitude they have towards one another. They often felt grateful, admitting that our interpretative clarifications helped them. They sometimes said they considered us now as relatives. If René finally was able to identify with a father figure, it was not necessarily just because I was there, but because of the analytical work our therapeutic couple achieved.

Even though the parents are very handicapped, their active function transmits the sense of parenthood: the notion of exchange between the generations here takes a very specific turn (devotion in exchange for being helped with mutual responsibility) and it reinforces the notion of the precession of generations, highlighting the tutelary aspect through the ethical reference to the grandparents: the cupola of the link. Therapy enabled the parental function to develop further. Lydie's control over the adolescent was highlighted during the last session. Anyway, René knows how to negotiate his freedom without too many clashes: the night is for the young, in spite of the camera. *It's being alone in spite of the presence of his mother.*

Our countertransference experiences and autoanalysis for two certainly contributed to this progress, as if in the fact that we should live in our own flesh the anxiety of separation and the impact of their affects had been necessary. Thus we might maybe have understood their message better, which was quite something: "For us, love is stronger than death."

Conclusion

Because of the focus on the worth of intersubjectivity, the concept of identification undergoes known amplifications. Furthermore, it showed itself to be a nodal mechanism of psychic functioning. It is even the cause of its energy and dynamism.

Identification appeared to be like a process which concerns the person in question as well as others, the one or those with whom the person identifies, at first. To reach reflexive identification, the person's subjectivity is a determining factor and his psychic autonomy must be mature enough to recognise himself as being different from others.

All three types of identification are active and each is as necessary as the other. Identification happens in continuity or contiguity with the other, although it is intersubjectivity which creates the conditions for its completion.

References

Bowlby, J. (1969). *Attachment and Loss: Vol. 1: Attachment.* London: Hogarth and the Institute of Psycho-Analysis.

Eiguer, A. (2002). *L'Éveil de la Conscience Féminine.* Paris: Bayard.

Freud, S. (1912d). On the universal tendency to debasement in the sphere of love (contribution to the psychology of love II). *S. E., 11:* 177–190. London: Hogarth.

Freud, S. (1915c). Instincts and their vicissitudes. *S. E., 14:* 109–140. London: Hogarth.

Freud, S. (1921c). *Group Psychology and the Analysis of the Ego. S. E., 18:* 65–144. London: Hogarth.

Klein, M., Isaacs, S., Heimann, P., & Riviere, J. (1952). *Developments in Psychoanalysis.* London: Karnac, 1989.

Lebovici, S. (1983). *L'Enfant, la Mère et son Psychanalyste.* Paris: Le Centurion.

Ogden, T. (1994). The analytic third: working in inter-subjective clinical facts. *International Journal of Psychoanalysis, 75*: 3–19.

Stern, D. N. (1985). *The Interpersonal World of the Infant. A View from Psychoanalysis and Developmental Psychology*. New York: Basic.

Winnicott, D. W. (1960). Ego distortion in terms of true and false self. In: D. W. Winnicott, *The Maturational Process and the Facilitating Environment* (pp. 140–152). London: Hogarth and the Institute of Psycho-Analysis, 1965.

Winnicott, D. W. (1971). *Playing and Reality*. London: Tavistock.

CHAPTER THREE

The mythic narrative neo-container in psychoanalytic family therapy: shame and treason as heritage

Pierre Benghozi

Introduction: little histories and big history

When we look at linking from a psychoanalytical perspective, we are interested in how the containers of the intimate, the private, and the public interface with each other, and how little histories of individuals, couples, and families overlap with big history, that of peoples, communities, and social transformation.

In this chapter, I continue my research into the genealogical transmission of shame and humiliation with the notion of "the inheritance of shame", or more precisely here the "inheritance of treason". I have described the concept of "shame-bearer" (Benghozi, 1994, 1995c, 1996a, 1998, 2010a, 2010b, 2011) as the symptom-carrier who is heir to and the ventriloquist of unconscious family hatred (Benghozi, 2006a, 2007a, 2007b, 2007c) that is passed on from generation to generation and within the generations by transgenerational transmission.

Starting with an account of a sequence of sessions of family therapy and a commentary on these, I will illustrate the work of narrative re-meshing and narrative figuration with the concept of the Narrative Neo-container (Benghozi, 1995a, 2004).

A family's capacity for psychical representation

It is difficult to show the singularity of a therapeutic practice as a singular kind of writing. There are as many therapeutic styles as there are therapists. It is mainly from our patients that we receive echoes of it. In the case of psychoanalytical family therapy, the writing is a group architecture. Often it is when we are doing post-session intertransference work with our co-therapists, and when we are sharing comments with our student interns, that we carry on this work of deconstructing group dream-work. The notion of "deconstruction", borrowed from the philosopher Jacques Derrida, is an attempt to capture both the creativity of therapeutic work as the elaboration of a new writing, and the critical analysis of it. It is "an operation performed on the traditional *structure* or *architecture*" (Derrida, 1998, p. 338, emphasis added).

I envisage the indication of psychoanalytical family therapy in pathologies involving genealogical containers of groups, families, and communities (Benghozi, 1995a, 2010a, 2011). It could provide access to a new familial psychical capacity for figural representation (Robert, 2007) when this has been lacking before. Psychoanalytical family psychotherapy is conceived of as an artistic, creative, emotional, narrative, and aesthetic experience that is renewed at every session in the field of the transference, in rhythm with the ritual of the therapeutic setting.

Illustration of psychoanalytical family therapy

We will begin with the second encounter with the family. The affiliating work of greeting is done as each of us introduces himself. Present at this session are: the mother, little Abdel and—for the first time—his sister Farida, along with the therapist, the co-therapist, and the intern who is being trained in family psychotherapy. Right away there is a discussion of family members who should be there but are not; an attack on the setting appears to be under way. They say that the sixteen-year-old son did not want to come. The mother says she forgot to tell the oldest son about it. "I'd lost the paper with the appointment time, I'm very forgetful, I have problems in that area …."

Transference onto the setting as container:
the attack on the setting

We think about the son's absence from the session, and the family's resistance to change. The mother's "forgetfulness" seems to be a manifestation of leaks in a psychical container that is a "sieve". This notion echoes Didier Anzieu's work in *Crise, Rupture et Dépassement* (Kaës et al., 1979). The attack on the setting is a symptom of what Bion (1959) calls an "attack on linking". It bears witness to a transference onto the setting as container. Through the transference, defects in familial group containment are projected by the family group onto the therapeutic setting (Bleger, 1979).

There is a correspondence between therapeutic setting, psychical apparatus, and familial group container. Individually, the mother's moments of "forgetfulness" may attest to a sieve-like psychical container; they may also indicate that there are holes in the family's group genealogical container, resonating with the attack on the therapeutic setting (Benghozi, 1995a, 1995b).

All of this is proffered, stated, listened to without verbalised interpretation.

The other important absence at this session is that of the husband and father. "*He* can't possibly come," says the mother. "He's no longer part of our household. He left. His life is elsewhere. I have to get that into my head."

In the therapy room several seats stay empty, unoccupied.

The absence of the father in the family is traumatic. But it seems he never found his place in the home as man and as father. He was always outside, though he forbade his wife to go out, except once a month to buy groceries. He often came home drunk. The couple is currently separated and going through a divorce. The atmosphere of emptiness and melancholy depression is palpable.

The presence of the big sister at this session is much appreciated. She has her arm around her mother's shoulders. She reassures her. She finds her mother "more lost and confused than sad". The mother confirms this: "I can't turn the page, I'm lost ... ."

For Farida, "forgetting the past" is not something he mother will be able to do.

What "page" and what "past" are we talking about here? The break-up, followed by her husband's departure, constitutes a loss. What makes her unable to elaborate a work of mourning is that, beyond object-loss, separation creates a narcissistic void in this case. The event of separation is, as we shall see, a breaking of links. In a sort of genealogically delayed action effect, separation breaches the genealogical group container. This jeopardises individual narcissism, as well as familial and genealogical group narcissism.

The breaking of the conjugal link is symptomatic of a break in the container of conjugal privacy. It heightens the vulnerability of the containers interfacing with intimacy and privacy (Anzieu et al., 1993).

Treason: a catastrophic unravelling

The father cheated on the mother. Everyone knew it, except the mother herself. It was an open secret. It is impossible for the mother to accept what her husband did—it is treason! She feels humiliated; she lost face in her eyes, in the eyes of her children and of her family.

For the daughter, there is a fault worse than that treason: he lied to her. He would not admit his misdeed. If he had, she could have forgiven him.

"Treason: it's being cheated on behind your back."

Though humiliated, she still feels guilty. "If he cheated on me it's my own fault!" she says.

Thus remarks about respecting the setting have led to central themes: trauma, mourning, memory, treason, shame, humiliation, incestuousness ...

These questions do not go any further now, but remain in the background. It is as though the essentials had already been there from the first moments of the consultation, stored away for later. But with time the therapeutic process will start to engage in elaborating work using the dimension of transference and countertransference.

Asking for therapy: a problem of links

The stated reason for the consultation is initially the clinging relationship between Abdel and his mother. "Since his birth, we have never been able to be separated. At the beginning, there was no room for him, so he slept between us. Now that I'm alone, separated from my husband, he's still sleeping in my bed. He's too attached to me, and I to him. Neither one of us can do otherwise".

What led them to seek help for this clingy mother–son attachment *now*? Their answer: "He's growing up, he's becoming a boy." Apparently, prepubescent sex drives pose a threat for the family's non-differentiation pact. The other children are growing up and leaving the house. Can the mother stay closed up in the house with her youngest son sharing her bed?

In fact, the problems Abdel and his mother have been having in distancing themselves from each other existed well before the father left the house. Abdel does not occupy the bed left empty by his father's departure: he occupies the place in his mother's bed that the father was never able to occupy in the marital bed. "All the children slept in 'my' room until the age of three ... Maybe that's why he went looking for someone else! I forgot my wifely role. I took refuge in my motherly role. I used the children to avoid sex. I didn't want it. I was more a mother hen than a woman. I neglected my relationship with my husband. My husband was living a separate life. In fact, he always slept in the armchair. He would watch TV sitting on the Moroccan seat in the living room, then fall asleep in the armchair. Nowadays it's my oldest son, when he's at home, who sleeps in the armchair. As for Abdel, I've coddled him too much," says the mother. "I thought only of him." Abdel lowers his eyes. At the last session, he said that he's afraid of having nightmares if he stays alone in his own room. Still, he does have a room of his own, apart from his brothers and sisters.

Family spaciogram and group imaginings
(Benghozi, 1996a, 1996b)

Hearing the description of the closeness of bodies and the confusion of intimate spaces gives my co-therapist and me an impression that is shared by the family: that of a discomfort that is difficult to put into words. In resonance with the countertransference, I ask the family to draw the spaciogram of their house. When I say spaciogram, I mean the set of representations of the group space as it is psychically experienced and inhabited. It is a form of mediation for a psychical work of representation. It leads to a mobilisation of the subconscious as if it were a child's drawing or a dream recounted in the session with the family.

Abdel draws his room and that of his mother. He goes into his own room during the day. At night he goes into his mother's room. Abdel introduces us to his "teddy" as "doudou", and his favourite soft toys: there is a lion, two frogs, a Marsupilami comic character, a rabbit, a bear ...

The therapist says, "So it's like a whole family of doudous, animal doudous?"

Each was a present from either his mother or his father.

The big Marsupilami was a present from his father. It stays in the mother's room. There are also doudous in the brother's room and one in the dining room. For Abdel, the difference between a doudou and a stuffed animal is that his doudous sleep with him at night. But what about *doudous* who sleep alone? How do they manage? "There's only one *doudou* that's real, and that's the cat!" says Abdel. Who does the cat sleep with? Abdel points to his sister's room on the spaciogram. With these narrative associations of the members of the family group, elicited by the spaciogram, we enter into the family's living space. Farida confirms: "The cat occupies my room when I'm not there". Thus the *doudou-cat* also occupies a place left empty by absence.

Spaciogram Abdel

Matrix daydream: *Abdel as a teddy in the bed of the mother. No place for the absent father.*

The *teddy* functions like a "*doudou*" for a child, as a transitional object. The transitional object is in Winnicott's (1971) sense, there and not there, present-absent. In the session it echoes the empty chair that represents the father's absence. When they were younger, Abdel's brothers and sisters had no *doudous*. "We were nearly the same age, so we kept each other company!" Are these the *doudou*-brothers/sisters of the sibling container?

The mother says that she never had any stuffed animal *doudou*. As a child, she never slept alone. The four sisters slept in bunk beds in the same room.

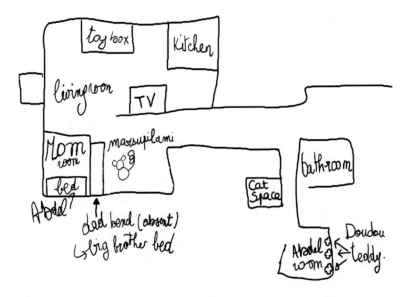

The mother is then asked to draw the spaciogram of her childhood room and house on the paperboard. She is troubled and fearful. Picturing the spaciogram of the house her family lived in when she was little brings on a regression, and a daydream into the world of childhood. She begins by drawing a big rectangle to represent her childhood bedroom … it looks like an undifferentiated whole. She says, "I don't know how to do the sisters' bunk beds."

Her daughter offers to help her. She will show her how to draw a bunk bed. But Abdel says he will do it. Abdel gets actively involved in the spaciogram. He is drawing the sides of the bed in perspective …

"It all comes down to what angle you look at it from," says Farida.

How are the representations that figure *the familial psychical body placed one on top of the other, like the bunk beds?*

In the mother's family, there were in fact twelve children, nine girls and three boys.

The geno-spaciogram is represented on a large sheet of paper. The drawing of the spaciogram is placed parallel to it, next to the family's genogram. The first names of the twelve children take up the whole sheet. But the mother's first name is not among them—she does not give her name. She writes "Me". Then she puts her first name in Arabic. It means "princess". She thus restores herself to the fraternal line, after her older brother and sister. While the mother is finding her way around her sibling relations, Abdel moves closer to his sister. Then he looks at himself in the mirror we have in the therapy room and says, "I was looking at the teeth I've lost. I've lost thirteen teeth." What is he trying to tell us with his lost teeth? What might he be saying about the siblings in the mother's family? Following the same ritual each time, he would wash the thirteen teeth, then place them in a piece of paper which he would in turn place under a pillow. This ritual comes at a cost. The little mouse that takes the teeth puts money under the pillow; but then the mouse puts the teeth in a box, and some of them get lost …

"But", says Farida, "now we have a cat, the cat scares away the mice. The mouse won't come anymore!"

Abdel knows who the "mouse" is that puts the money under his pillow. "It's Mom!" Then he waxes nostalgic: "They are milk teeth, my first teeth, my baby teeth." Abdel is afraid to grow up. Fortunately he has still got four baby teeth left!

Everyone is invited to comment on the geno-spaciogram and make associations about this group object. The mother draws a single branch of her family tree, that of her mother's side, showing her maternal grandparents.

She has "forgotten" to write down her father's parents.

Farida says that she, too, would only show her mother's side of the family.

The paternal line is not shown.

Abdel points out the generational confusion, the fact that the order of the generations has not been respected in his mother's drawing.

Farida remarks that the way her mother draws reflects the way she is inside her head: "She talks the way she thinks; it's jumbled up. That's what comes naturally to her."

The mother confirms this: "I do mix things up a lot in life."

Abdel seems to get his bearings more easily.

Farida thinks that the way the parents and children have been placed in the genogram makes it look "as if the father and mother were the children".

In the genogram made by the mother, father, mother, brothers, and sisters seem to be at the same generational level. The horizontal level of affiliation—collateral relations—prevails over the generation gap of filiation.

"*My father*", says Abdel's mother, "always took care of us. He played with us or else he was in his garden. He was so nice that he had no authority. *My mother* disciplined us all by herself. She's the one who had the authority. My father would never make a decision. She'd argue with him. She would have preferred a real man!"

Group dreaming and neo-imaginings

The therapeutic space becomes a space for group play and imagining. It is a veritable dream-workshop where group daydreams are co-created (Benghozi, 1995b). The loom on which dreams are woven is co-created: "There are twelve brothers and sisters in Mom's childhood room, in bunk beds … Papa is not in the bed … In the bedroom, there is a lion, two frogs, Papa's Marsupilami, a rabbit, a bear … Abdel hides his thirteen teeth under the pillow … Mom-the-mouse places money under the pillow and takes away the thirteen teeth hidden under the pillow by Abdel. Farida is not there. The cat is there. The cat eats the mouse! Teeth get lost … In the mirror, Abdel's mouth is wide open. He still has some baby teeth left! Abdel plays mouth-games with chewing gum. He blows in the bubble which bursts around his mouth ...." Dream fantasies and neo-imaginings in a session of family therapy mean that work of inter-linking is taking place "here-and-now" in the group's subconscious metapsychical space.

Boundaries and interfaces between the territories of containers for the intimate and the private (Benghozi, 1997)

At the age of eight, Abdel still sleeps in the same bed as his mother. He also seems to be a bit of a dreamer, with something about him that is both immature and very serious, "parentified". The clinging behaviour of mother and son cannot be reduced to individual intra-psychical symptoms of Abdel; rather it represents a problematic of the mother–father–child link within a genealogical formation of links and the transmission of the psychical heritage of the parents' birth-families.

The filial link is a dual link which holds together both the father's side of the family and the mother's. It bears witness to the paradoxical nature of the conjugal pact of alliance, which meshes together the gene-alogical containers of the partners' original families. What about male and female filiation? What happens to the construction of masculinity and femininity, and issues of the conjugal alliance pact?

Thus, in a consultation concerning the difficult separation of little Abdel and his mother, we met impasses in connection with the construc-tion of Me/Not-Me, and the construction of sexual identity (in this case, the mother's womanhood). The way the unconscious image of the sin-gular body and the body image of the family group overlap echoes the blurred outlines of the boundaries between the territories of intimacy, and those of conjugal and familial private life (Benghozi, 1999a, 1999b).

The singular little history in the context of the big collective history: a page from the Algerian war which never spoke its name. Being a child of the harki community (Benghozi, 1996a)

It happened in Algeria ... at the time of the events in Algeria!

The descriptions that emerge in relation to the spaciogram give us access to a tale from the family history, the history of a *harki* family, of the war in Algeria, of repatriation, immigration, and exile.

The therapy unfolds like a series of history containers that are nested inside each other like Russian dolls.

The maternal grandfather of Abdel is actually a forest ranger. The mother's family is from Algeria. They came to France after Algeria gained its independence. "I don't know the exact history," says the mother. This period of the family's history seems blurry, evaded, rejected. It is Farida, a child of the second generation, who can best describe it

What is essential at this point in the interview is the re-inscription of the dyadic problem of Abdel's clinging to his mother, first in a conjugal history, then in a childhood history of the mother, finally into the history of the family and the community. The narrative of the avatars of the filial link and the parent–child relations are played out in a historical transcription that is familial and communitarian.

Farida says of her family "They're *harkis*!"

But who are the *harkis*? They came to France, often hidden among the French soldiers they fought alongside during the war in Algeria. Many were killed. They are the families of Algerians who fought with the Algerian army to keep Algeria French. *For the Algerians, they are traitors;* for the French, they are Algerians.

Treason and identity hatred: wounded family identities

Abdel's maternal grandfather was a soldier fighting for France. He was taken prisoner by the *fellaghas*, Algerian soldiers fighting for independence.

At this moment when family history is mentioned, Abdel moves closer to his mother. He was still before; now he is starting to move.

The members of the same family have trouble defining their own national and ethnic identity. Farida considers herself Algerian like her grandparents, but she is bitter about the rejection of *harkis* and the children of *harki* families by the Algerian community. Her mother says without conviction that she is of Algerian origin. Here "Algerian" signifies both having a national identity, that of a country, Algeria, and belonging to an ethnic group, the Algerians.

Abdel does not know how to tell the difference between Algerian, Moroccan, French.

The mother's family is of Algerian origin. The father is of Moroccan origin but he lived with his family in Algeria, near the Algerian-Moroccan border.

In fact both the mother's and the father's side are *harki* families that had to leave, flee Algeria after the independence.

Abdel seems to be discovering this family and ethnic history for the first time. He had never heard about this *"harki* stuff". There is a silence, something unsaid, concerning this part of the family history.

Farida goes over these stories with her grandparents. "I listen to my grandparents, because in the history books it's too simplified. It's not that they meant to betray Algeria. They were Algerians who went to live in France. But now, if they go to Algeria, they're not welcome."

The mother remarks that they are rejected on both sides, by the Algerians and by the French.

Treason is also what would later happen to *harki* families at the hands of the French government after Algerian independence. Many of them were abandoned by the French army and lynched as traitors after Algeria became independent.

The inheritance of treason is what has been passed on to children whose parents fought against the independence of members of the Algerian community and whose parents were betrayed in turn by the French they had served.

Even now Farida can still feel the stigma of this and she feels rejected even by other Algerians living in France. To be Algerian, and the grand-daughter of *harkis*, is *shameful*.

It is *shameful* for everyone, for the whole family and for the whole *harki* community. And this gets passed on from generation to generation.

For the mother, the separation and her husband's departure, her winding up alone, discarded and abandoned by her husband, is just one more humiliation, a new act of treason.

"I'm already the daughter of *harkis*—I didn't need this on top of it!"

Abdel touches his mother's shoulder. He straightens the necklace she is wearing.

She also feels rejected and excluded by her husband's family.

Farida puts it like this: "I am the daughter of their son. I am not their granddaughter; it's as though they were not my grandparents." She clearly expresses the suffering of the filial link, and the uneasiness she feels about her identity that goes with it. How, then, can the children become the grandchildren of the paternal grandparents, who call themselves Moroccans and reject Algerians? The maternal grand-father, a former *harki*, no longer shines as he used to. He takes refuge in his garden. The grandmother occupies the place of father and mother. What happens to the sons and grandsons, when the mother acts as both mother and father? Girls hold a particular place in filiation. The mother is important, but girls are alone. Oedipal fixation is attached to nostalgia for a fallen paternal imago.

Abdel and Farida's two brothers have played a paternal role. The big brother "does" the father. But who takes the father's place in the mother's bed? How can Abdel grow up when links are configured like this? He says he is afraid to grow up: "After that, you die." Growing up is associated with death and emptiness.

The mother seems to elaborate on the relation between Abdel's presence in her bed, his difficulties in growing up, and her own link to the father. The father figure is the figure of Abdel, but also that of her husband, and of her own father—her mother's husband, her siblings' father, an Algerian, a veteran of the army of a country that did not acknowledge him … At the end of this interview, she says that she is relieved she didn't throw away the Marsupilami, the great, big *doudou*, that funny animal with the huge tail, a gift from the father. "Fortunately I didn't throw him away!"

How can we understand the symptom of a child that clings to his mother, the sieve-memory of a mother, as an incestuous oedipal fixation and as a symptom of an attack on linking, of inherited treason, and of a breech in the containers of family and community?

There is a psychic collapsing of shame among the topical levels of the intimate (a woman's body cast aside), the private (a marital bed abandoned), and the public (a family and a community scorned and rejected).

Dream deconstruction

We work on the drawing of the genogram, taking a psychoanalytical approach. It complements the spaciogram (Benghozi, 1996b, 2006c), mediating the representation of the image of the familial and genealogical group-body.

In addition to being a search for information about the family in the present and the preceding generations, the drawing of the genogram invites current representations of the family from a group and genealogical perspective.

The genogram is to the psychical temporality of the family body what the spaciogram is to the psychical space of the family body.

It is also very instructive for the therapists, helping them to think more clearly about the group and genealogical issues within a new epistemology that is not a linear, cause-and-effect one. The family and the therapists work together in the session to construct a new whole, in accordance with Von Bertallanfy's rule of totality, an emerging entity, different from and greater than the sum of its parts. With the help of the geno-spaciogram, that is with the bringing together of the narratives being elaborated around the drawings of the genogram and the spacio-gram, the therapist is able to receive what comes to him in associative bits and pieces. Evocations—perceptual, sensory, auditory, olfactory, visual, kinetic, of forms, of colours—mobilise mental images. At the meta-group level, *neo-imaginings, mythic scenarios* emerge. This receiving-work helps support the work on the ability to figuratively represent the containment of dream deconstruction, vague impressions, bodily sensations, the construction of imaginary sequences, affects, emotions, sensations, bits of memories, and fragments of images, the production of proto-representations of images—sensations, proto-words, proto-neo-histories. It shores up the work of pre-symbolisation.

The topical field in question is present here in a group way, and the co-presence of the family and of the therapists produces an effect essen-tially of the *subconscious*.

The associations and commentaries about the geno-spaciogram bring into play the knitting, unraveling, and knitting-up again of the filial and affiliate links.

The mesh-palimpsest: the family's genealogical fresco and the mythical narrative neo-container

The set of links knit a containing mesh. The genealogical mesh is both a link and not a link. The link is the support of and vector for psy-chical transmission. The genealogical transmission of prints and traces of the family group's psychical heritage generates a mesh-palimpsest. Palimpsests are old manuscripts inscribed on parchment which has already been used; the old inscriptions were erased so that the parch-ment could be reused for other texts. Some palimpsests still bear the indented traces of the former text. The mesh-palimpsest is an effect of the work of unravelling and re-meshing, re-knitting the links. It is a psychical object constructed through a succession of deconstructions and reconstructions. The narrative deconstruction retains the memory of the old traces. The palimpsest is a neo-container wherein the ruins of erased images and forgotten memories are stored, as well as new inscriptions. The effect of palimpsest-transmission mobilises the capacity for figurative representation of the work of the unconscious in the genealogical transmission of mnesic traces and of the layer of imprinted "negatives". Associations, daydreams, and dream fantasies contribute to the therapy, to the deconstruction of the palimpsest of genealogical transmission and the co-construction of a mythic neo-narrative of the family saga. This epic family romance is the creative group expression of the narrative re-meshing of familial containers that have been breached. It plays out the meta-therapeutic group space of the session: the *genealogical family fresco*. It figures the emergence of a *mythic container*, alongside the therapeutic saga of the session (Benghozi, 1994, 1995a).

This is an illustration of narrative deconstruction. Following in the footsteps of Derrida, family members' words are looked at as fragments of a family text. Words from the writing of the family group and the community group, along with the removal and the addition of phrases, are used to put together a new writing, a new family story. It is not a matter of researching the reality of historical truths, but of receiving and sustaining this process of putting into narrative form the family's psychical traces and imprints, which it was troublesome to represent and figure. From our perspective, narrative deconstruction generates a new organising mythical narrative which will buttress the defective family and community containers. *This is the mythical narrative neo-container.*

Topical collapse of the intimate, the private history, and the public History: historicity and group narrativity

How does one listen to a history that re-actualises suspended fragments of one's own private "history", which is itself contained within public History of the peoples, "History", written with a capital H?

The traumatic experiences of the war in Algeria, migration, uprooting, mourning, and national treason still resonate, and overlap with the therapist's own family history.

In pathologies like this which affect the family genealogical container, we are under the control of an oscillation between overwhelming excess and emptiness that cannot be filled. The containers of intimacy, privacy, community, and society are nested inside each other like Russian dolls.

I have tried to illustrate the isomorphic equation between space, group psychical body image, the genealogical container, and identities based on belonging.

In this situation, the community container of the Algerian *harkis* is suffering.

The filial link in the *harki* community has to stand the transmission of shame and the humiliation of being stigmatised as traitors, or as the child or grandchild of a traitor. The children of treason have shame as their inheritance. The suffering familial container receives no support from the container of the Algerian community.

The pact of conjugal alliances is cemented with the paradoxical nature of the link. Not only the children of *harki* families, but the husband and wife share a common humiliation that at the same time unites and separates them.

This is also a psychical return of the humiliation and of what cannot be avowed, a memory that carries the family's unconscious shame (Benghozi, 1996a).

How do myths crisscross and overlap between the original families of each partner? How does this echo the family myths of the therapists? The subject inscribed in social and familial group psychical space contributes to the narrative elaboration of a new familial mythic romance.

Founding myths are built from the set of values and beliefs shared by the group. They define the contours of identity based on belonging, the boundaries of inner and outer worlds, of inclusion and exclusion. The treason scenario includes both betraying and being betrayed, the traitor as well the one(s) being betrayed. Treason is an attack on linking; it is a form of violence. It is a form of discrediting which destroys trust. The group ego ideal is vacillating. Trust is a belief and a value that organises the alliance. To betray someone's trust is to betray the rule that structures the boundaries of the group one belongs to. If the pact of trust can no longer be relied upon, then the boundaries between the Me and the Not-Me are no longer guaranteed, because this is an attack from inside. The alliance and the link of solidarity implode. The treasons most to be feared are those that arise from systems that are meant to ensure protection.

The containers of the intimate are broken into. Intimacy is threatened. When the links are broken, there is an intrusion into the territory of the intimate. The stigmatising gaze that is turned upon this territory is persecutory and a source of shame. The environment, in Winnicott's

(1971) sense of the maternal matrix environment, no longer provides a sense of security. One's ability to be alone is compromised. To betray is to stop respecting the distance that comes with difference. Here we are in the area of incest, when a transgressive act occurs, or in the area of incestuality, when there is a confusing encroachment on the differences between the topical levels of containers. This is a topical collapse of the respective containers of the intimate, the private, and the public. There is a dropping of the reciprocal trans-containing functions.

"It's the suitcase or the coffin!": transmitting the murmurs

They had to leave their country or die. There were no other alternatives for the *harkis* who were considered traitors by those who fought for Algeria's independence. For a long time in France, people said "the Algeria events" when speaking of a war for independence that was not recognised as such by the French government. In correspondence with what was unnameable about the war, there were the silences and the shadows on a page as yet unwritten in the history of decolonisation. The *harkis*, the community composed of the families of Algerian soldiers who fought in the French army, inherit the stigma of this history. We find it when the family saga is narrated in therapy.

Intrafamilial transmission is characteristic of what one finds in contexts where a community has been catastrophically traumatised.

Parent–child transmission acts as a barrier. What happens is rather what I call the "transmission of murmurs"—the murmurs of sobbing, the murmurs of lamentation (Benghozi, 1996a). Something unsaid, shared by the parents but hidden from the child, is making this enigmatic background noise. It is not really a secret but the systematisation of a set of elements that are being avoided. It is a deafening silence. The rule is that one must above all not ask questions about histories which are so sensitive and painful for the parents and grandparents.

The child often experiences this as a puzzling alliance with a traumatic event that has repercussions for him but from which he feels excluded.

The movement of transmission often skips a generation.

It is striking to observe how everyone's little history—singular and familial—is inscribed in and transmitted across "History", written with a capital H—the "big" history of societies, peoples, and cultures.

Interpretations that break into neo-imaginings

It is always interesting to ask the question: what is currently at stake in the symptom and in the request for therapy? How do they find a place both in the diachronic psychical function, and in a synchronic economic function? In other words, how have they been constructed within the history of links and how does the present demand for change contribute to an economic readjustment in the family's psychical equilibrium? Listening sensitively to both the diachronic and synchronic dimensions prevents us from getting caught up in a cause-and-effect linear mode of understanding. It makes us more open to what is being played out at the crossroads of actual resonances and those that cannot be predicted. How can one learn to be receptive to surprises? Therapeutic intervention is no longer reduced to an interpretation of symptoms enclosed within preconceived codes from theoretical reading models. We share Janine Puget's reference (2005) to the principle of indetermination. This conception of a therapeutic approach raises questions about how to train psychoanalysts to be open to incertitude and indetermination. Most often, psychoanalysts are trained to listen to repressed psychical material, such as is found in neurotic pathologies, using theoretical-clinical reading models to guide them. I think that situations characterised by psychopathology of the genealogical justify an approach to psychoanalytic family therapy that embraces the unpredictable. This presupposes empathy towards the narrative emergence. In such families, there are suffering links and broken links. Now, the link is what ensures genealogical psychical transmission. Suffering of the link corresponds to a flaw in the psychical elaboration and an impasse in transmission (Kaës, 1995). Reciprocally, an impasse in transmission corresponds to suffering in the link. Unelaborated familial psychical material cannot fail to be transmitted (Abraham & Torok, 1978). So how does the psychical transmission of unelaborated material occur? The psychical material is not introjected; rather, it is incorporated and diffracted in the family's group psychical apparatus. It does not provide access to repression and the products of fantasy. Unbinding attacks show that at the level of the psyche inter-fantasising has been stunned, fantasy production is under attack. *It is an attack on fantasmapoiesis.* Interpretative interventions are wrong when they claim to be working on illusory latent content. Such interpretations are at risk of breaking into narrative neo-containers that have been co-constructed in the space of the therapeutic meta-group's imagining. Any work of an interpretative type centred on the content of the group's dream neo-productions could cause a catastrophic unravelling. For this is not fantasised psychical material. These are group fantasies emerging during the session. They do not involve psychical material that has been repressed. They are narrative dream containers that are grafted and superimposed onto each other to shore up the holes in the familial containers.

An attempt at interpretation could break through the protective shield that is the narrative neo-envelope. The work of transforming stored-away, non-representable experiences and incorporated elements is carried out thanks to the therapist's ability to be empathically receptive. The work of reception is essentially that of listening-as-container in Bion's sense (1961, 1963). Its fundamental function is to support the processes of psychical transformation.

Transferance: emergence in psychoanalytic family group therapy

It is in the here-and-now of the real, but also imaginary, encounter between family and therapists where what I call the *transferance* emerges (Benghozi, 2006b). The *transferance* indicates that there is a new, auto-poietic psychical entity in the therapeutic meta-group. It is different from, and greater than, the expression of the sum of transference and countertransference. The *transferance* is a group emergence of the dialectical movement between transference and countertransference. It is more than a simple interaction between the two: it is a transferential co-production that emerges in the meta-group space. The unconscious life of the group in therapy involves the psyche of everyone who is psychically engaged in the setting of the therapeutic process.

The pre-transference and the pre-countertransference are already present in the anticipations (Benghozi, 2006b), in the representations and psychical investments, beyond the reality of the therapeutic encounter.

Everybody's psyches—those of therapists and family members—are not in an undifferentiated state. The therapist/family relationship is differentiated and asymmetrical. But this shows that there is a mobilisation of new group defence mechanisms in the space of the therapeutic meta-group. Fractures in our own individual and family histories help to deconstruct and co-construct, with the support of the therapeutic meta-group, "the genealogical family fresco" (Benghozi, 1994), the family's neo-romance. This is an epic figural representation emerging in therapy, out of the *transferance* movement.

The containing function of family therapists who are analysts is essential for providing the guarantee of a therapeutic "holding" and "handing" in the Winnicottian (1971) sense.

Topical approach to trans-containing, kaleidoscopic support for individual identity, family identity, and community identity

I thought it interesting to work on the resonances between an individual destiny and a group history. How do the cultural container and the community container provide mutual and reciprocal support for each other?

The therapy's evolutions give the family's and the individuals' psychical issues a new context within the social and community containers. This step is considered from the perspective of the genealogical mesh, a reflection that has to do with a trans-container support approach.

Social, familial, and individual containers provide mutual support for each other.

The containers of the intimate, the private, and the public respond to those of the individual, the conjugal, the familial, the societal, and the communitarian.

Each person's identity is constructed with a trans-psychical topic of the intimate, the private, and the public.

How do the individual container and the group, family, and community containers co-construct themselves and each other?

How are individual identity, family group identity, and community identity interconnected?

How do individual narcissistic flaws resonate with the narcissism of the family group and the community?

This approach leads us to think psychoanalytically about the trans-container co-support among individual identity containers and group identity containers of families and communities.

How can we rearrange the unconscious image of the individual body and the unconscious image of the family group body and the societal and communitarian body?

We can characterise the Russian doll embedding of these levels of containment by saying that *there is reciprocal support among the individual container, the familial group container, and the community container.*

I describe the existence of an isomorphism, that is, of a formal analogy between the limits of the unconscious body image and the limits of psychical containers.

A new capacity for figural representation: the kaleidoscope metaphor

It is as though there were a dynamic co-construction of new images. Like in a kaleidoscope, a new figural representation is created with the kinetic movement of each cylinder until a stable enough image has taken shape. In keeping with this metaphor, each cylinder represents a psychical container and the body image. The kaleidoscope metaphor aims to show that the co-construction of a reorganisation of the image of the individual body, the image of the familial genealogical body, and the image of the communitarian genealogical body is a dynamic process that engages in a twofold envelope, the singular level and the group level of family, community, and genealogy. I suggest that we conceive of individual psychical reorganisations in the individual and family life cycle as an opportunity for the individual container, the genealogical family group container to which one belongs, and the community container, to engage with each other. I propose that we think about the psychodynamics and the psychopathology of "containers in transformation" (Benghozi, 2010a).

Conclusion: a meta-setting for elaboration

The shame-carrier is the transgenerational inheritor of unconscious shame; in addition to the content of secrets and what is left unsaid, this is a problematic of linking, and thus of the container, for the ego ideal manifested by shame organises the limits of outside and inside, of psychical containers, and of identity construction (Benghozi, 1994).

Therapeutic deconstruction work makes it possible to elaborate the narrative neo-container, from which a scenario may arise, one that provides an alternative to the genealogical scenario according to which one is destined to shame and humiliation (Benghozi, 2000, 2002, 2003).

But in this type of situation, where the little history and the big history are interwoven, we must think using the logic of the meta-setting. I speak of meta-setting when the therapeutic setting is necessarily connected with other systems, like the justice system in cases of incest. Recognition of the legal status of *harki* families is a necessary step not only for communities of former *harkis*, but also for the identity containers of the French nation and the Algerian nation. These container-nations cannot function as supports or containers of the *harki* community as long as there is no work of elaboration of shameful things that cannot be avowed, and which are still in suspense, like the issue of torture during the Algerian war.

Historical group memory-work cannot rest on the forgetting of a past left in silence (Benghozi, 2000, 2003). Repression of the history of wounded identities boomerangs back, appearing with a vengeance in later generations, when genealogical community containers are still torn apart …

References

Abraham, A., & Torok, M. (1978). *The Shell and the Kernel: Renewals of Psychoanalysis*. Chicago: University of Chicago Press, 1994.

Anzieu, D., Haag, G., Tisseron, S., Lavalle, G., Boubli, M., & Lassegue, J. (1993). *Les Contenants de Pensée*. Paris: Dunod.

Benghozi, P. (1994). Porte la honte et maillage des contenants généalogiques familiaux et communautaires en thérapie familiale. Le groupe familial en psychothérapie. *Revue de Psychothérapie Psychanalytique de Groupe, 22*: 81–94.

Benghozi, P. (1995a). Approche psychothérapique familiale et psychoses infantiles, en autisme et psychoses infantiles. *Cahiers du CTNERHI, 67–68*: 101–112.

Benghozi, P. (1995b). Effraction des contenants généalogiques familiaux, transfert catastrophique, rêveries et néosecrets. *Revue de Psychothérapie Psychanalytique de Groupe, 24*: 91–99.

Benghozi, P. (1995c). L'empreinte généalogique du traumatisme et la Honte—Génocide identitaire et femmes violées en ex-Yougoslavie. In: M. R. Moro & S. Lebovici (Eds.), *Psychiatrie Humanitaire en ex-Yougoslavie et en Arménie—Face au Traumatisme* (pp. 51–64). Paris: PUF.

Benghozi, P. (1996a). L'image du corps généalogique et le génospaciogramme. *Image du Corps, Du Groupe à la Famille*. Actes du colloque AFPC, Besançon, France.

Benghozi, P. (1996b). L'attaque contre l'humain, attaque contre la dignité—Traumatisme catastrophique et transmission généalogique. *Nervure, Journal de Psychiatrie, 9*: 39–45.

Benghozi, P. (1997). Conceptualisation et clinique de l'effraction. In: M. Broquen (Ed.), *L'Effraction* (pp. 149–159). Paris: L'Harmattan.

Benghozi, P. (1998). La honte. In: Y. Pelicier (Ed.), *Les Objets de la Psychiatrie* (pp. 250–253). Paris: L'Esprit du Temps.

Benghozi, P. (1999a). *Adolescence et Sexualité—Liens et Maillage-Reseau*. Paris: L'Harmattan.

Benghozi, P. (1999b). *L'Adolescence, Identité Chrysalide*. Paris: L'Harmattan.

Benghozi, P. (2000). Scénario généalogique de la violence et de l'inceste. In: A. Yahyaoui (Ed.), *Violence Passages à l'Acte et Situations de Rupture* (pp. 15–30). Paris: La Pensée Sauvage.

Benghozi, P. (2002). *Violence et Champ Social*. Rennes, France: ENSP.

Benghozi, P. (2003). Résilience sociale et communautaire: pour un travail de pardon. *La Santé de l'Homme, 366*: 25–29.

Benghozi, P. (2004). Esthétique de la figurabilité et néocontenants narratifs groupaux, médiations d'expression. *Revue de Psychothérapie Psychanalytique de Groupe, 41*: 7–12.

Benghozi, P. (2006a). Honte, haine, ritualisation du pardon et complexe d'Antigone. In: G. Decherf, A. -M. Blanchard, & E. Darchis (Eds.), *Amour, Haine et Tyrannie dans la Famille* (pp. 67–78). Paris: In Press.

Benghozi, P. (2006b). Pré-contre-transfert, cadre et dispositif. *Revue de Psychothérapie Psychanalytique de Groupe, 47*: 25–29.

Benghozi, P. (2006c). Le spatiogramme en thérapie psychanalytique de couple et de famille. *Dialogue, 172*: 5–24.

Benghozi, P. (2007a). Le leurre comme symptôme des contenants généalogiques troués, dans la psychothérapie familiale à l'épreuve de l'adolescent. *Le Journal des Psychologues, 245*: 35–40.

Benghozi, P. (2007b). La transmission généalogique de la trace et de l'empreinte: temps mythique en thérapie familiale psychanalytique. *Cahiers Critiques de Thérapie Familiale et de Pratiques de Réseaux, 38*: 43–60.

Benghozi, P. (2007c). La trace et l'empreinte: L'adolescent héritier porte—l'empreinte de la transmission généalogique. *Adolescence, 62*: 755–777.

Benghozi, P. (2010a). Remaillage et Résilience Familiale et communautaire de la honte, et de l'humiliation. In: M. Delage & B. Cyrulnik (Eds.), *Famille et Résilience* (pp. 87–110). Paris: Odile Jacob.

Benghozi, P. (2010b). La violence n'est pas l'agressivité. Une perspective psychanalytique des Liens. *Revue de Psychothérapie Psychanalytique de Groupe, 55*: 41–54.

Benghozi, P. (2011). Le scénario généalogique porte la Honte, Honte et transmission. *Dialogue, 190*: 25–39.

Bion, W. R. (1959). Attaque contre les liens. *Nouvelle Revue de Psychanalyse,* 25: 285–298.

Bion, W. R. (1961). *Experiences in Group, and Other Papers.* London: Tavistock.

Bion, W. R. (1963). *Elements of Psycho-Analysis.* London: William Heinemann Medical Books.

Bleger, J. (1979). Psychanalyse du cadre psychanalytique. In: R. Kaës (Ed.), *Crise, Rupture et Dépassement* (pp. 255–274). Paris: Dunod.

Derrida, J. (1998). *Psyche: Inventions of the Other.* Stanford, CA: Stanford University Press, 2007.

Kaës, R. (1995). *Le Groupe et le Sujet du Groupe.* Paris: Dunod.

Kaës, R., Missenard, A., Kaspi, R., Anzieu, D., Guillaumin, J., Bleger, J., & Jacques, E. (1979). *Crise, Rupture et Dépassement. Analyse Transitionnelle en Psychanalyse Individuelle et Groupale.* Paris: Dunod.

Puget, J. (2005). Dialogue d'un certain genre avec René Kaës à propos du lien. *Le Divan familial, 15:* 59–71.

Robert, P. (2007). La thérapie familiale psychanalytique: questions techniques. In: J. -G. Lemaire (Ed.), *L'Inconscient dans la Famille* (pp. 57–107). Paris: Dunod.

Winnicott, D. W. (1971). *Playing and Reality.* London: Tavistock.

CHAPTER FOUR

Where is the unconscious located? Reflections on links in families and couples

Anna Maria Nicolò

After fifteen years of individual psychoanalytical treatments (three different ones, discontinued after a few years each) for Camilla, a patient living in a therapeutic community, and fruitless despite her use of antipsychotic and antidepressant medication, the team in charge of her therapy decided to refer her parents to couple treatment. Each parent, in turn, had already undergone individual therapy during the long years of their daughter's illness, but this experience seemed to have only reinforced their intellectual defences and had not freed them from their distress at having such a problematic daughter.

Camilla has been living in this therapeutic community for three years now and is reaching the end of her treatment. After this period (already extended for six months beyond its standard length) she will no longer be entitled to having social security pay her fees, but it seems that her parents' couple treatment has changed something right away.

After the dramatic session described in detail below, Camilla too seems to have changed.

Fourth session in a once-a-week treatment[1]

They arrive on time. M, the father, seems more composed. F, the mother, starts by saying that they just met two couples they are friends with. M instead talks about the difficulties and the pain he feels all the time during the day, including when he meets friends or relatives, and says that he remembers the obsessive thoughts that made him fear he could throw his wife down a cliff.

One of the co-therapists, Francesco, says that one throws ugly things into the abyss but at times also beautiful things, and adds how difficult it is for M to distinguish beautiful things from ugly things. M remembers that he used to be jealous of his brother, especially when his brother was making jokes with his wife. In those moments, he did not think of an affair, but that his brother was better than himself.

Francesco tells M that thoughts about active violence could be related to violence suffered as a victim.

This spontaneous interpretation by the analyst, based on his counter-transference, seems to act like lightning that rips a veil. M is silent, and then recounts that he was abused when aged about ten in the boarding school he attended and that after the event, he was sexually promiscuous, only to later become a strict moralist; judgemental, punitive, and violent towards the other boys at the boarding school. Later he always found it difficult to cope with obsessive fantasies of raping and killing the girls attending his school. His wife listens and starts crying. She looks at him intently and says that in their story there are many unsaid things. She confesses that she had never known the details but that he had mentioned them in generic terms.

The therapist mentions the strong emotional impact he feels in his countertransference but thinks during the session that this couple has always remained on the borderline, as if they had never shared emotions and experiences, worries and passions.

The co-therapist Maria adds that probably these unsaid things were used to maintain a "safe zone", to keep a distance but also to protect. She mentions the great autonomy from each other that this couple maintains, and talks about how the father used to retreat to his workplace while the mother had the keys to some friends' flat where she too could retreat and spend some time on her own.

The mother agrees and says she remembers that Camilla is ambivalent about being hugged, fearing and wishing it at the same time, and how at the beginning of couple therapy she had dreamed that she and her husband were going to make love.

The analyst comments on the mother's dream as an opening to hope also for their new therapeutic experience.

M adds that before being sent to boarding school he had a sexual obsession and often masturbated with friends. He says that now, after retirement, his life no longer has any value …

F connects her husband's distress to their daughter's distress and wonders if Camilla is waiting for her father to get better before getting better herself, as if in hidden agreement. The session ends.

Shortly after this session, news from the community is that Camilla seems less in anguish. She had two dreams and recounted them to anyone willing to listen. One of the dreams she had almost at the same time as the session: a woman, an educator (the job of her parents) was going to kill a lot of young women and wanted to kill her too because she was a serial killer. In another dream, her father raped some young women and she was very scared.

Later work unearthed family problems in the father's early life. He had been sent to boarding school at a religious institution very early in life because his mother was depressed.

Comment

I think that this is an interesting case history[2] useful for highlighting the startling coincidence between the content of Camilla's dreams and her father's confessions, in particular his obsessions and the abuse that he had apparently kept secret. Just as significant is the fact that Camilla spoke about her dreams at all, since she had not reported many dreams before and started dreaming at the same time as the session took place in which her father revealed his past.

M had kept his past experiences of abuse and his obsessive fantasies hidden for many years, but these were present within him as dissociated or rejected parts, even while he appeared outwardly to be a brilliant and careful educator.

These persecutory and obsessive ideations, in which he had located his hate for the abuse suffered, for his female passive parts that had exposed him to indelible trauma in pre-adolescence, as well as his identification with the aggressor, could not be expressed openly but had affected his internal defences and the quality of the link to his daughter who used to keep saying endlessly (it was one of her main delusional ideas) that her parents wanted to kill her body or her soul. His wife too was part of this system of apparent denial of problems and of pseudo-normality; she too had with him an unconscious agreement aimed at rejection because she also denied aggression and defended herself from death anxieties with her story. Camilla's dreams seem to be evacuations with which she tries to get rid of transgenerational impingements, showing a paranoid persecutory level, typical for her but also for her family's experiences.

Developments in this case history

Two years after the beginning of couple therapy there is an improvement in the general situation. The father has to undergo surgery for prostatic cancer. Here follows an excerpt from a meaningful session one week before the Easter break.

The father made a powerful parapraxis: he had wanted to call his wife and dialled Francesco's number instead. So the therapist hears him imperiously asking him to go straight away to see him with the incontinence pads he needs because of his situation after surgery. In the session after this parapraxis, the parents talk of their daughter's improvement. However, the father complains that she has turned her attention to her mother and that she has a budding relationship with a young man she met in the community.

For the first time there is a differentiation between the parents. The mother says she thinks about hope and seems to be more capable of contacting emotions, feelings, fantasies, and thoughts. She also adds that her daughter told her she is sorry "because she abused the house where she had lived before living in this community".

While the father displays his persisting depression, the mother says she imagines that in the future their daughter can move to live in a little flat they own, but the father again comments on the innumerable mistakes they made.

Francesco comments on the parapraxis that had already been mentioned at the beginning of the session and gives the interpretation that M feels the lack of a container for all that he feels to be wrong, negative, depressive, and deathly inside himself. As his daughter opens up to hope, he is afraid that she is moving closer to her mother, recovering a good relationship with her, and he feels very alone. Maybe not only is his daughter moving away, his wife might also be finding a new space and he is feeling the lack of his mother and his wife.

To this, he replies: "If my daughter rejects me, I don't exist any more and my worn-out body does not work any more. Believe me, it's horrible!" The session is over. F asks to go to the bathroom and while waiting for her to come back M remarks to the therapists that a newspaper article he wrote is considered good by everybody except himself, who thinks it is not good.

This session is significant for various reasons. We can see the displacement on the analyst in the transference of the tyrannical requests for massive care made by the patient. He demands the containment of internal persecutory objects that he has to face now that his wife and daughter seem more autonomous and less available to him. An earthquake is taking place. The father feels that if the container for his sadistic deathly anal objects fails him, he no longer exists. There are still doubts by the psychotherapist as to the extent of the implication of his body in this powerful attack, which might have helped develop his cancer.

Of the many questions posed by this case history, I choose to discuss two:

1. How do we explain the startling coincidence of unconscious contents in Camilla and her father? Is there a shared unconscious? An extraterritorial area of the unconscious located in the other, in the family, or in the couple?
2. What are the mechanisms that regulate these phenomena?

Is there a shared unconscious? The opinion of a family therapist

Almost all psychoanalysts working with seriously ill patients and their families have encountered similar case histories. In Argentina, in particular, the pioneering work of Garcia Badaracco (2000), Roberto Losso (2000), Isidoro Berenstein and Janine Puget (2008) and in France that of Alberto Eiguer and André Ruffiot (1981) among many others, showed the mutual links that tie each person to the family she belongs to from the very beginning of life. Although Freud (1914c, 1916–1917) showed with startling clarity the links tying children to their mothers or how the baby's narcissism is based and leans on its parents' investment, he merely hinted at the importance of the family as a group in its entirety, with rules and mechanisms of its own, for the construction of individual identity.

Serious pathologies, like Camilla's, make this mutual interdependence especially evident, that between the patient's internal world and the fantasy world of the family where the patient is located and to which she belongs.

The theory of the intergenerational transmission of unconscious, unelaborated traumatic contents weighing on the identity of subjects in later generations formulated by Haydée Faimberg and René Kaës (1993) is well known. But before it, Garcia Badaracco's pioneering conceptualisation of a "maddening object" (2000) and the related theorisations by some French authors (such as Cahn) on alienating identifications help explain the phenomena described in our case history in terms of identification. The patient has to host alien introjects or fantasies alien to the ego that belong to her parents and that the parents have not been able to work through and which act inside them like parasites. Badaracco talks of mutual interdependence among family members. These notions suggest that the global functioning of a family can be considered as an organisation of emotional and fantastic links, transpersonal defences, ghosts, and myths that coexist at various levels. The construction of a myth, as I discuss elsewhere in this book, is a good example and can be seen as the family's collective product, in part conscious and in part unconscious.

The family as a unit, with its specific identity, story, myths, and transgenerational secrets belonging to the family for generations, represents the basis of our internal functioning. And to this we can add each member's position in the family history, which is especially important in terms of siblinghood: to be the first born or the last, to be born after a dead sibling, to bear a grandfather's name, all these elements play a role in the organisation of identity, as we can very well imagine.

A stipulation

Without fear of disproval, we dare say that no one today questions the radical impact of the earliest baby–mother interactions on the organisation of personality. Problems may arise, however, when we move outside the mother–baby dyad. Only recently have we been able to stress the importance of the parents' relationship in front of the baby that it is witness to (Britton, 1989) and which it internalises. But we do not have much research in developmental psychology or psychoanalysis on the family as a network of relationships and interactions mutually affecting one another during the essential development phases from infancy to adolescence and later.

Based on existing research we can quote the authors (myself among them) who practise family psychoanalysis. For them the basic matrix for the formation of the individual self in a process of continuous differentiation, recovery, and transformation is the family as fantastic organisation and not only the relationship to each parent that is included in it. This brings to mind what Ruffiot (1990) argued for when he wrote that there exists a family psychic apparatus (see also Kaës, 1976, 1994), and that group thinking is the matrix of individual thinking. For the individual this represents that extraterritorial part of the ego that is always available for group experiences.

A few years later, in the article,, "The family as a matrix for thinking", I dwelled on the same issues and defined the family as a fantastic multidimensional organism made of various levels. I also added that at the most primitive level of a family that some called group self, the differentiation between somatic and psychic states vanishes just like the differentiation between self and other (Nicolò, 1988). Within these dimensions a member can react with a somatic state or with action to the psychic state or to a dream of another member and vice versa. The continuous interchange between the internal family that everyone has inside themselves and the external family with its fantastic links that we contributed to build from the inception of our lives, is a continuous process lasting all life long and progressively organised from birth onwards.

More recently, research in the area of developmental psychology has started to widen its interest to the relationships between a person and her family. The pioneer in this field has certainly been Daniel Stern who argues (1985) that object relations and relational patterns originate in social interactions. Relational patterns from the beginning of life are constructed in the interactions of two or more persons. In this sense they are at the same time objective events and subjective experiences.

According to Stern, how an interaction is perceived and interpreted depends on the fantasies, hopes, fears, traditions, and myths of the family of the participants in this interaction.

In a work in developmental psychology, Beebe, Lachmann, and Jaffe (1997) suggested the existence of a pre-reflexive unconscious that is different from the dynamic unconscious. According to these authors, the representations an infant is organising will become symbolic through a system of non-verbal representations that might not be translated into verbal representation. These mother–baby relationships—I would add mother–father–baby relationships—transformed by the baby, represent a pre-reflexive unconscious that each person will carry along with them all life long, sometimes translating it into verbal representations, at other times leaving it unspoken. Is this position really different from that which family psychoanalysts take when they suggest that the unconscious dimension is shared by all family members?

So, in addition to an individual unconscious, there also exists a complex and multidimensional fantasy world created by the family as a unit, as a group that shares a story, space, and time, and by the links that each member builds together with the others. Each family has its own identity and shared functioning that affects each member. Each member will progressively differentiate through an oscillating elaboration and a continuous shuttle movement from one's internal world to the external family that was co-constructed by all family members.

This is the reason why we must always focus our work on the relation between the intrapsychic and the interpersonal, observing repetitions, identities, discrepancies, fusions, confusions, differences, and oppositions between our internal world and the interpersonal world of families or couples. This is especially clear in the observation of children and adolescent patients and in serious cases, such as psychotic onsets in adolescence where action prevails over thought and there is a pathology of the boundaries of the self, not only in the patient but in all family members.

This is what I focus on in my work, observing coincidences and divergences between the intrapsychic and the interpersonal, between identities and differentiations, since each person belongs to a family that provides the context for emotional learning and organises her personality, but in which she is subjected to change day by day under the process of subjectivisation.

The work done in this area of intersection and complementarity between the internal world and the co-constructed interpersonal world allows us to distinguish various levels in our observation:

1. intrapsychic dynamics
2. the effect of projections on the other
3. the effects of splittings, projections, and externalisations that are especially meaningful in childhood and adolescence.

What are the mechanisms that regulate these phenomena?

We can try now to answer the second question I posed above: what are the mechanisms that regulate these phenomena in a family: what tools do we have to understand the phenomena underlying the development of an individual mind and that of collective organisations like families, in which a child is engaged in building a world of internal relations and of interactions with external objects?

The first answer can be found in Freud (1921c, 1933a) who argued that identification is the mechanism that connects the ego and the others. According to Freud, we all belong in a generational chain thanks to our capacity for identifying with our parents or grandparents and counter-identifying with our children. An interesting study of families and their educational role by Meltzer and Harris (1983) distinguishes various types of family functioning based on the prevailing quality of identifications.

But identification and projective identification—which could be considered a bridge for connecting oneself with the other, with the parent or the child, the analyst and the partner—are in reality seen as mechanisms internal to individuals. Still, psychoanalysis has always investigated the other, what effect we have on the other, and what effect the other has on us, and how the other changes us and vice versa. Freud too observed phenomena such as crowds and folie-à-deux, stating that they follow different rules from the ones we see at the individual level. There is still much to understand in answering significant questions. What use do we make of others? Can we use the other to defend ourselves? To heal ourselves? To change? And who are we for the other?

Many analysts have discussed these issues. Meltzer (1979), for example, argued that we should not only investigate the ways in which we defend ourselves from mental pain, but we must also assume that there is a displacement or transport of it. If repression makes us unaware of our internal pain, we can also get rid of it by locating it in objects in the external world. Instead of denying or disowning pain, we can displace it onto someone near us.

I find this mechanism quite important because it highlights quite a few pathological modes of functioning such as transgenerational dynamics, i.e., non-elaborated traumatic experiences that can affect later generations and require the displacement of psychic pain onto another person, usually a child, who has to perform the painful elaboration that the first actor (usually a parent or grandparent) was not able to make.

In a sense, this mode of functioning could be considered one of the mechanisms called "interpersonal or transpersonal defences" by couple and family analysts. These defences are shared by family members and are used to cope with unthinkable catastrophic anxieties of annihilation, guilt, and so on. In my opinion, transpersonal defences are a collective product, relatively stable in time and often activated through a specific context. They are a collective product to the extent that they "meet" the needs of the participants in the relationship. They cannot be used if the partner does not agree, or flees, or does not need that relationship. We can see what happens in a situation like Camilla's case.

We know that her father suffered a very intense early trauma. In cases like this, the personality organises itself with the help of peculiar defences: first of all, dissociation allowing the subject's psychic survival and providing optimal functioning under the impact of very difficult experiences. Other mechanisms can also work, such as the disowning (*Verleugnung*) (Freud, 1927e), rejection (*Verwerfung*) (Freud, 1894a, 1914c), or denial (*Verneinung*) (Freud, 1925h) of external reality. Freud argued that rejection is a form of self-defence that is stronger and more efficient than repression and consists in the fact that the ego rejects any incompatible representations along with its affect and behaves as if this representation had never reached it. These mechanisms take part in the genesis of psychosis, but the case history mentioned above shows that these mechanisms are active in one person, the father, covering up and masking the anxieties and conflicts that have been transmitted, transported, and transferred to the daughter, subtly affecting her functioning and that of the whole family. These very traumas also determined the organisation of other specific links and functionings that have been learned in the family by Camilla, who can thus be considered the repository (Bleger, 1967) or spokesperson (Kaës, 2007) of the conflicts her father and the parental couple denied and rejected, but she can also be seen as the witness of a family mode of functioning that is organised around these traumatic cores.

As couple and family analysts we can assume that these aspects that have been split off, dissociated, or rejected by one subject, if they remain at more primitive non-verbalised levels, can however contribute to determining the family's functioning and organise the links that each member co-constructs with the others in the course of time.

I think that at pre-symbolic and pre-reflective levels families organise co-constructed links. Some of them connect the couple's partners and others connect with each sibling in turn. Some of these links are made out of split-off, dissociated, or rejected elements, at times offsetting them with elements taken from the other. Here I am talking about the defences organised unconsciously by creating compensatory links, as we can see in the folie-à-deux or in those couples where one becomes a parasite of the other in order to be supported by the other. In some families, for example, somatisation becomes a privileged response, transferred from one generation to the other and used by various members (Nicolò, 1990, 1992, 1997, 2009). In such families we often see that any one member is looking for a container for evacuating anxiety and a sense of loneliness and non-existence, deep shame, and humiliation into, and in order to achieve this, he makes use of various transpersonal defensive strategies. In working with these families, we observe not only individual defence mechanisms such as repression or denial, but also collectively constructed defences, such as a malignant fusion with the other, the colonisation of the other's mind (with the resulting cancellation of the other's subjectivity), or the disowning of the other and of his autonomous existence, or of his identity from birth onwards. We frequently hear unbelievable stories hiding unspeakable secrets often left unspoken: children left like dead, offspring and generations kept secret and characterised by secrecy, abuse, or other traumas.

Interpersonal and transpersonal defences are a way to express the link that ties the members of a family together. But we could wonder if they work only from one generation to the other or if they are active also in couples.

But what do we mean with the term link?

To Pichon Rivière (1980) we owe the first elaboration of this concept that he called "vínculo", a complex structure that includes the subject, the object, and their mutual interaction. He distinguishes the link from the object relation, and argues that a link forms a pattern of behaviour that tends to be automatically repeated both in the internal and in the external world with the other.

But obviously there may be other antecedents of this concept. First of all, Bion (1992), while commenting on what takes place in a dual context, argued that the patient's relationship is mainly with the couple in the room: any couple, but more clearly the couple made up of patient and analyst. One is with oneself only in some peculiar way, since one identifies both with oneself and with the couple. Albeit equipped with somewhat different features, and owing to his experience in working with psychotic families, Racamier (1990) also highlights a very interesting relational pattern that he calls "ingrainment". He argues that this term defines a relational mode and a form of psychic functioning of mutual connectedness, characterised by a double connection between the intrapsychic and the interactive, just like between one person and another. Ingrainment processes engage the ego and perpetuate a deep mutual dependence. They are characterised by reversibility and invertibility which make it possible for one person to do something to the other and to receive it back from the other. According to Racamier, at the fantastic level the most representative configuration is Anzieu's ghost of a common skin. But ingrainment is enacted and experienced rather than fantasised. While acknowledging that it can come in different degrees, Racamier assigns to ingrainment an exclusively pathological value which differentiates it from the attunement of mother and baby or from sexual relations that are also intense relations based on powerful interactions. So he shows various pathological situations where ingrainment is present: "The subjects that make others enact parts of themselves; those who use it to put in the other their phallic or narcissistic complement or their unacknowledged drives; those who keep this 'forced delegate' [Jacobson, 1967] available; those who expel on the other their denied losses and repressed depressions; those who walk on with *paranoid intimations* and some families that designate one among them as the *predestined enacter*. This latter one at the end of the chain and all the others, what could they be if not supporters of ingrainment?" (Racamier, 1990, p. 67, emphasis added).

Among the authors who have more recently discussed this matter, I would like to mention Berenstein and Puget (2008) who, starting from the same view, discussed the concept of link and its implications also outside family settings. These two Argentine psychoanalysts argue that in a relationship between two or more persons, there exists at least one element connected with the external reality of the other that remains foreign, unknowable, and that weighs on the relationship, co-determining it. The inability to tolerate this element that is felt as being alien to the mutual projective identification, this irreducible presence of the other as external subject can lead to an attempt at denying or cancelling it by various means, such as impingement on the other or imposition of thoughts and fantasies, as it often happens in psychosis, where we observe at the same time a failure to see the other as differentiated, as an autonomous person with his own mental functioning, as well as an impingement on the other's mental space with secret and, at times, transgenerational thoughts and fantasies.

Another relevant author who developed this issue is René Kaës. This French analyst argues that we can see the creation of one or more links "in the places of memory, crypts, cultural monuments, myths and inhabited spaces that represent forms that we inherit from previous generations and carry on to later ones" (2001, p. 167).

He describes the existence of unconscious alliances as "psychic formations constructed by those who build a link in order to reinforce their processes, functions and structures. They form a cluster of links that tie the subjects to the function of the role they play in the group. The idea of unconscious alliance implies that of duty and submission" (ibid., p. 168).

I will try to clarify this concept with the help of a clinical vignette.

Case history

With a couple I had in treatment any pretext was seized upon to start a fight. They came to see me because they could neither stay together nor live apart. Their dynamics was the following: psychological violence tended to be used by the wife and induced suicidal thoughts in the husband. For example, the husband, a brilliant businessman, had not dedicated his whole afternoon to helping their adolescent son with his homework, as his wife had requested, because he was busy at work; or he had not eaten the dinner she had left for him in the fridge, preferring to eat something else. This made his wife attack him in his sensitive spots. This led to him fantasising about suicide. After two years of treatment things were going better, but a partial relapse shows again this dynamics, as described below.

There has been a clear improvement, but the patient comes to the session in great distress. His wife cannot come, but he asks me to see him all the same because he feels dejected. (I decide to see him alone because I see his distress. At some later point I will have a session with the wife alone to restore neutrality.) He has had a temperature because of cystitis, but he also has high levels of PSA and the doctor has prescribed a scan that he will take the following week. For the time being, the doctors have detected a colibacillus in his faeces. His wife told him he has it because he had anal intercourse with someone. He could not stand this accusation, turning him almost crazy, and he exploded. They had a physical fight and after a while he started his revenge. This is his only relief. He has recurring ideas. He did not let her sleep all night because she can't stand the lack of sleep. At every hour and a half he turned the light on. She moved to another room and he followed her there and turned the light on again. He must have his revenge or he will kill her or himself.

I have the interpretation that maybe he and his wife had death anxieties and reacted with persecution in order to deny anxiety and evacuate it in the other. I say to him that he creates a confused situation where one cannot see who is persecuting whom.

He seems not to hear and repeats that he needs revenge, that it is his only relief. I feel helpless, just as he felt with his wife, and I see he cannot even hear my words because of his growing anxiety.

I ask him (probably enacting my need to flee from this situation) why he did not try to go out with a friend to distract himself from his obsessive thoughts. He tells me he has no friends. In the past few years it has become difficult to go out with his wife. He says his wife has made her mother become an alcoholic and then she killed herself.

I say again that they are building a vicious circle in which one partner's persecution will reinforce the persecution of the other.

He seems to calm down a bit and to listen. I tell him that and he agrees.

He asks for explanations and I remind him of his difficulties in deciding on a separation or at least on reaching an emotional autonomy. He says it is not possible. Now he has convinced her not to call him four times a day and not to control the hotels he goes to when he is away for work. At least now he can work.

When these events happen he feels suicidal: he says at least he won't see her any more and he will be free.

I say that if they separate he could feel the same and remain alive.

He reflects on this. He is calmer and says he knows it, but he also knows he can't separate from her.

Comment

How does the session begin? There is a death anxiety that the couple cannot contact and that is turned into the anxiety about the alleged affair. The anxiety of abandonment and the fear of death or of something that cannot be controlled trigger in both an unbearable tension. An explanation must be found, any explanation, often an unreasonable one: you betray me with another woman, with my son, with your mother, you betray me because you don't obey me. This crazy explanation has several consequences.

When the intrusive projections, typical of this type of functioning, work because the other is unable to defend against them, they generate a peculiar situation that in my opinion has a confusing and claustrophobic quality. They generate a sort of claustrum in which each partner feels trapped with a sense of impending catastrophe. Meltzer (2008, p. 119 it. ed.) describes something similar in a play by Sartre, *No Exit*. When these projections are massive and recurrent, the outcome is the creation of a fantastic climate where no room is left for a true experience of the other, but most of all there is no room for imagination and fantasy. A concrete functioning dominates interpersonal relations, while at a split-off level, neither partner can see the reality of the other but imagines the other as a persecutor. The lack of doubts or uncertainties about who the other is and who the subject is, according to Fisher (1999), and to Meltzer (1979) before him, is inspired by the imaginary knowledge of an internal mother and has the quality of a delusion of the clarity of insight.

We see here a peculiar relationship based on the conscious or unconscious induction of suffering in the other in order to control, parasitise, and completely possess the other and to block his subjectivity. This is the unconscious goal unrealised by both partners. The fear of abandonment underlies it and generates a link where, in order to avoid the anxious void of abandonment, one has to expropriate the other's consciousness. Seen in this light, the terror of abandonment is only a superficial explanation, because in these couples dynamic "abandonment" can also mean just to do something autonomously: to cook something different, to see an old friend, to wear something the other does not like, to escape control somehow, even unawares; to stop being at the mercy of the other who needs that part of the partner to be able to exist.

The crucial question then is: why does the other not leave? What is his response? It is in fact the other's response that creates or solves the problem.

But how should we consider this functioning?

In the case I presented we can ask if we are observing either a core of delusional jealousy or a perverse personality structure that has not been enacted until then, or on the other hand, as I suggest, a sort of folie-à-deux shared by both partners.

In my opinion we see in some situations something similar to what happens in the case of some diseases, where a genetic defect is expressed only when environmental conditions determine its outbreak, as for example in favism, a genetic defect that translates into haemolytic anaemia only when the subject eats something that triggers the disease. The perverse or crazy element would have had a different outcome if the encounter with the other had not allowed the passage from a potential psychic dimension to a tangible enacted reality. After that encounter, the perverse fantasy of one or both partners becomes concrete, existing in reality and no longer in fantasy. The other is engaged as in a confirmation of the reality of that content and the impossibility of repressing it in a relationship that perverts and extracts something which would otherwise have remained forgotten, hidden, apparently repressed, dissociated, or split-off.

It is clear that some types of pathology appear clearly and openly from the beginning. And equally, that there are strong personalities that are unaffected by the destructive impact of pathological relationships.

Still, we will not be able to get out of this conundrum unless we understand and highlight not only their relational need for being involved in this relationship or their masochistic identification, but also the link that ties these partners and that represents the true problem. In fact all this is possible because the open violence of one is countered by the relational violence of the other. When his wife accuses him of betrayal because of the colibacillus, the husband reacts with revenge.

In reality, in everyday life, my patient, who comes from a better social milieu and has a higher professional standing than his wife, despises her clothes and always comments negatively on her wrinkles or on her unrefined behaviour, which obviously humiliates her. So a vicious circle is started, where the one induces suffering in the other who then reacts with physical and psychological violence. But who is this other from whom one cannot separate? What does it represent for both?

These situations really remind us of the patterns of folie-à-deux and I do not think we should describe events in causal terms, i.e., in terms of what induces what in the other, but rather we should describe the links that tie or imprison the interacting subjects.

Specificity of links

Their object relation too describes a functioning level between two subjects, but while this relation originates in one's infantile history and is intertwined with another who is the object of projections, we must confer to the link between two subjects a status that is independent from them but at the same time is produced by them and affects them. The nature of the link then is that of a third in a relationship, usually located in the background and not dominating the scene (except in pathological situations), while the actors play their roles in the drama. Nino Ferro's (2009) concept of field and the idea of an intersubjective third can be equated with this even if there are relevant differences between the two concepts.

This point of view should not sound unfamiliar to a group analyst, used to working with the unconscious basic assumptions produced by the group and not by its individual members, so that they will interpret the productions of each group member also as expressions of the whole group's mental functioning.

The link created in a couple, for example, even if triggered by the unconscious motives for the choice of a partner, is however a new element generated here and now in the encounter. We can assume that a meaningful link is able to extract from each partner a version of the self that is complementary to the other and functional to the link.

To treat oneself in the other

Clinical experience with couples and families has shown once and for all that there are ways of treating and falling ill that use the other, that are a way of treating oneself in the other, and of falling ill instead of the other.

Freud too, in commenting on marriage, considered its spontaneously therapeutic aspects and, in discussing his hypothetical response to a husband, said that his wife's improvement could have caused the couple's dissolution.

In particular, clinicians who work with very serious pathologies know that psychic disorders are in fact an "interactive folly" (as Racamier calls it) that has always at least another person interacting with it. These disorders underlie a specific "traumatic organisation of links" and psychosis is not an individual disorder but a problem of the whole organisation.

I assume that in psychotic families the primitive links constructed in a sort of vicious circle affect the life of all members. They are characterised by mutual control of death anxieties, by persecution, by the prohibition to think, and by a concrete pre-operational functioning.

To fall ill in the other is one of the aspects of the link pathology that we have to treat in these contexts.

We will not be surprised then by the startling changes that take place in individuals when links that imprisoned them are broken or solved by events in their life or by therapeutic work. The emergence, or better the sudden end of serious depression, of claustro- or agoraphobic symptoms can be considered as the outcome of the breaking up of significant links that had clearly been constructed as a compensation for the fragile functioning of one member. We can see how a specific link activates levels of mental functioning in the other or the states of the self that are enacted in accordance with that link. These types of functioning, like those of the case history I presented, must work by maintaining other aspects and other ways of being split off, dissociated or foreclosed.

But to answer these yet unanswered questions we need to understand better the status of the other in our psychic life, we must go beyond the positions that always focus on our unreachable self, to observe not only our upsetting unconscious but also the other in ourselves, the many others that are present in us and that we express from the origin of our life.

Notes

1. The treatment is made by two therapists, a man and a woman, under my supervision.
2. I neglect, for the moment, the question of the timing of interpretations.

References

Beebe, B., Lachman, F. M., & Jaffe, J. (1997). Mother–infant interaction structures and pre-symbolic Self and object representation. *Psychoanalytic Psychology*, 5: 305–377.
Berenstein, I., & Puget, J. (2008). *Psychanalyse du Lien*. Paris: Erès.
Bion, W. R. (1992). *Cogitations*. London: Karnac.
Bleger, J. (1967). *Simbiosis y Ambiguedad, Estudio Psicoanalitico*. [Symbiosis and ambiguity, psychoanalytic study.] Buenos Aires, Argentina: Paidòs.

Britton, R. (1989). The missing link: parental sexuality. In: R. Britton, M. Feldman, & E. O'Shaughnessy (Eds.), *The Oedipus Complex Today: Clinical Implications*. London: Karnac.

Faimberg, H., Enriquez, M., & Baranès, J. J. (1993). *Transmission de la Vie Psychique entre Générations*. Paris: Dunod.

Ferro, A. (2009). *The Analytic Field*. London: Karnac for EFPP.

Fisher, J. V. (1999). *The Uninvited Guest: Emerging from Narcissism towards Marriage*. London: Karnac.

Freud, S. (1894a). The neuro-psychoses of defence. *S. E., 3*: 45–57.

Freud, S. (1914c). On narcissism: An introduction. *S. E., 14*: 73–100.

Freud, S. (1916–1917). *Introductory Lectures on Psycho-Analysis. S. E., 15–16*: 9–238.

Freud, S. (1918b). From the history of an infantile neurosis. *S. E., 17*: 7–119.

Freud, S. (1921c). *Group Psychology and the Analysis of the Ego. S. E., 18*: 69–143.

Freud, S. (1925h). Negation. *S. E., 19*: 235.

Freud, S. (1927e). Fetishism. *S. E., 21*: 152–156.

Freud, S. (1933a). *New Introductory Lectures on Psycho-Analysis. S. E., 22*.

Garcia Badaracco, J. (2000). *Psicoanálisis familiar: los otros en nosotros y el descubrimiento del sí mismo*. Buenos Aires, Argentina: Paidòs.

Jacobson, E. (1967). *Psychotic Conflict and Reality*. New York: International Universities Press.

Kaës, R. (1976). *L'Appareil Psychique Groupal. Constructions du Groupe*. Paris: Dunod.

Kaës, R. (1994). A propos du groupe interne, du groupe, du sujet, du lien et du porte-voix dans l'œuvre de Pichon Rivière. *Revue de Psychothérapie Psychanalytique de Groupe, 22*.

Kaës, R. (2001). Il concetto di legame. *Ricerca Psicoanalitica, XII*(2): 161–184.

Kaës, R. (2007). *Un Singulier Pluriel*. Paris: Dunod.

Kaës, R., Haydée, F., Enriquez, M., & Baranes J. -J. (1993). *Transmission de la vie psychique entre générations*. Paris: Dunod.

Losso, R. (2000). *La Psicoanalisi della Famiglia*. Milan, Italy: Franco Angeli.

Meltzer, D. (1979). Un approccio psicoanalitico alla psicosi. *Quaderni di psicoterapia infantile, 2*: 31–49.

Meltzer, D. (2008). *Claustrum: An Investigation of Claustrophobic Phenomena*. Karnac Books [trad. It. Claustrum: Uno studio dei fenomeni claustrofobici. Milano: Cortina, 1993].

Meltzer, D., & Harris, H. (1983). *Child, Family and Community*. Paris: Organisation for Economic Co-operation and Development.

Mitchell, S. A. (1991). Contemporary perspectives on Self: Toward an integration. *Psychoanalytic Dialogues, 1*: 121–147.

Nicolò, A. M. (1988). La famiglia come matrice del pensiero. *Terapia Familiare, 28*: 5–16.

Nicolò, A. M. (1990). Soigner à l'intérieur de l'autre: Notes sur la dynamique entre l'individu et la famille. *Cahiers critique de thérapie familiale et de pratique de réseaux, 12*: 29–51.

Nicolò, A. M. (1992). Versioni del Sé e interazioni patologiche. *Interazioni, 0(1)*: 37–48.

Nicolò, A. M. (1997). L'importanza diagnostica delle interazioni nella valutazione della famiglia e delle sue difese trans personali. *Interazioni, 10(2)*: 53–66.

Nicolò, A. M. (2009). Subjectual links and transpersonal pathologies. *International Review of Psychoanalysis of Couple and Family, 6(2)*. www.iacfp.net.

Pichon-Rivière, E. (1980). *Teoria del vínculo*. Buenos Aires, Argentina: Nueva Vision.

Racamier, P. -C. (1990). A propos de l'engrénement. *Gruppo, 6*: 83–95.

Ruffiot, A. (1990). Le groupe-famille en analyse. L'appareil psychique familial. In: A. Ruffiot, A. Eiguer, Litovsky de Eiguer, D., Gear, M. C., Liendo, E. C., Perrot, J., & Morel, B. A. (Eds.), *La Thérapie Familiale Psychanalytique*. Paris: Dunod.

Ruffiot, A., Eiguer, A., Litovsky de Eiguer, D., Gear, M. C., Liendo, E. C., Perrot, J., & Morel, B. A. (1981). *La Thérapie Familiale Psychanalytique*. Paris: Dunod.

Stern, D. N. (1985). *The Interpersonal World of the Infant*. New York: Basic.

CHAPTER FIVE

The frightened couple*

Stanley Ruszczynski

Working clinically with patients, individuals, couples, and families, who actually act out their difficulties through delinquent, violent, or sexually perverse behaviour, is probably the biggest challenge now facing contemporary psychoanalytic psychotherapy and psychoanalysis. Until recently it was thought that such patients could not benefit from in-depth psychoanalytic work. This view is now changing and increasingly such patients are seen in psychotherapeutic clinics for treatment, and not just for management and supervision.

In the clinical work with such patients it becomes clear that their actions are often driven by anger and hatred. Robert Stoller's description of perversion as "the erotic form of hatred" (1976) could be equally applied to much delinquency and criminality and more obviously to violence. These are all acts of violation and hatred against another.

---

*An earlier version of this chapter was published (2006) under the title "Sado-masochistic Enactments in a Couple Relationship: The Fear of Intimacy and the Dread of Separateness", in *Psychoanalytic Perspectives on Couple Work, 2*: 107–116.

However, clinical experience also suggests that this *external* expression of destructiveness and hatred is often a desperate defence against overwhelming *internal* feelings of humiliation, vulnerability, and terror—a fear of becoming overwhelmed by unmanageable anxiety of annihilation. The histories of most of these patients show that they themselves were very often victims and were now in identification with the aggressor as a defence against further feared abuse and violence (Rosenfeld, 1975). In addition, they may also display what Mervyn Glasser refers to as "identification with the neglector" and through projective processes get themselves caught up in situations where they do not gain help, support and care but experience further neglect (Glasser, 1998; Ruszczynski, 2010).

Patients who act out in this way may be thought of as having no internal psychic space within which to manage their anxieties, impulses, and conflicts and, as a result, have to use, through processes of splitting, projection, and projective identification, external space into which they evacuate these unprocessed feelings. The patients find themselves behaving in ways that raise fear, horror, and terror in their external environment, not only in their relationships and in their victims but also in the community in general, including in their clinicians. They do not expect anyone to listen to them or understand them. Their terror about being a victim is unconsciously dealt with by evacuating this and creating a victim in the other person.

Violence is related to destructiveness and aggression, but aggressive feelings themselves do not lead to violence. Aggression is in fact necessarily part of the life-force and, when connected to concern for the other, is the engine behind passion, potency, and authority. In violence, the concern for the other is absent, primarily because there is often a very powerful sense of a desperate need to protect the self (Ruszczynski, 2007).

In this chapter I will discuss how aggression and violence in a couple relationship may be understood as dealing with profound states of fear and anxiety, coupled with disbelief that any help is actually available. The violent couple is always also a very frightened couple and the violence, emotional or physical, is used as a perverse solution to their difficulties in facing their fears and anxieties.

John and Jane are in their thirties and have lived together for three years. They came into treatment because of increasing arguments between them, resulting in physical fights, with Jane usually attacking

John. John usually responded to the violence by trying to ignore it or by briefly leaving the house. When he eventually found himself fighting back—he began to slap Jane—he became very frightened that he might lose control and hurt Jane badly. This brought them into treatment.

In the assessment I learned that the couple's relationship had been unstable from the beginning, with times of sadomasochistic and violent exchanges followed by periods of more reasonable and loving inter-actions. Sex had always been very poor. Not long before coming into treatment Jane had had a brief sexual affair with John's best friend. Knowledge of this affair, as a result of Jane telling him, contributed to John's beginning to physically attack Jane.

Both came from families that broke up during their childhood. From the age of ten Jane had to look after her ill mother, with her father mostly away from the home because of his work. Jane's mother died when she was thirteen and she and her brother were brought up by her father and an aunt. The two children were subject to very strict rules and expecta-tions. Though the father gave all the appearances of having their inter-ests in his mind, Jane and her brother felt that they had no choice but to do exactly as their father wanted, with no discussion about what they needed or wanted.

John was an only child and at the age of five was sent to boarding school because his parents' work often took them abroad. When he was nine his parents divorced and he spent his summer holidays either with friends or moving between his divorced parents' two homes. He described how both his mother and father seemed to feel threatened by his visits to the other parent, and each anxiously questioned him about the other parent. Both assumed that he preferred to be with the other parent, but never actually asked him. John says that he always felt that his parents related to him on the basis of *their* worries and anxieties rather than being aware of or concerned about his fears or concerns.

John remembers that when he was in his early teens, his father had parties in the house and on two or three occasions a drunken female guest came into his bedroom at night and tried to wake and sexually seduce him. He remembers feeling terrified by this intrusion: the fear "froze" him, he said, and he learned to pretend to be asleep as a way of creating a barrier against the sense of sexual attack.

Given these histories and the very anxious atmosphere created dur-ing the assessment, it became clear that neither John nor Jane had the experience of a parent or of a parental couple who could contain their fears and anxieties. In fact the opposite was true: *both John and Jane were obliged to be the recipients of their parents' unprocessed anxieties and fears.* This is a highly disturbing reversal of the usual container-contained relationship. Such an experience creates not simply the sense of absence of a good object, and therefore no containment of anxieties, but the presence of a persecutory and intrusive bad object with all the terror that goes with it.

John and Jane could both be described as having primitive anxieties about their psychic existence and hence their defences and object relations remained primarily paranoid-schizoid, with terror about abandonment and intrusiveness central. Frightening anxieties and negative emotions remained unprocessed and were experienced as toxic, humiliating, and persecutory. Jane tended to expel these states externally into John, either through her sadistic attitude towards him or in a physically violent way. Projecting her terror she creates a very frightened and persecuted John. John, in contrast, more often projected these negative emotions into an internal object and tended to be more masochistic and could easily feel demeaned. Both were terrified about their internal states.

As treatment began, it quickly became clear that the couple both feared for their psychic survival and defended against this by living out a sadomasochistic relationship. Jane is very controlling and demanding of John, whilst at the same time being very dismissive of him. She does not allow him to put his point of view in any discussion and insists that he do as she wants. She demands to know everything about his past, especially about his previous girlfriends. She attacks him verbally and, at home, physically, telling him that he is not really a man because if he were he would stand up to her. Her need to expel her own fears into him and there control them became increasingly clear.

In my emotional reaction to Jane I often felt overwhelming anger as she regularly dismissed John, the therapy, and me. She said that the treatment was a waste of time and all men were useless, clearly including me in that view. I found myself feeling anger physically in my body and, when I eventually became aware of it, my countertransference was one of being unsure about my clinical work, of being dismissed and so feeling anxious and humiliated. This could result in an agitated desire to attack the couple or, in despair, to terminate treatment and abandon them.

It was as if any state of anxiety and uncertainty could only be dealt with by an attack or by withdrawal and abandonment, not only in my countertransference but also in the couple's behaviour to each other.

I came to learn that behind Jane's sadistic and violent presentation, there was a terror of separateness which for her unconsciously represented a life-threatening abandonment. John's uncertainty and hesitance about their relationship produced for Jane the presence of a persecutory object that might desert her. Unconsciously, this may be linked to Jane having had the responsibility and anxiety of caring for her ill mother with the constant fear of failing her and of being abandoned as a result of her death.

In a desperate attempt to triumph over this terror of being abandoned, Jane tries to establish an omnipotent and narcissistic phantasy that she and John were the same, and that he wanted what she wanted with no difference between them. She colonised John via intrusive projective identification. When she felt she was failing in this, he was then experienced as a toxic and persecutory presence such that she had to violently attack him to protect herself.

In comparison, John is passive, withdrawn, and sometimes struggling to find his words. In the face of Jane's verbal assault he withdraws into a frozen state. Like Jane, he too is responding in a manner that is driven by a fear for his survival. The story of the approach from the drunken sexual women who, in his terror, John dealt with by pretending to be cocooned in sleep, represents a narcissistic retreat which enables him to fend off the horror of other people's intrusions and demands on his vulnerable self.

John was not consciously aware of how his passivity provokes Jane, brutally feeding all her terrors about being abandoned.

The sadomasochistic atmosphere in the consulting room made my attempts to have a thinking therapeutic mind very difficult. When I did come to try to offer an observation, I was openly dismissed by Jane and received in a passive way by John. Jane described what I said as meaningless or irrelevant, or she attacked me for trying to undermine her. For her, my thoughts and comments were at best empty, but often toxic, making me in her mind sadistic and damaging. John would say that my comments were "quite interesting" but what he actually conveyed was an overwhelming sense of being impenetrable and unmoved. There was no internal model for either of them of a concerned or helpful object.

I often found myself feeling very unsure about my clinical capacity to manage this couple and would sometimes then get caught up in sadistic fantasies, or feel physically disturbed and agitated. This countertransference was an important indicator of how the couple managed their fears and anxieties. An atmosphere had been created whereby I could find myself feeling impotent and hopeless, fearing that my analytic identity was being threatened or even destroyed. I would find myself struggling not to be provoked into being aggressive in my comments, joining them in their sadomasochism. At other times, I wanted to attack them or attack the relationship by terminating the analytic treatment. As for the couple, fear and anxiety felt unmanageable and could only be dealt with by aggression.

This helped me to understand the structure of the couple's unconscious marital fit and object relationship: overwhelmed by unprocessed internal fears and anxieties the couple are both preoccupied with a terrorising internal persecutor, which, in both of them, is sometimes projected outwards, leading to a sense of murderousness, or identified with internally, leading to a self-destructive passivity.

Jane projects her vulnerability and fear into John and through projective processes has to keep him frightened and controlled so that she does not have to face that terrifying vulnerability in herself. John projects his aggressive and therefore more potent self into Jane. He, too, via projective processes, has to go on seeing her in that way, otherwise he would have to become more aware of his own feared aggression and destructiveness. It was when John started to respond violently to Jane's violence that they became concerned about the danger in their relationship and came into treatment.

You will recall from their histories that both of the couple had no containing parental objects but also each had to deal with the terror of the intrusion of a demanding and persecutory object. This vicious and ceaseless movement between colonising closeness and abandoning separateness is a central experience for many patients who act out perversely or violently. Mervyn Glasser has described this in his discussion of the "core complex" (1964), and Henri Rey in his discussion of the "claustro–agoraphobic" dilemma (1994).

One of the difficulties of working with this couple was that if I showed any interest or curiosity about them they both experienced this as highly intrusive and violating. To defend against this they would often verbally dominate the therapy hour, colonising the therapeutic process, but in so doing I would be rendered impotent and in effect, specifically in my curiosity and thinking, I would be destroyed. Jane used to accuse me of having a perverse interest in the way they related, and used to ask why I could not simply let them be the way they were. In the transference, I was, at best, dismissed as useless but more often seen as a dangerous figure whose curiosity and desire to understand was experienced as hostile and aggressive and hence had to be made silent or destroyed.

In working clinically with this couple and other violent patients, couples, and individuals, I have come to find it essential to have in mind the idea of the patients' anxiety and terror of violation as a central element in the meaning of the sadomasochistic behaviour and violence. The perpetrator's sense of being humiliated, diminished, and violated, physically or emotionally, is at the core of that state of mind, which protects itself by activating the psychically or physically violent behaviour towards the victim. The victim then becomes the terrified, hurt, and frightened person, freeing the abuser from experiencing these terrors. In a sadomasochistic or violent couple this psychic constellation is likely to be shared.

Mervin Glasser, in his writing on aggression and violence (1964, 1998), makes an important distinction between what he calls "self-preservative violence" and "sadistic violence". In *self-preservative violence* the overriding aim is to eliminate anxiety, fear, and a sense of threat by attacking and destroying its source. In *sadistic violence* the aim is to gain control and vengefully gain pleasure and relief from dominating and inflicting pain on the threatening object. Sadism suggests *some* capacity to imagine the emotional reaction of the other person and also, through the sadomasochistic interaction, some investment in sustaining the relationship. This differs significantly from self-preservative violence where the fate of the object is irrelevant, as the overriding aim is to simply annihilate the perceived threat to the self.

This difference in the nature of the relationship to the object is important. The capacity to imagine or have some awareness of the other is in contrast to the much more primitive and narcissistic personality for whom difference and boundaries between selves are absent. Sadistic violence, by definition, involves some awareness of the separate other, and self-preservative violence is characteristic of much more primitive and narcissistic states of mind.

In reality, of course, as we can see with John and Jane, these different states of mind are never that distinct, and are certainly not fixed structures. There is always movement between the anxieties, defences, and types of interaction belonging to these two types of object relations. Attempts to manage unbearable fear and anxiety are at the heart of both, with domination and control being essential features in both. Sadistic violence, based on sadomasochistic object relations, may break down into the more dangerous self-preservative violence if the object continues to feel persecutory and psychically toxic. Narcissistic and borderline patients rapidly *oscillate between these states and this oscillation itself* comes to add a further disturbing dimension to the persecution and threat. The act of violence might sometimes be enacted in the attempt to stop this highly disturbing oscillation.

Glasser's concept of the "core complex" (1964), similar to what Henri Rey describes as the "agoraphobic–claustrophobic dilemma" (1994), as mentioned above, refers to the inevitable human dilemma between the deep-seated longing for intimacy and closeness, and the need for autonomy and separateness. The closeness may come to feel claustrophobic or like merger, and the separateness may come to feel agoraphobic or like abandonment. This struggle between individuality and partnership is, of course, central to the constant and inevitable tension in any and every couple relationship, between legitimate and necessary separateness and appropriate and desired intimacy.

Both states therefore might raise fear and anxiety about separateness and loss, either the loss of the self or the loss of the desired and/or required other. The capacity to achieve and tolerate this anxiety suggests a move towards the depressive position, which is only really possible if there has been a reasonable resolution in infancy of the anxieties of the oedipal situation. In a couple relationship, this means coming to tolerate the anxieties provoked by both dependence and independence, and to manage the anxieties of sometimes being included and sometimes excluded.

In a relatively mature relationship, with depressive position functioning being more predominant, this oscillation will be contained and tolerated. If this depressive capacity has not been achieved, as with John and Jane, the conflicts are experienced at the border of the more primitive, persecutory, and threatening anxieties. In a psychic structure that is more paranoid-schizoid, or if there is a regression to that state, the sense of difference is experienced not as separateness, with the ensuing sense of mourning and loss, but more as an intrusion by a terrifying persecutor. The experience is not primarily one of *loss* but of the *presence* of something persecutory, humiliating, and unbearable. It is this persecutory invasion that has to be dealt with by its annihilation.

If there is some fragile capacity to imagine the feelings of the other, a more sadistic reaction might emerge with domination, control, and possibly revenge, actively or passively, becoming primary. In this situation, however, the ongoing presence of the other is essential and so defensively the aggression is sexualised as a way, in phantasy, of binding the object into the relationship, albeit a sadomasochistic relationship. As already suggested, it is likely that there will be an oscillation between these two states of mind and ways of object relating, as became a familiar part of my experience with John and Jane.

Is it possible to understand why some patients actually act out their violent feelings as a means of dealing with their deep anxieties and fears? Various authors have suggested that enactments of aggression, violence, and murderousness are induced by the psychic toxicity resulting from certain impulses, anxieties, and conflicts being unprocessed as a result of a failure or lack of containment, or because of a lack of a capacity for mentalisation (Fonagy & Target, 1995). Without the experience of containment, no development of a *psychological self* can take place, of a self that can process and think about experiences and psychic states. Such development requires the primary experience and perception of oneself, with all one's fears, anxieties, and conflicts, being present in *the mind of someone who is able to feel these feelings and try to think about them*. Without this, what results is "mindlessness", an empty, inanimate, and even malignant sense of the self rooted, not in the mind, but in the body. The inability to reflect on and integrate mental experiences results in only the body and bodily experiences being available to be used to provide a sense of relief, release, or consolidation. If this threatening object is projected into another, as with Jane, it may result in a sadistic, violent, or murderous attack on the body of the victim. If identified with, as with John, it results in a masochistic or suicidal attack on the physical self.

With violent and perverse patients, there has very often been not just a lack of parental containment but of violent or perverse parents with a predatory aspect to their relationships, emotional, physical, and sexual. Such patients often display a desperate urge to evacuate their psychic states into the mind and body of the other so as to expel their own toxic states. This might lead to sadomasochistic interactions, and it might also be more destructive, violent, and murderous.

In thinking about failure in containment or the lack of a capacity for mentalisation we should keep in mind the nature of the death instinct, which, at its strongest, attacks and distorts the capacities for perception and judgement, both in the potentially available containing object and in the self. Clinically, the concept should be thought of as a destructive *psychological* force. Michael Feldman says that what is deadly about the death instinct is the way in which meaning, and specifically difference, is attacked (2000). Bion describes this process very powerfully, saying that it is characterised by experiences being denuded of their meaning and value (1959). As a result of these attacks, ordinary developmental processes, which would eventually result in the development of a thinking psychological self that is able to manage and contain most fear and anxiety, are retarded or undermined. This understanding seems clinically helpful when thinking about perverse attacks on the emotional facts of vulnerability, neediness, dependence, separateness, and loss. All these experiences need to become tolerable in the mind, so as to allow for the capacity to develop relatively mature couple relationships.

Working with such patients has to take their violence and destructiveness seriously. However, this can probably be done more easily if *in addition* such patients are also understood as attempting to manage anxiety and fear which feel unbearable and which have to be evacuated externally and so creating a victim in the other, thereby to ensure that they themselves do not again become victims. I hope that the phase of work with John and Jane described above illustrates that struggle.

References

Bion, W. R. (1959). Attacks on linking. *International Journal of Psychoanalysis, 40*: 308–315.

Feldman, M. (2000). Some views on the manifestation of the death instinct. *International Journal of Psychoanalysis, 81*: 53–65.

Fonagy, P., & Target, M. (1995). Understanding the violent patient. *International Journal of Psychoanalysis, 76*: 487–501.

Glasser, M. (1964). Some aspects of the role of aggression in the perversions. In: I. Rosen (Ed.), *Sexual Deviation* (pp. 279–300). New York: Oxford University Press.

Glasser, M. (1998). On violence: a preliminary communication. *International Journal of Psychoanalysis, 79*: 887–902.

Rey, H. (1994). *Universals of Psychoanalysis in the Treatment of Psychotic and Borderline States*. London: Free Association.

Rosenfeld, H. (1975). Negative therapeutic reaction. In: P. Giovacchini (Ed.), *Tactics and Techniques in Psychoanalytic Psychotherapy, vol. 2, Countertransference* (pp. 217–228). New York: Jason Aronson.

Ruszczynski, S. (2006). Sado-masochistic enactments in a couple relationship: the fear of intimacy and the dread of separateness. *Psychoanalytic Perspectives on Couple Work Issue, 2*: 107–116.

Ruszczynski, S. (2007). The problem of certain psychic realities. In: D. Morgan & S. Ruszczynski (Eds.), *Lectures on Violence, Perversion and Delinquency* (pp. 23–42). London: Karnac.

Ruszczynski, S. (2010). Becoming neglected: a perverse relationship to care. *British Journal of Psychotherapy, 26*: 22–32.

Stoller, R. (1976). *Perversion: The Erotic Form of Hatred*. Brighton, UK: Harvester Press.

CHAPTER SIX

Adoptive families: what pathways for subjectivisation?

Daniela Lucarelli and Gabriela Tavazza

D. W. Winnicott used to say that when a child is given to parents, it does not represent a nice diversion, but something that changes their whole life. If all goes well they will spend the following twenty-five years trying to solve the problem they now have, but if it goes wrong, then it can go really wrong: they will have started on the path of disillusionment and the tolerance of failure (1996).

Winnicott was perhaps a bit pessimistic, but his statement introduces us to the difficulties in the relationship between a child and its new parents. In this encounter we see different modes of mental functioning and mutual stories at play.

In this sense we would like to present some reflections on the complexity of the subjectivisation process in adoptive families, where all members have experienced traumas that marked a break in their continuity of being. For an adopted child this break is an early uprooting, while for the parents it is the wound struck by not having been able to reproduce.

In our clinical experience, adoption has put us in direct contact with a wide range of problems: from difficulties in identification and mutual recognition, via the rupture of the sense of an original "we" built on the feeling of belonging to a unity (Lemaire, 2010), to the complicated construction of a new family "we", and ending with the difficulties in the subjectivisation process and the creation of an ego. Reflecting on these questions we felt that concepts such as the subjectivisation process, intersubjective psychic space, and the subjectivising function of the family environment could be useful for exploring the complex intrapsychic and interpersonal aspects of adoption.

In consultations with parents, we touch upon the distress they feel together with their adopted child over the effort of building a sense of belonging from which they would be able to start a deep elaboration of the trauma, caused in the child by having been abandoned, and in the parents by their infertility. But this elaboration is difficult and cannot but be incomplete. In fact, Artoni Schlesinger (2006) argues that in this case one is bound to mourn a void, an absence, a lost object that refers to other existences from which the subject is excluded.

The parents experience difficulty at elaborating the unconscious reasons for the dismissal or prohibition to give birth, at integrating the foreignness of the child, and at sharing with the child the traumatic experiences pre-dating the adoption or in affiliating a child whose origins also elicit a sense of rejection.

On the other hand, we do know the complexity of the parental function, which cannot be considered only in relation to the physical event of birth, but which is related also to the complex process of psychic transformation that starts in the parents (as individuals and as a couple) at the very moment they feel they want a child. This paves the way for a long process of affiliation that includes fantasies, wishes, and projections that create a psychic space for a child in the family and allow the creation of a family "we". Nicolò (2005) suggested the term "symbolic parenting" for the parental function, a term that conveys symbols and describes an affiliation which in turn will produce a capacity for symbolisation. This process is even more meaningful in the case of adoptive parents, where there is no biological event.

We would also like to argue that parenting should be a continuously changing function that is built by parents and child, each with their own reactions. In this sense it is an intersubjective function.

The problems that can emerge in a biological or an adopted child should be considered as part of a more or less complex intersubjective cluster of affective relations.

However, in particular in the case of adoption, it is quite frequent that parents, when faced with serious situations, come to therapy with the request "to treat" the child, as if they wanted to eliminate something unexpected, disturbing, and extraneous in their child that changes him and makes them feel he is different from them and does not correspond to their expectations.

In these situations, the parents often seem not only worried but also surprised, as if what is happening could not have anything in common with the child they had fantasised about and wished for. They are invaded by a sense of foreignness: the new unexpected behaviours of this child evoke in them ghosts related to the negative impact of his origin that represents the trace of the child's identification with its biological parents.

This fear can be expressed consciously, but at times it cannot even be thought and immediately produces a feeling of devaluation and rejection of the child, whose difficulties cannot be thought, let alone understood.

They then feel the re-emergence of that feeling of "foreignness" that might have been perceived at the moment of adoption but was kept at bay by various defence mechanisms, such as the denial of the child's story before adoption, the idealisation of the child, the projection of parental narcissism, the projection onto the child of their reproductive problems, and the displacement of deep emotional experiences onto the material issues of upbringing and organising their everyday life.

But beyond the defences, traumatic experiences are still present in the family. On the one hand, those of the child who was abandoned, had to spend short or long periods in an institution, and had to undergo the traumatic inclusion in this new family with its habits, environment, and sensations that are quite different from the child's original ones. On the other, those of the parents who are burdened with an experience of helplessness, failure, and loss of self-realisation, and of the fantasy of continuing their life in their offspring. "They have to mourn a part of themselves felt as damaged, destructive for the self, for the other member of the couple, for the couple itself and the family and its generational continuity" (Nicolò, 2002, p. 86). Adoptive parents have suffered and are suffering still because they are different, just like the child who also feels different because he has been abandoned.

In order to be able to integrate these traumatic experiences, so well described by Artoni Schlesinger (2006), it would be necessary for parents and child to build an affective and mental bond that allows the construction of a shared emotional narrative where fragmented memories could be located. Often the reconstruction of a traumatic memory is not possible for the child because abandonment caused a change that has become a break (Bion, 1992) "in that network of primitive mental relations that can be shared and allow the self to form and see itself as belonging to a context that fed the original experience" (Artoni Schlesinger, 2006, p. 116). The continuity of being has been interrupted (Winnicott, 1965) during a period when the child's immaturity did not allow the formation of explicit memories. The break in continuity experienced at an early age can evoke anxiety and a loss of meaning due to the lack of affective memories related to one's origin and to the feeling of belonging to a whole that is the basis of the original "we".

The intersubjectivisation process can thus be hampered by the distress felt by all family members: "… the child's subjectivization always requires the subjectivizing function of the mother" (Carel, 2006, p. 186).

The new adoptive family should be able to build a new affective plot, an intersubjective psychic space that can contain the child's experience of loss of continuity and loss of ties with his biological parents and his origins, and/or the lack of an internal image of his biological parents.

But in order to perform this function, adoptive parents need to elaborate their own trauma in the face of their loss of reproductive capacity and/or any existing obstacles to reproduction. Elaboration can be particularly complex due to the deep narcissistic wound defined by the loss of a part of oneself and the deprivation of continuity through offspring (Luzzatto, 2002, p. 35). The parents too must then face "breaks" in the continuity of their self-representation. Being in one's skin starts with the internalisation of a continuity of being and a feeling of trust that is supported by an intersubjectivising matrix of the family group (Richard & Wainrib, 2006).

At the time of adoption, parents need to feel reassured that these destabilising and distressing experiences have been overcome and that the arrival of a child will help to put them aside. Most parents massively invest in the child, trying their best at making him feel at home, so that the child too can overcome and forget his experience of abandonment as fast as possible. Their feeling of not being the "real" parents can then be erased by the concrete reality of daily care. They can build a bond with their child (in particular one parent, usually the mother) with fusion features that represent the need for constant reassurance to fend off anxiety.

The most immediate aspect we see is the one related to the need for creating a "glue" that allows parents and child to tie themselves together while repressing or denying wounds and losses. At a deeper level, especially in the case of infertility without a specific physical cause, there can be the ghost of a mother that did not play the function of "psychic incubator" and did not internally support the possibility of pregnancy (Neri, Pallier, Petacchi, Soavi & Tagliacozzo, 1990). In these cases the concrete need for fusion can express an anxiety and an inability to think the fantasies and mental states underlying anxiety. The concrete becomes a substitute for relational feelings, for good emotional symbols, fantasies, and representations (ibid.). In these cases we see a break in subjectivisation.

In many cases a fusion relationship can also last for a long time and allow a quiet period until puberty when the child is faced with the new developmental tasks of adolescence. The onset of differentiation processes and the search for identity bring the complexity of identification back on the scene. In addition, pubertal changes and the emergence of a sexual body put the parents in contact with the question of fertility and revive the pain of their infertility/sterility.

Puberty challenges the solidity of internal resources for the construction of identity. Kaës (2002) writes: "The sense of our origin, along with the environment that brought us up and that still surrounds us with relations and affects, is essential for completing our identity" (p. 185).

If their child behaves in offending ways, adoptive parents can feel guilty because they were not able to produce the child from themselves and therefore think that they might not be good parents, also due to the unconscious fantasy of having taken the child from his real parents. Strong abandonment anxieties can also emerge because they are not truly sure of the child's love, as they themselves doubt their bond with him.

Adoptive parents can experience a threat to their identity as parents when the parenting process is not based on a completed mourning and on an affiliation process allowing them to integrate the "foreign" aspects of their child that, not having been generated by these parents, is in fact a "foreigner". In order for this to take place they need a mental and affective contact with the unknown world of origins (Artoni Schlesinger, 2006).

Clinical vignettes

We present two clinical vignettes, one concerning a recent adoption (having lasted so far only three months) of a seven-year-old boy; the other of a girl, now fifteen, who was adopted at age eight. With the first case we want to show how the parents' difficulty in integrating the boy's diversity and the emergence of a sense of foreignness have created obstacles to a mutual recognition and to the establishment of a subjectivising function in the family. With the second vignette we want to focus on the situations where after adoption an apparently positive and harmonious climate is formed, as well as a family "we" that is disrupted by the emergence of violent behaviours and of pathological symptoms in adolescence, showing that subjectivisation of traumatic experiences has not taken place.

Diego

Diego is seven and was adopted three months ago by a relatively old couple (he is forty-seven and she is forty-five) who no longer had any hope of becoming parents. Although not much time has passed since the boy has entered their home, the parents ask for help in managing his behaviour that they cannot understand.

The mother comes to the first interview with a folder containing the boy's story, and giving it to me she says: "This is Diego," signalling that probably they don't yet have an internal image of the child and that their representation of him coincides with the paperwork contained in the folder.

The interview time is almost completely taken up by the detailed and enraged narrative of the long procedure they had to undergo before they were finally told that they were adequate for becoming parents.

Mother defines herself: "I am a manager and I know all the steps necessary to overcome the numerous bureaucratic hurdles. That certainly did not scare me!"

She shows a mental functioning characterised by very concrete thinking and a narcissistic set-up in the absence of any contact with the complexity and the psychic contents typical of parenting. The central issue of our first interviews is lying and how many lies Diego tells.

"We told him he should not tell lies, they are useless and just as we don't tell lies to him, he should not lie to us. In the end, are we a family, or not? And in a family lies are not necessary." They recount that the first time they met him, he said he liked to go to school and to study English, but later neither of these statements turned out to be true.

When asked why he had said that, Diego replied: "The nun suggested that I say something surprising that would induce you to take me. Are you going to change your mind now?"

For Diego, lies have the function of protecting a true self that cannot be seen; they are a way of complying and mediating with the environment, of exploring the emotional responses he elicits in the people around him. We could define them as tools for his work, for his search for the proper distance/proximity to the adults that also masks his most authentic part without uncovering too much of himself.

Ferenczi (1928) argued that in a child, lies meet the need for avoiding unpleasant experiences and for imagining and inventing.

For the adoptive parents, instead, lies are a deception of their narcissistic ideal and a testimony to the child's hostility. So they ask: "Why doesn't he understand? He does it on purpose. The earlier we do something, the earlier we recover."

But what is there to recover, if not that image of a child that is as similar as possible to what they had fantasised about? Otherwise the feeling of foreignness prevails and brings back the idea of a link to a past that is not well known and can evoke ghosts.

It seems impossible to reach the mutual recognition that is not symmetry or narcissistic union. A subjectivising link cannot truly be formed because there is no recognition of the otherness and of differences (Richard & Wainrib, 2006).

"Diego upset our life, we were like lovers in a Peynet cartoon and now the hurricane Diego swept everything away. It has become hard even to say good morning. I can't even take a shower without him knocking on the door to know when I am finished. At times I feel like I am suffocating. Diego is always in my thoughts, I can think of nothing else."

It is clear that the child is experienced on one side as the element that destroyed the couple's union and on the other as an object whose otherness becomes persecutory.

The father also admits his inability at managing Diego and says: "For me it is inconceivable that he can refuse to consider what adults tell him." The father seems lost, unable to find a possible identification with a son who does not identify with him. So the process of cathexis that is essential for a mutual recognition cannot take place (ibid., 2006).

His admission to school is the problem that most challenged the parents' ability to manage the child, as the normative aspect is the only one they know how to use and it made them feel helpless. Diego behaves badly at school, is restless and cannot concentrate, so he upsets lessons, but at the same time he shows a good learning ability. The parents admit that he is a clever boy and this aspect is certainly meaningful for them: it is now the only area where they can identify with him.

Melissa

Melissa is fourteen and was adopted at age eight. She is the eldest of four siblings who were adopted by different families. The environment of her biological family was run-down; her father used to abuse her mother even though he lived with another family. Her paternal grandfather was a pimp, lived with the family, and made the mother walk the streets along with other prostitutes. Probably one of Melissa's siblings is his son.

At home the situation was one of violence and promiscuity, witnessed daily by the children, with the mother totally unable to protect them. At age six, Melissa was left in an institution with her siblings by her mother, who at first visited them and later vanished.

Her adoptive parents seem very engaged: mother shows a more narcissistic set-up while father seems more able to contact the depressive experiences and current difficulties of his daughter. They say that when she arrived, she was a smiling, quiet, loving, and obedient child. They spent a lot of time with her, each one of them taking time from work in turns. An early puberty at ten changes everything. Mother soon finds out that Melissa chats with older men using very explicit and seductive sexual language. She also posted some pictures on the internet of herself naked in exciting positions. Mother is scared and leaves her job to take care of her daughter.

The parents ask for a consultation together with their daughter. In the first interview mother is plagued by a terrible headache; she is taken to the casualty department and is diagnosed with a cerebral haemorrhage and hospitalised for two weeks. Until that moment she had never had symptoms of a cardiovascular disease. After this event she decides to postpone her return to work. The second consultation interview is also postponed, but after a while the parents discover that on the school bus Melissa is blackmailed by schoolmates to whom she pays large sums of money she steals at home. So the parents take Melissa's computer and mobile phone from her, she no longer takes the school bus, and mother again stays at home with her.

The parents are upset and very worried and decide to ask for a new consultation and this time it seems possible to start the interviews with them as well as sessions with Melissa.

In one of her first sessions Melissa says that the sentences she is writing in chats are the same ones she heard as a child at home said by her biological mother.

Melissa's psychotherapy has been going on twice a week for a year and her parents accepted to see a therapist once a week.

What we know so far invites some considerations.

First of all, the coincidence of mother's haemorrhage with the interview suggests that it has been unbearable for her to face the problem of integrating Melissa's violent infantile experiences, giving up the image of a sweet child that met her ideal and allowed her to repair her own infantile experience.

Melissa's parents, in fact, do not seem to have integrated the split-off dramatic aspects of their adopted daughter's life, due to their narcissistic need for protecting an ideal form of parenting and an ideal daughter. So Melissa has not been supported by a parental subjectivising function in integrating and elaborating her violent infantile experiences, which re-emerge when separation is imposed by adolescence.

Her psychic functioning does not yet allow her to touch these painful experiences without threatening her ego. She therefore needs her parents' psychic support to beable to continue her subjectivisation process. How can adoptive parents succeed in favouring a greater differentiation and separation, if they cannot contain in the relationship the traumas she suffered and share her anxiety for having been abandoned? As they are currently helped by treatment to learn how to play this role, maybe their response will give her an adequate narcissistic confirmation that allows her to tolerate her need for dependence.

What psychic work will this "foreign" daughter, arrived from another world, need to do to be integrated in her new family?

Concluding remarks

In closing we would like to stress that the process of adoption highlights that only the establishment of a family "we" can favour the emergence of an ego supported by a subjectivising environment that is formed in a mutual recognition of otherness and difference of places, and not of symmetry and fusion. The mutual recognition of subjects will favour the birth of subjectivising bonds that cannot be developed only in the intrapsychic, but also in the logic of object relations where only one person is a subject and the other becomes automatically an object (Richard & Wainrib, 2006). The link, instead, is more than an exchange of mutual projective identifications: it is established as an entity experienced unconsciously as a third element that can affect other internal and external relations. Subjectivising bonds therefore develop in the interpersonal space between subjects that are capable of recognising the other, differentiating him/her from other internal objects and evaluating his/her similarity or otherness. A subjectivising bond needs to lean on a facilitating bond with the other that allows for differentiation. Subjectivising, in fact, goes through a progressive recognition/appropriation of basic differences (and how many there are in adoptive families!): between oneself and the others, and between sexes and generations. When the loss of having to accept this limit is not felt as a pure loss, it can support the subjectivising bond that allows for differentiation and guarantees the continuity of being.

We can think then of subjectivisation as a process that leans more on mutual recognition than on object relations, that is established thanks to a continuous exchange of what is organised in the child's psyche and what the child finds in his relationships with his parents. The parents in turn must develop a self-reflection that allows them to appropriate their psychic functioning and let the capacity for representation emerge.

Starting from this theoretical stance in thinking of adoption, clinical work with the parents will become essential.

In fact, therapeutic work with adoptive parents, when it can get started, can facilitate the development of relationships and allow the integration of traumatic experiences.

Already in 1956 Winnicott suggested that adoptive parents should be therapists for their children. In saying this he was certainly aware that it is extremely difficult for adopted children to be assigned to persons other than their biological parents and what deep emotional implications this has. Experience tells us that children too can be helped by keeping in mind their fragility and the specificity of the developmental phase they are in. It is important, however, to take into account that the problems of a child are always part of a cluster of affective relations in the family and that it is possible to activate functions that the parents must first discover in themselves in order to convey them to their children.

But as Vallino (1997) argues, it is also important to keep in mind that when working on adoption, a psychotherapist risks feeling a decrease in her own reassuring unity and can be forced to face the anxiety deriving from a loss of meaning.

In the process of adoption we should re-establish a process of creation of affective bonds first of all in the parents, so that they can build an internal world belonging to all the members of the new family from which subjectivisation processes can begin to take place.

References

Artoni Schlesinger, C. (2006). *Adozione e Oltre*. Rome: Borla.

Bion, W. R. (1992). *Cogitations*. London: Karnac.

Carel, A. (2006). L'inter subjectualisation. In: F. Richard & S. Wainrib (Eds.), *La Subjectivation* (pp. 185–201). Paris: Dunod.

Ferenczi, S. (1928). The adaptation of the family to the child. *British Journal of Medical Psychology, 8*: 1–13.

Kaës, R. (2002). La costruzione dell'identità in correlazione all'alterità e alla differenza. *Psiche, 1*: 185–195.

Lemaire, J. -G. (2014). *Couple and Family Psychoanalytic Psychotherapy's Contribution to Current Psychoanalysis*. IIn: this volume (pp. 171–185).

Luzzatto, L. (2002). L'adozione tra azione e pensiero. *Interazioni, 18*: 35–48.

Neri, C., Pallier, L., Petacchi, G., Soavi, G. C., & Tagliacozzo, R. (1990). *Fusionalità*. Rome: Borla.

Nicolò, A. M. (2002). Identità e identificazione nelle adozioni. *Interazioni, 18*: 82–94.

Nicolò, A. M. (2005). Nuove forme di genitorialità. Riflessioni a partire da un caso di procreazione assistita. *Interazioni, 23*: 43–52.

Richard, F., & Wainrib, S. (2006). *La Subjectivation*. Paris: Dunod.

Vallino, D. (1997). Commento al lavoro di Claudia Artoni Schlesinger— Memorie delle mie "non-memorie". In: M. L. Algini (Ed.), *La Depressione dei Bambini* (pp. 153–156). Rome: Borla.

Winnicott, D. W. (1956). *Through Paediatrics to Psycho-Analysis*. London: Tavistock, 1958.

Winnicott, D. W. (1965). *The Maturational Process and the Facilitating Environment: Studies in the Theory of Emotional Development*. London: Hogarth & The Institute of Psychoanalysis.

Winnicott, D. W. (1996). *Thinking about Children*. London: The Winnicott Trust.

CHAPTER SEVEN

Transformations through repetitions of female and male representations in reconstructed families

Diana Norsa

Introduction

When reflecting on psychotherapy cases of couples in their second or third marriage, I asked myself: what is it that drives people who have suffered over previous broken relationships to get married again? Why are some couples success stories and others not?

The rich material that has emerged from the cases I have handled has stimulated my reflection on the hypothesis that the desire to remarry, despite the suffering caused by repeated separations, can depend both on a compulsion to repeat previous traumatic situations, and on an increased self-awareness—what we normally call "learning from experience"—that drives us to a new sexual, romantic relationship.

Kernberg (1993) reminds us that divorce and a new marriage are ways of giving us a new opportunity to reach maturity: people share a period of their life with one partner and the following with a different one in a satisfactory way.

Nonetheless, despite the desire to have new opportunities to grow, some couples are motivated by the urge of repetition compulsion. As Enid Balint pointed out: "Over and over again people come back to their failures in an attempt to remedy them ... we could say that in marriage we unconsciously hope to find a solution to our intimate and primitive problems, particularly to those that we cannot communicate socially" (1968, p. 41).

The couple relationship implies a physicality which is not only sexual but also involves care and tenderness, and, as such, reawakens those memories that are written in one's body, the traces of more primitive experiences of the Self. My own findings in clinical practice have brought me to value the body in emotional, cognitive, and psychic events in the lives of infants and adults. Melanie Klein (1957) uses a suggestive term: "memories in feeling" to underline the nature of memories which go back to the beginning of bodily experiences that are endowed with psychic value not yet converted into a psychic language, but nevertheless ageing in the present object relations. Winnicott (1966) studied the importance of bodily experience in the first phase of the maturational process that implies a mother–baby dual unit: he speaks about unintegrated phenomena distinguishing it both from integration and disintegration. Not only in the sexual relationship of the couple, but also in parental issues, regression is implicated at the deepest levels of the psyche-soma: from oedipal conflict identification, to partial sexual identification, to the primal female and male components as "being" and "doing".[1] The regressive phenomena that occur in a couple relation, whether in the sexual relationship or in parental tasks, imply an undifferentiated level of "being" that is seeking to be in relation with the object. When we say, "I feel good when I'm with you," it means we have reached an even balance between these two basic affective states (Norsa & Baldassarre, 2008). The absence of one or both of these components making us "feel good on our own or feel good with our partner" can generate distress, causing the breakdown of the relationship and the search for a new intimate relationship with a new object, in the hope that it will be more successful the next time. If the new object responds in a different way to the scene already staged in the past, the Self of the subject is also induced to respond differently and a virtuous circle thus sets in.

In the following two clinical cases I will describe a male whose female partner requires him to fulfil a repairing function of the internal models concerning the triadic relation, inasmuch as the relationship with her children imposes the urgent need of bringing about this change.

In the first case, this urgent need concerns the adolescence of Anna's daughter whose development is hindered by bouts of bulimia. In the second case, Elena's subjective urgent need appears in the form of a sudden falling in love, a short time after the birth of her second son, which will be instrumental in upsetting the whole family, as we will see.

Sexuality in psychoanalysis

The sexual instinct for Freud is the force moving every psychic dynamic: from the search for a relationship with the other, as an object of desire,[2] to the dream, which, while satisfying the instinctual desire in an illusory form, creates representations and metaphors. In its pre-oedipal form, oral, anal, and phallic, it constitutes a powerful source of psychopathology that drives individuals towards regressive forms of satisfying desire through the creation of collusive and sado-masochistic relationships. One of the most obvious elements distorting relationships found in families with a psychotic, perverse structure is the negation of differences: adults are not differentiated from children, male not from female, sexuality not from sensuality/tenderness. Clinical material often shows how, in place of a sexed and generative couple, the "male" and "female" are certainly present but in partial, regressive, and dissociated forms and how they act as "partial objects" which, on entering into a relationship, instead of generating life in all its symbolic meanings, release a potentially highly destructive force, animated by anxiety for survival or desire to dominate.

The parental couple of origin

"... the fate of the human psyche is to have always two objects and never one alone, however far one goes back to try to understand the earliest psychic structure" (Green, 1980, p. 24).

On a primitive level, the "female" and "male" represent that "home where we start from"[3] without which the subjective Self remains silent, incapable of using all the acquisitions of a body and a mind which, growing, develop highly differentiated functions. Instead of integration, development will therefore be characterised by dissociation. The primal bisexuality here refers not only to sexual identity, female or male, but rather to the female as "being" and to the male as "doing", as a transformative force.

Holding is an abstract concept that becomes a concrete reality in the handling of the baby by the mother. The term "going concern"

(Winnicott, 1966), describes how the mother, through her actions of looking after her baby, communicates her ability to combine cathexis and selfless concern and care. Not only the mother needs to integrate "being" and "doing", the male and female elements, but the father also needs to do the same.

The Italian author Gaddini has greatly contributed to clarifying these aspects of development with two major works: "On Father Formation in Early Child Development" (1976), and "Formation of the Father and the Primal Scene" (1974) in which he elaborates some elements of Winnicott's thought. Gaddini refers to the father as a figure who appears on two different levels in the perceptive sphere of the child: on one level as the first external object which, in contrast to the mother, remains excluded from the dual unit of mother and child and therefore comes to represent for the child the prototype object "outside the Self" on which gradually all those perceptions of extraneousness experienced by the child towards his mother converge, enabling him to absorb them not as threatening elements buy simply as external ones. On another level, the father is also an internal element of the mother, indissolubly connected to her. The crucial point of Gaddini's theory is to perceive the personality structure in strict relation to the parental figures, also on very precocious levels. Gaddini sets aside reference to elements pertaining to adult sexuality, preferring to concentrate instead on the psychosensory experience that characterises childhood sexuality. The author speaks of an "imitative identity" organised on the basis of psychosensory activity according to a functional model of the type "imitate for being": imitate the object to become subject, the purpose of such activity being to reinforce the integrity of the Self. This activity in a small child develops from the relationship with his mother and father in their role as a couple in a complex series of presentations which Gaddini calls the "primal scene process", it being the central representation through which the child develops internally his definitive separation-discovery of the maternal body.

First clinical case

I will now discuss a consultation with a couple that represents an excellent illustration of what I have been affirming. The couple brought a classical sexual conflict, betrayal, into the first session, whereas in the second a more primitive and complex psychic trauma appears which shows us just how much the parent function and the couple relationship are interwoven, up to the point of affecting the couple's individual unconscious issues.

First session

Anna telephoned, pressing me for a consultation for herself and her partner. They were both in their early fifties, with successful careers, well dressed and affable.

At our first encounter, I was presented with a "non-couple" situation, considered as such from the beginning of their relationship—two years of cohabitation for contingent reasons rather than through choice, characterised by pleasure in doing things together, a recent crisis attributed to another of Aldo's habitual betrayals, a situation tolerated in the past, however, in the context of a general philosophy of life shared by both, along the lines of "we won't be influenced by conventions". Both appeared to be unhappy, Anna frantic, aggressive, attacking Aldo and saying he had betrayed her trust. Aldo was visibly in difficulty and defended himself with the hit-and-run method, maintaining that he was unfaithful by choice, that he had always told her so, that he had made various attempts to satisfy her needs but that she was too possessive and he was unable to put up with her. Both stated they were distressed about the thought of ending the relationship but when asked about how they had been before they met, she maintained that she undoubtedly had felt more confident, whereas now she felt insecure and fragile. He said that he had been able to establish with her moments of togetherness and sharing which he had never experienced before for such long periods with other partners. Apart from a comprehensible attitude of initial diffidence, what characterised our first meeting was a tendency to use me as the public in front of whom to act, to reveal negative things. As the reason for their request for a consultation was not clear to me, and being unable to identify any common ground on which to develop therapeutic work, I told them about my perplexity and suggested we had another meeting to clarify matters. The fact that I referred, at the end of the session, to their obvious personal distress and my doubts that their relationship was a significant answer for either of them in the face of such suffering, had the effect, however, of eliminating their diffidence towards me and to make them behave more cooperatively.

Comment on the first session

During the first session, both partners in conflict with each other were convinced that it was necessary to prevent dependency setting in. The domination of a narcissistic couple axis and the instrumental use of the therapist's listening to reinforce this narcissistic collusion were obvious. I think their fear of being dependent on each other veiled a regressive need they feared because it was out of control. Control and the need for dependency were therefore defensively attributed by each to the other.

Second session

The next time they presented me with another side of the problem: Anna had a daughter who had always lived with her, an eighteen-year-old girl who had been suffering from bulimia since childhood. Recently the situation had become alarming as in a very short time she had reached a weight of ninety kilos. The girl had currently been making attempts to solve her situation but had then stopped. Her mother felt guilty about this state of things and attacked the problem defensively, saying that her daughter was doing it on purpose because she, her mother, had never dealt with the problem, preferring to pass weekends with her current boyfriend rather than with her daughter.

Aldo instead had a different version of the story. According to him, the mother–daughter relationship was a good one, open and frank, and that it wasn't true that she neglected her daughter. On the contrary, from what he had been able to see, she looked after her daughter a lot and it was for this reason that the daughter had chosen to stay with her mother, even though she could have lived with her father. Aldo added that the first fracture in their relationship came about when Anna had first asked him to stay in order not to traumatise her daughter, even though he had always made his refusal to be a father clear. At this point, Anna turned to the therapist and said that the other evening she had been in a very difficult situation with her daughter and had been very happy that he was there. His presence had enabled both to talk more calmly and try to understand each other better. Aldo, on the other hand, talked about his love for music when he was a boy and how he had decided to abandon it because it was too demanding an occupation and required total involvement. From a very young age he had decided that for the same reason he would never have children. Both talked to me about the project they had had when they were happy together, which was to get a large house in the country and to go and live there.

Comment on the second session

With the appearance of the daughter, mother, and father/non-father, we have a presentation of the "core complex": the phantasy which recurrently appears is the "primal triangle" where uncertainty reigns over the female as environment (is this mother a sufficiently good mother for this daughter or not?), and over the male with its transformative potential (if Aldo were identified as a father), thus denying access to the oedipal triangulation and consequently to full independence.

Use of the analyst in the transference

As can be seen, the two sessions showed two different scenarios within which the same drama was being played out, but with diverse affective colourings: we are dealing, however, with relations based on the need to take care of the Self through the Other in the sense of being able to use the object to reach a degree of integration of the self sufficient to maintain personal well-being, which, however, does not succeed in reaching full autonomy, as the health of the relationship is continually being put into doubt.

In the first session, thanks to the transference, the couple expressed a collusive, narcissistic attitude: they both used, in fact, my presence as the public before which to exhibit their anti-conformist ideology.[4] My intervention, which served to point out the state of unhappiness of both and the critical situation of this axis, forced them to adopt, in the second session, a less superficial attitude. Then, as was observed, the core complex appeared, constituted by the daughter as symptom but above all by a triangular issue deeply involving all three. And at the same time, in their free associations a surprising connection arose between parenthood and creative passion—an object of negation on which both were colluding.

One of the salient features of second and third marriages is in fact represented by the affective implication extending to the entire family nucleus of previous marriages.

As often happens in these situations, Aldo's affective cathexis not only regards Anna as an object of sexual desire but the relationship between Anna and her daughter also provides him with the opportunity of living these three different roles (of husband, lover, and father) in the present and at the same time, which is a problem requiring a solution also on the inner stage. At the same time, when her daughter began a process of detachment, Anna felt the loss of that sense of strength and certainty which being a mother had given her ("before she felt more confident") and had felt perhaps a more pressing need to attach herself affectively to someone other than her daughter, thus drawing near to an oedipal problem. "I would like to recognise you as a father who enables me and my daughter to separate without destroying each other." The daughter's bulimia, Anna's aggressive and possessive greed, Aldo's stubborn refusal hiding a strong fear of being wrapped up by an all-enveloping female figure, from whom he has always defended himself by hit-and-run tactics, different behaviours and acting out at different levels of functioning of the Self, they all concern exactly the same focal point: dependency. These symptoms had become entwined seeking a balance between various needs and functions, in an intersubjective dependency. However, I would like to emphasise the reciprocal attempt at repairing the Self or the damaged object. I refer to the moment when Anna and Aldo both valorise each other's maternal and paternal functions, and their nostalgia for music and for the countryside returns. This occurred after a more benevolent atmosphere had been restored and a more capable analyst was called upon to play the role of a third party able to listen to the reasons for their distress, but who could also be a witness to moments of transformative potential.

After a subsequent session I learnt that the couple were living with each other again and that the daughter had finally decided to undergo therapy. We agreed on a date for another appointment, and Anna, as she was leaving said laughingly, "Suppose instead of coming here, we get married?"

The paradox which we are witnessing in this and other similar cases concerns the power of both fascination and fear that dependency, an inevitable component of family bonds, continues to exercise over people even when they have refused such involvements in the past. Evidently an internal motivation exists which drives them to try again in the hope that they can unlock a capacity for autonomy which they have never completely acquired, and which can be reached only through a relationship involving them at a primitive level.

Winnicott, in considering the "capacity to be alone" in the presence of the Other as the highest level of an individual's maturity, says: "One could say that an individual's capacity 'to be alone' depends on his ability to deal with the sentiments roused by the primal scene. In the primal scene an aroused relationship between parents is imagined and accepted by the healthy child capable of dominating hatred ..." (1958, pp. 158–165).

Aldo, Anna, and her daughter clearly display an incapability to integrate sexuality, dependency, and the capacity to be alone, in order to discover more constructive ways to deal with the aggressiveness. They are also trying to resolve this enigma in their relations with each other, at times two of them, at other times all three of them together.

Second clinical case

The second case deals with a psychoanalytic psychotherapy I conducted with a couple, Elena and Hugo. The couple is bringing up Elena's children born during her previous marriage. I have been following this case for many years now and it has given me the opportunity to explore an aspect of gender identity often ignored in psychoanalytic theorisation. I am referring to the sexual and parental double component existing in both the woman and the man. In clinical work it is becoming more common to observe that men, just as it has been observed for women before them, are beginning to be represented by a double gender identity: sexual identity and fatherhood. When a woman starts to feel the desire for maternity, the oedipal conflict that she has often faced during the previous phases of her development, in particular with her mother, reappears on the scene. The same thing happens to men; a reoccurring of the oedipal conflict triggers off identifications and disidentifications with the father and mother alike.

Pregnancy and birth, even more so than puberty, clearly bring to the fore the physical differences between female and male bodies. Apart from this biological data, the cultural influence is important in determining the roles of the male and female genders. The reshuffling of the gender identities of the couple is played out on two tables: on the one, we have the identification/disidentification processes with the father and the mother, as mentioned above, and on the other, a powerful identification with the baby, thus triggering off regression in both partners.

When the married couple becomes a parent couple it can expect the reoccurrence of partial male and female elements of the personality based on those "memories in feeling" and unconscious themes that concern primal bisexuality.

Falling in love with a woman already with children and accepting to be part of the family is due to a lack of elaboration of the oedipal complex. Standing in for the biological father and exploiting an existing context safeguards the man from archaic fears of desire of becoming a father in his own right. On the other hand, a woman who decides to change partners, above all when the children are still very young, is involved in oedipal issues and other even more archaic elements. In the following case we will see how the lack of elaboration of the Oedipus complex brings an urgency to construct a family more from need than from desire. By creating a symbiotic relationship, both partners attempt to repair the traumatised primal Self. In point of fact, the couple both suffered abandonment and trauma in early childhood, resulting in grave repercussions in adolescence, as we will see. The decision of the couple to form a family in order to feel strong and secure was taken in the light of their past, experienced as intimately harmful, and at the same time in order to repair the Self through affective cathexis.

A brief account of the couple's story follows. Elena, mother of two small sons, falls in love with Hugo. A series of events come about rapidly: the husband leaves and Hugo moves in with Elena and the two children. For the moment, neither the one nor the other of the couple is capable of elaborate reflection for themselves or the other components: the passion sparked off between them imposes itself on everything else. In the past Elena had suffered from anorexia; she led an intensive, promiscuous sexual life and had been married twice, giving birth during the second marriage. Elena is an only child of a couple who denied her need for love and affection in the name of a strict upbringing. Elena's parents divided their home into twin apartments when Elena first got married, to enable her to live near them. Elena suffered and suffers still from depression and is under medical treatment.

Hugo's family is composed of his parents and a younger brother. When Hugo was three, at the birth of his sibling, he was sent to live with relatives in another city for two years. During adolescence he broke off his studies, thus becoming painfully dependent on his family until he left for the army—a forced separation that enabled him to separate from an oppressive mother. Afterwards, he was able to take up his studies again, to graduate, and acquire a job socially superior to that of his own father. Hugo had never had a sexual relationship before he met Elena. Hugo disrupts all ties with his family when they disapprove of his relationship with Elena.

Both Elena and Hugo are diligent workers in their respective jobs. After some years together, the couple seeks help for a reoccurring problem that is hobbling the family life. The following account describes the vicious circle that has set in.

Alex, the firstborn, is eight, very rebellious and intolerant of the rules set down by the couple who believe in a rather strict discipline. As a rule, it is the mother who will try to bring the boy into line, who then reacts badly. At that point, Hugo, who normally keeps his distance from family issues, will become furious and treat Alex very harshly. The more Elena's urgent concern for her children and her parents grows, the more she tends to become depressed (turning her anger against herself). Elena's depression provokes an exaggerated concern in Hugo. Usually a gentle and helpful person, Hugo's explosions reactivate Elena's depression; she also accuses him of not loving her children. Hugo in those moments becomes aware of the suffering he has provoked in the woman he loves and loses heart. Both end up in a state of prostration, united in the belief of not being good parents, and the vicious circle repeats itself.

If one observes a little closer, at the level of parental function none of this is so dramatic. Elena is the classic protective mother, the opposite of her mother, and Hugo the classic superego father, rigid and demanding, the opposite of his father. In the family dynamic, Elena and Hugo show themselves as adequate and valid parents and the children grow well. In particular, Alex does not seem to be perturbed by Hugo's outbursts, rather he starts to see Hugo as a father who does not shrink from facing his parental duties, but instead imposes limits, thus recognising the importance of Alex on his own, not through Elena's eyes. Clearly Hugo will not tolerate any harm done to the relationship of the sexual couple. The couple link, even though characterised by deep suffering is at the same time a strong partnership of love.

On a different level we can observe the family "mise-en-scène" of internal partial characters. Elena sees herself in Alex's shoes: a child badly treated by the father and not protected enough by the mother; on the other hand, Hugo in Alex's shoes sees himself as a firstborn male, torn between selfishness and devotion towards his mother—in complete conflict. The scene reaches its climax when, after the "orgasm" provoked by the outburst of anger (Hugo's towards the son, and Elena's towards Hugo), it results in the two finding themselves spent with the shared belief of failure.

It is clear therefore, that the intensity of the affective dynamic concerns the couple, and in particular a theme on which their deep relationship is engaged: in other words, what can be observed is an effort to deal with the suffering and deficient parts of the Self as a result of harmful primal experiences with the primal parental couple.

Why did Hugo and Elena choose each other with such determination: a type of deep and unexpected recognition, ending up in each other's arms? Can we define this as a symbiotic link? What makes a couple continue in their reciprocal commitment when a great deal of suffering exists? Is there perhaps a sadomasochistic component? One unconscious reason for their mutual attraction could be that Elena and Hugo felt they were well matched because depression was a characteristic peculiar to both of them. Subsequently, the couple was able to establish itself only after the exclusion of Elena's previous husband and Hugo's family, to create the illusion that the symbiosis lacking in both their childhoods could be reconstructed. At the same time the existence of Elena's children constantly reminds the couple that a third component is asking to be taken into consideration. The tension that emerged was almost intolerable, but a new opportunity for internal development came about. We could define the couple's relationship as being a pseudo-symbiosis, if compared to a more common symbiotic pathology of the couple. In fact, the existence of Elena's children at the inception of the couple demands libidinal cathexis on different levels. The parental tasks with real children requires a sort of daily exercise of differentiation between "me" and "non-me", between tenderness and sexuality, between the functions of the ego, between the desires and the needs of the Self. Furthermore, those phantasies that still dramatically inhabit the unconscious with respect to the failure of the primary triadic experience, leaving a profound impression on the Self of both partners, have to be considered. Even though it is extremely painful for both partners, the fact that aggressiveness can now be expressed and that at the same time the survival of the object is secure makes a substantial modification on the internal set-up of each one. Elena, who suffers from migraines that confine her to her bed for entire days, observes that these episodes are gradually diminishing and have become less intense. Hugo for his part is attaining desired results in the office.

After three years of therapy

At the conclusion of the annual summer holidays the couple appears more relaxed. The youngsters, who rarely see their father, were invited to stay with him for a month during the holidays. Elena and Hugo have moved away from living next door to Elena's parents and bought a house. They speak about their plans with enthusiasm. Hugo oversees the renovations to make sure that all the members of the family have the space they need. Elena recounts a dream: they are in the new house, to evaluate the feasibility of the project; there is also a man in a kilt, something they did not find at all surprising, rather, he seems a familiar element. From their associations emerges a figure dressed as a woman but with male attributes. Elena associates the figure with Hugo, who in appearance seems meek and attentive, above all towards her, maternal, yet all the same, when it is necessary to discipline the boys, Hugo manifests potent, male attributes, no less than what is expected of him. Hugo, on the other hand, associates the kilt-clad figure with Elena who appears so fragile, but is also endowed with great strength and determination, for example when she allows time in the family menage for the couple to enjoy each other's love. Hugo compares the couple to an elephant and a mouse in a hostile land. The metaphor he uses speaks of a small but dynamic mouse (Elena) leading the big slow-moving elephant (Hugo), who in turn protects the mouse from outside aggression.

This scene represents the couple in regressive terms characterised by partial male and female aspects in which the duo's active/female and passive/male elements prevail: Hugo is presented as a trustful, solid, stable elephant, while Elena is a dynamic, mobile, active mouse. Together they compensate for each other, and are able to face the outside world that gives rise to their traumatic, regressive experiences. The Scottish figure in the kilt and the metaphor of the mouse and the elephant reveal primal bisexual aspects. Unintegrated males and females appear, juxtaposed or superimposed in a risky, disorderly confusion that also caused the problems that each partner had during adolescence and early adulthood. The same confusion tends to repeat itself today in the couple's link, although at times beneficial variations come about through the switching of roles; especially when the couple are obliged to assume father and mother roles, they seem to be more capable at falling in line with their gender roles.[5] The new house can become the place where the various adult, regressive parts find containment. A better knowledge of the Self and the Other helps to recognise the different subjective particularities. Furthermore, the Scottish figure in Elena's dream represents the role of the analyst in the transference like a combined parental figure who facilitates integration by means of differentiation. The capacity to face the different phases of the children's development with the help of the therapy constitutes a fundamental element that is deeply felt in the symbiotic couple as a means to heal the traumatised parts.

"The link between love, life and pleasure is very powerful. This connection implies the existence, sooner or later, of the awareness of the other ... moreover, the inexorable passage of time will lead to an even more dramatic consequence: the finding that the object has its own object, which I call the *other of the object*, in other words the third element which the father symbolizes" (Green, 1996, p. 882).

In conclusion

Our principal aim is to demonstrate how the lack of elaboration of the Oedipus complex is only the tip of the iceberg regarding an issue that implies confusion between male and female roles, above all on a primal level of bisexuality. It is clear, therefore, that the intensity of the affective dynamic concerns the couple, and is a theme on which their deep relationship is engaged: the dealing with suffering and deficient parts of the Self as a result of harmful primal experiences with the primal parental couple, that enact in the natural transference on the partner, affectively involving the entire family nucleus (Norsa & Zavattini, 1997). If we observe newly formed families where the links are freely chosen and not dictated by social conventions, we have a wonderful opportunity to comprehend not only projective identification, but the more archaic levels that contribute to the link connecting the intrapsychic to the intersubjective. Dependency can last in time only if a third entity is recognised (Nicolò, Norsa, & Carratelli, 2003), which involves a lot of conflict, however. Indeed, the primal triangle reappears in the various developmental moments in the life of a family, where we find the female as "being" and the male as "doing" whether it is in the sexual relationship or in parenthood dynamics. In particular, the vicissitudes of parenthood involve profound aspects of gender identity in the man and the woman, because maternity and paternity are elements that constitute the primal bisexual Self.

In the couple therapy we have shown how the "mise-en-scène" of the central conflict between Elena, Hugo, and Alex is a source of malaise and devaluation for each member. We have shown how the situation reveals a useful transformative potential with the help of therapy; that is to say, the analyst assumes the role of witness that participates internally in this process of transformation, thus becoming a new object that the patients can use by exploiting the potentiality of regression. Finally, we believe that constant psychoanalytic work with couples and families gives us the opportunity "to add a few words" to the vast literature relating to the libidinal development and integration of the Self.

Notes

1. "Psychoanalysts have perhaps given special attention to this male element or drive aspect of object-relating, and yet have neglected the subject-object identity to which I am drawing attention here, which is at the basis of the capacity to be. The male element *does* while the female element *is*" (Winnicott, 1971, p. 81).
2. "Experiences of love are supported by the interplay between subject of desire and desired object, but the poietic concept of desire breaks up potential stabilization in positions absolutely associated with either the feminine or the masculine. A productive and positive notion of desire enables us to illuminate singularities in the field of subjectivity, beyond rigid gender assignments in terms of passive-active or subject-object polarities. The relationship between two subjects in the field of sexuality exceeds strict dualities" (Glocer Fiorini, 2007, p. 102).
3. "Whatever definition we arrive at, it must include the idea that life is worth living or not, according to whether creativity is or is not a part of an individual person's living experience. To be creative a person must exist and have a feeling of existing, not in conscious awareness, but as a basic place to operate from.

   Creativity is then the doing that arises out of being. It indicates that he who is, is alive. Impulse may be at rest, but when the word 'doing' becomes appropriate, then already there is creativity. (…) Creativity, then, is the retention throughout life of something that belongs properly to infant experience: the ability to create the world" (Winnicott, 1986, pp. 39–40).

4. "… the desire of the transference would be marked by the figure of the witness rather than by that of the analyst as accomplice … In the ensemble formed by the pervert, the victim, and the witness, each is different but has a role within a collective logic. Within the group, the roles are distributed. The *witness* has a significant function in the way that he observes the pervert. The latter 'requires of him' that he function as a mirror, which gives the pervert an image of himself that he can otherwise not achieve, in the absence of an integrated capacity to see himself as another. Most importantly, the pervert maintains a relation with the witness, which has to do with his unconscious link with the paternal function, comprising revolt, provocation of the father and challenge to the foundation of the attachment to the law, which the father represents" (Eiguer, 2007, p. 1147).

5. "There is a structure in the name of the mother and a structure in the name of the father. These structures, in turn, are composed of their functions. When referring to the separate set of functions, we may refer to the maternal and paternal orders, especially if we intend to emphasize the functional difference between the two. The psyche is not unisexual, but bisexual, and a self will be utilizing separate but equal sets of functions … we refer to the mosaic function" (Bollas, 2000, p. 71).

References

Balint, E. (1968). Unconscious communications between husband and wife. In: S. Ruszczynski (Ed.), *Psychotherapy with Couples: Theory and Practice at the Tavistock Institute of Marital Studies* (pp. 30–43). London: Karnac, 1993.

Bollas, C. (2000). *Hysteria*. London: Routledge.

Eiguer, A. (2007). The intersubjective links in perversion. *International Journal of Psychoanalysis, 88*: 1135–1152.

Gaddini, E. (1974). Formazione del padre e scena primaria. *Rivista Psicoanalisi, 23*: 157–183.

Gaddini, E. (1976). On father formation in early child development. *International Journal of Psychoanalysis, 57*: 397–401.

Glocer Fiorini, L. (2007). *Deconstructing the Feminine: Psychoanalysis, Gender and Theories of Complexity*. London: Karnac.

Green, A. (1980). *The Dead Mother: The Work of André Green* (G. Kohon, Ed.). London: Routledge, 1999.

Green, A. (1996). *The Work of Negative*. London: Free Association.

Kernberg, O. F. (1993). The couple's constructive and destructive super-ego functions. *Journal of the American Psychoanalytic Association, 41*: 653–677.

Klein, M. (1957). *Envy and Gratitude*. London: Tavistock.

Nicolò, A. M., Norsa, D., & Carratelli, T. J. (2003). Playing with dreams: the introduction of a third party into the transference dynamic of the couple. *Journal of Applied Psychoanalytic Studies, 5*: 283–296.

Norsa, D., & Baldassarre, L. (2008). Intimacy, collusion and complicity in psychoanalysis with couples. *AIPCF Journal*. www.aipcf.net

Norsa, D., & Zavattini, G. C. (1997). *Intimità e Collusione. Teoria e Tecnica della Psicoterapia Psicoanalitica di Coppia*. Milan, Italy: Raffaello Cortina.

Winnicott, D. W. (1958). The capacity to be alone. In: *The Maturational Process and the Facilitating Environment* (pp. 29–36). London: Hogarth and the Institute of Psychoanalysis, 1965.

Winnicott, D. W. (1966). Split-off male and female elements. In: *Psycho-Analytic Explorations* (pp. 169–183). London: Karnac, 1989.

Winnicott, D. W. (1971). Creativity and its origins. In: *Playing and Reality* (pp. 65–85). London: Tavistock.

Winnicott, D. W. (1986). *Home is Where We Start from*. London: Penguin.

PART II

OEDIPUS IN THE NEW FAMILIES

CHAPTER EIGHT

The Oedipus complex and the new generations

Philippe Robert

When the primal pack became a group and began to be structured by the prohibition of incest, guilt and a feeling of belonging came to provide the framework for bonds of alliance and friendship. Have couples and families really changed since this founding event? As we try to answer this question, let us first recall many psychoanalysts' views on the supposed changes in psychopathology. As early as the 1950s there seemed to be far fewer cases of hysterical pathologies, and even of so-called "classic" neuroses. Conflict between the ego and the superego seemed to have been replaced by a depressive relationship with an unattainable ego ideal. People were already speaking of new pathologies, as Ehrenberg points out in his work (2010) *La Société du Malaise*.

In a parallel movement, but one belonging to the same register, a more and more culturalist has been developing. This was already present in the work of Erich Fromm (1971) and Karen Horney (1937); it becomes very significant—though there it takes a different form—in the works of Alexander (1930) and Hartmann (1939).

From the outset the interest in character and ego psychology included environmental issues, that is, the weight and influence of external reality.

Consequently, other psychoanalytic settings appeared. By "other settings" I do not mean the adjustments necessarily made for children, groups, or psychotic patients, but rather a modification of the analyst's inner setting, in other words, a difference in his way of listening to the material the patient presents.

One of the reasons why Freud was not really interested in the couple and the family was his fear of the over-possible return of a psychology that would cover up metapsychology. Any reference to external objects could endanger what he had worked so hard to demonstrate and to "get accepted" about drives, repression, and the role of the dynamic of the unconscious. Though Freud certainly never ignored the parents' influence, he considered it in its unconscious dimension, its aspect of superego transmission.

In such conditions, the revelation of the Oedipus complex in Freud's work should be understood less in family terms than for what it signifies about the construction of the individual psyche. But though Freud very clearly showed intrapsychical space and its dimension of structural conflict, and even though he implicitly showed the importance of family history in the elaboration of the individual fantasy scenario by firmly anchoring the psyche in biology, he probably underestimated the porosity of the boundaries between the individual and the group.

Working with families inevitably leads us back to these questions, particularly the question of the link between external reality and psychical reality. I should point out, just for the record, that we are often confronted with issues very similar to those psychoanalysis had to deal with in its early days. The question of trauma attests to this. Some analysts working with families still believe in their "neurotica". When speaking of trauma, especially with regard to transgenerational transmission, it is sometimes tempting to imagine that there is a trauma in reality that could have caused the current pathologies. It even happens that the ancestors' reality gets mixed up with their imagos. So there is a risk in speaking of new couples and new families, thus confining ourselves to formal changes in reality.

Changes or invariables?

It is true that there have been more demographical, technological, and geopolitical changes since the Second World War than in all of human history before. The industrial revolution already considerably modified social relations and lifestyles. In so-called "developed" societies, urbanisation has overtaken rural life, upsetting both standards and family structures.

But two changes have undoubtedly had an even more direct impact on representations of our work. The first was spectacularly expressed in 1968. It was not so much social organisation that was called into question, but conjugal and family links. Contraception, abortion, women's access to the workplace, more sexual freedom (apparently, at least)—all presented links as shackles rather than supports. It was the era of free love and the "death of the family".

There emerged a demand for the right to happiness and autonomy, and each individual had to release himself from what had been imposed upon him. In a certain way, this was a great comeback for Reich's thinking, with suppression being mistaken for repression. People were clamouring for outward freedom, while disavowing the importance of inner reality.

From this perspective, perceptual reality, greedy for excitation that makes it feel alive, takes centre stage. Children are no longer allowed to be bored; they must constantly have "activities" planned for them. Lack and frustration become less and less tolerable, and continuity is under assault from the culture of "zapping". Everything becomes consumable, disposable, and immediate.

But in what ways do these changes affect the structure of the couple and the family?

Ethnopsychiatry—at least at the beginning—had thought itself capable of showing that the cultural environment played a starring role in individual personalities. It is obvious that representations of time and of death, for example, differ according to culture. But what are we, as psychoanalysts, really interested in? Is there not confusion here between signification and meaning, decoding and interpretation? The analyst can try to understand his patient—as much as possible—within a given culture that he more or less shares. We know how difficult it can be to work with patients who are too close to us, or with others who are too removed. But understanding is not the analyst's resource, or at least not his only one. The psychiatrist or psychologist must be able to understand his patients. The analyst must be able to listen to them, and that is not the same thing. To do this, he must rely on the invariables that make up the human condition, to which he is himself subjected.

So what has not changed revolves around the dependence that is part of human existence, the human need for dignity and thus for a feeling of belonging, humans' fear of death and need to believe …

From the Oedipus complex to transformation

If anything has really changed in the family psyche, it would perhaps be that inner conflict is avoided and projected onto the external world, or else disavowed. It is thus possible that from this perspective, the Oedipus complex can help us to see more clearly, especially in light of the question of generations.

The Oedipus complex is not a son's rivalry with his father. Nor is it the son's desire to take the mother away from the father. It is not the generation of children who want to take the parents' place, but the fear that the gods have of human beings. It is the creator's anxiety about being dispossessed. At the origin of the Oedipus complex there is no difference between the sexes, but there is a difference between generations. To get rid of Oedipus, Jocasta maintains her solidarity with Laius.

By anchoring his model in biology, Freud *ipso facto* defended the universal nature of his metapsychology. But it also transcends the cultural through the universality of the generational boundary marked by the Oedipus complex. And when he wrote "The Dissolution of the Oedipus Complex" in 1924, he was of course not talking about dissolution but, on the contrary, about the introjection of its organisation.

The organisation of boundaries between generations structures not only the family, but also the entire social body. It is the same boundary that enables identifications and fosters the process of transmission.

The psychoanalyst is not a sociologist. Nor is he a philosopher or anthropologist. He nevertheless has the right to wonder about the evolution of generational boundaries. For many years, people spoke of the "child-king". This expression thrived, managing to prevent, and even subvert, any truly psychoanalytical discourse. Masquerading as listening to children—which is of course a legitimate pursuit—it entailed giving in to their desires. Authority was perceived as arbitrary and any command had to be justified. This movement may be understood in different ways.

First of all, what one generation has not settled with the preceding generation will reappear in the following generation. The child-kings are none other than parent-kings who make their children replay their own childhoods, thus causing problems for the processes of identification. When parents take their children to an amusement park, are they enjoying their satisfaction or are they themselves the children?

Asking children to evaluate their teachers has the same meaning. This opens the way to all kinds of confusion and, worse, to perverse seductions.

A second factor that can attest to the attack on generational boundaries is expressed in the weakening of authority. Of course, one should not confuse authority and authoritarianism, as do some television reality shows where families expect someone to come and "be the police" in their home.

In France the possibility of enacting an "anti-spanking" law has been evoked. Besides being an incursion of public authority into the private life of the family—about which much could be said—this is without a doubt a counter-investment of parental violence. If we are afraid of our children, it is because we are afraid of ourselves and of our violence towards them. Unconscious infanticidal desire, which is consubstantial with the Oedipus complex, is always there. But the need to combat it on the social stage through laws and/or behaviours may bear witness to a weakening of its repression. It is, however, this repression that is useful to the inner conflicts of the family psyche, and it is what allows for a work of mentalisation and representation.

If a thought is to be put to work, there must be tension and psychical conflict, which can occur only inside an envelope.

This case concerns a family who came to consult me in the following context: two sisters and two brothers who are all between the ages of forty and fifty come with one or two of their children, who are around twenty years old. The cousins used to get along very well, "like the rest of the family", they say. But at a family party a cell phone belonging to a female cousin was stolen, and one of the male cousins was strongly suspected. Since then there has been much tension.

I point out that not one of the spouses is present at this meeting. They reply that it's because everyone considers the problem to be between them. "Them" means a family whose parents came to France in extremely difficult circumstances, fleeing a country at war. In order to survive they needed to stick together in the face of hardship. It was unthinkable that any member of the family should break this sacred union.

After a few sessions, it appeared that the purpose of the scandalous theft was to release subsequent generations from this vital pact. What had been a sacred bond risked becoming a controlling bond. Little by little the spouses could participate in the sessions, finding what they needed to say, and how to appropriate a family in which they were at least co-founders.

This family had the ability to benefit from third-party intervention; in this case, well-spaced family interviews were enough to restart the processes of filiation and affiliation.

For passages to occur, boundaries must be sufficiently defined. But this is not enough. In this case a crisis was needed to get the processes of filiation going again.

The human being is born into dependence. This creates *ipso facto* expectation and tension with regard to the other person. But this dependence cannot be conceived of individually. It should always be understood as part of interdependence. Difference creates tensions and a form of energy. The permanent tendency towards homeostasis generates movement through the alternation of balance and unbalance.

From group to family

There is now a weakening of organising meta-frameworks. The organising and regulating character of institutions is in difficulty; more grave still, instituting procedures are being mismanaged. Laws seem to be voted into existence in reaction to something without any attempt to view them in context. We can observe the deleterious effects of this process as much in the area of health care, as in the justice system and in education. The processes of maturation and integration are short-circuited in favour of immediate gratification, or simple release. Although we should be cautious in our appreciation of the weakening of the social bond, I think we can agree with more certainty that there has been a decline in parental imagos.

In France between the wars, the teacher and the nurse were respected figures. Little by little their image has been weakening and this same weakening of prestige has affected the medical doctor and the professor. New images which could potentially serve the purposes of identification would nowadays be figures who experience fast success and earn a lot of money. So a process of competition starts which, behind surface stimulation, slows or even blocks genuine identifying processes. Images replace imagos and imitation replaces identification.

If the generational boundary no longer provides structure to, or structures at least only poorly, the organisation of the family, then there will be fewer oedipal families; in other words, there will be fewer families wherein otherness can be recognised.

AFT (analytic familial therapy) is still principally recommended for narcissistic pathologies and psychotic organisations, as any psychoanalyst working in this field knows. The rise in these pathologies can only increase the number of patients. But the problem is that in these situations, the psychoanalyst does not work alone. The clinician has long known the importance of the setting and its transformative effects. This setting is made up of the analyst's inner setting, his own history, his filiation, and his own analysis—but not only these. He must be able to rely on a much bigger container, composed first of all by his peers—especially members of an analytic society—and by the institution he works in. The setting also depends on a larger envelope which goes from the network of professionals involved in the situation, to the community. We know that with incestuous families, for example, it is imperative that one be able to work together with judges, doctors, educators, social workers … Now, if social links and organisers are defective, all of this networking will be compromised. The narcissistic issues of each partner, of each participant, will defeat the necessary "conflicted solidarity". We could cite an example of two co-therapists who seem juxtaposed in a narcissistic placement. Any conflict that could enliven otherness would be blocked off.

So if the group envelope—to which the psychoanalyst cannot be impermeable—is defective, is there not a risk of wanting to "reinforce the setting"? The psychoanalyst feeling that the thing he should look to for support is giving way, may want to increase—in an illusory way—his containing function. Then we fall back into omnipotence, the dual relation, and the absence of triangulation.

But families want the setting we offer them to act as a container. It is an implicit demand that we cannot shirk. Indeed, what keeps coming out as a result of the discourse of sociologists, anthropologists, and some psychoanalysts seems to be change in favour of excess and overkill. This is exacerbated in the behaviour of what Cournut (2004) calls "les défoncés"—people who force themselves to go to extremes. I myself share this point of view, and think that this excitation can no longer—or only with difficulty—be checked by familial or social containers.

A family started therapy with its two children, a sixteen-year-old boy and a twelve-year-old girl. The parents say they are overwhelmed by the behaviour of their son who absolutely refuses to listen to them. During one session, the son takes a felt-tipped pen and says, "If I want to, I could use this to put graffiti on the wall; or I could smash it into the carpet." When I ask the family as a whole about this, the father says: "In either case, what would you have me do? Anyway, he's bigger than I am!" The teenager instantly repeats his threat, snatching up a felt-pen. I ask again what he means by this. He then says: "I don't say—I do." Then he takes the pen and smashes it into the carpet. I stand up and tell the family: "Not everything is permitted here; I'm stopping the session for today and we'll meet again in two weeks." Everyone looks stunned, including the teenage boy. After a few moments of hesitation, they get up and leave. Two weeks later, the parents and the sister come, but the boy is not with them. I had made it clear from the start that—and this is another issue—the sessions would take place only if everyone were present. So I inform the parents that I cannot receive them without their son, and the daughter that I cannot receive her without her brother. I tell them that I'll be expecting them in two weeks.

On the appointed day, all four of them are back. As soon as the son enters, he says: "Wow! You left the felt-pens there!" The mother adds: "We talked about whether you would, and I didn't think you would either."

The therapist is asked to hold a position of authority, not only for adolescence, but for the whole family, as though it were lacking the support of a containing and reassuring imago.

Conclusion

In the face of such changes, questions must be asked about the technique used in psychoanalytic couple and family therapies. It cannot be reduced to a "veneer" of the classic treatment or to a transposition of the overall setting of group analysis.

The treatment setting must be adapted to the type of patient. Some techniques, like psychodrama, have managed to elaborate their technical consistency. But family therapy is not merely an adaptation. We are not—and I would insist on this—using the group to treat the individual; rather, we are treating the group itself. The specific nature of the family group calls into question the analyst's legitimacy—why is he meddling in their affairs?—and his ability to listen competently.

With families we are dealing with a group that has common experiences and interests. It is not just a question of what the other represents, but also of what he or she is "in the flesh". Sometimes we are missing pieces of the reality that gives different structures to patients gravely traumatised in childhood and those who become "ordinary neurotics".

Though Green (1980) emphasises that in the "dead mother complex", the mother may be present physically but not psychically, real parents are very important, especially—as Pasche (1975) notes—in the formation of the superego.

"The Superego is never internalized right away; this happens gradually, and it remains partly externalized for a long time, perhaps for the rest of one's life. The real parents and parent substitutes (including Society) continue it on the outside, which explains why their real behavior, as well as what happens to them, has such an impact on the subject" (Pasche, 1988).

In these conditions, the legitimacy of the psychoanalyst comes from the feeling of being, or not being, intrusive. If one does not feel like a legitimate witness—not a voyeur—to the couple's and the family's intimate life, then one had better not work in this format. There is certainly a "starting point" in this which is not linked to countertransference but to whether we can authorise ourselves to enquire into private life.

References

Alexander, F. (1930). The neurotic character. *International Journal of Psychoanalysis, 11*: 292–311.

Cournut, J. (2004). Les défoncés. In: N. Aubert (Ed.), *L'individu Hypermoderne* (pp. 61–71). Paris: Érès, 2010.

Ehrenberg, A. (2010). *La Société du Malaise*. Paris: Odile Jacob.

Freud, S. (1924d). The dissolution of the Oedipus complex. *S. E., 19*: 171–180. London: Hogarth.

Fromm, E. (1971). *The Crisis of Psychoanalysis*. London: Jonathan Cape.

Green, A. (1980). The dead mother. In: A. Green, *Life Narcissism/Death Narcissism* (pp. 265–303). London: Free Association, 2001.

Hartmann, H. (1939). *Ego Psychology and the Problem of Adaptation*. Madison, CT: International Universities Press, 1958.

Horney, K. (1937). *The Neurotic Personality in Our Time*. New York: W. W. Norton.

Pasche, F. (1975). Réalités psychiques et réalité matérielle. *Nouvelle Revue de Psychanalyse, 12*: 189–197.

Pasche, F. (1988). *Le Sens de la Psychanalyse*. Paris: PUF.

CHAPTER NINE

When the fraternal prevails over the oedipal: a possible interpretative model for modern couples

Massimiliano Sommantico

It is becoming more and more evident how right in the unconscious partner choice and in the development of the couple relation, the importance and sometimes the centrality of what we might define as a sort of transference on the couple, characterised by some archaic and undifferentiated aspects of the fraternal complex, may emerge, as the analysis of both theoretical and clinical literature on the specific subject shows (Abend, 1984; Conrath, de Butler, Lagrand, & Lemaire, 1991; de Butler, 2000; Jaitin, 2008; Kaës, 2008; Kancyper, 1991; Morley, 2006; Nicolò & Imparato, 2000; Sommantico, 2008).

Our aim is to propose a solution to the problem posed by the infiltration of the fraternal into some couples' psychic dynamics, which seem to characterise today's clinical scene (Sommantico, 2009).[1] In this we follow Kaës (2008), when he asserts that the complex is "one of the *unconscious psychic organizers* of each link: familiar, couple, group" (p. 45, emphasis added) and, in a narrower sense, that the fraternal complex becomes the organiser of the fraternal link.

In the light of the above-mentioned, I propose a reflection upon something which may be defined as a *fraternisation* of the couple's link through the presentation of a clinical case related to a couple psychoanalytic psychotherapy led in co-therapy,[2] and based on the most recent contributions about the fraternal in psychoanalysis (Coles, 2006; Kaës, 2008; Kancyper, 2004; Mitchell, 2003; Trapanese & Sommantico, 2008). By this I refer to a functioning in which the fraternal link's mirror-like and narcissistic dimension seems to prevail (Eiguer, 2000), and where it has worked like the foundation and bonding agent of the couple's link since the moment of the partner choice, and where it holds the partners, locked in a "game of rivalry and fight for the power" (Conrath, de Butler, Lagrand, & Lemaire, 1991), in the status of a *brother* or *son*, which for this reason makes them unable to take their genuine and framing parental function.

These are therefore circumstances in which both maternal and paternal functions are impoverished, and where parents live dynamics characterised by a sort of fraternal "boxing" (de Butler, 2000), which is typical, as mentioned, of a filial attitude towards the respective families of origin.

The B couple

Mr and Mrs B consulted us because of their clear incapability of exercising their parental functions. Mr B came to us via an individual psychotherapy, which, as he affirmed, had led him to mature and understand better some elements of his past. He added that he didn't want to face that past again because it had shattered him.

Mrs B had already started an individual psychotherapy before coming to us. Her previous therapist sent her and her husband to us after asking for a couple consultation, making it clear that at that moment their priority was to take care of their pained parenthood, and telling Mrs B she would be able to come back to the individual therapy only after the couple one.

From the first meetings, we have been facing a situation which seems still and stagnant for a long time in all its violence and mortal charge, and leaves us feeling powerless and unable to gain even the smallest possibility to intervene.

Indeed, communication during the sessions seemed to be characterised only by mutual charge and complaint.

A pause followed our request to Mr and Mrs B to reconstruct their story as a couple. They did not know when and if they had chosen each other, that is, when they had become a couple: "Actually I've never understood why you wanted to see me again after our first date. You've always said that you like a different kind of woman," said Mrs B;

Mr B did not seem to find an answer to that question, which he in return also asks his wife: "And you? Why did you accept to meet again when you had immediately understood I was a spoiled brat?" Nor did it seem to be the case that they had chosen to have a child and to be a family. It was as if everything in their lives had been lived with an increasingly comprehensive passive attitude. They had suffered events, rather than living them. Then they started telling their individual stories, which eventually took up the whole time of the consultation.

Mr B comes from an ancient upper class family; he is the heir to a family company, now bankrupt, the fact of which constitutes such a loss for him that he has not been able to get over it. He also did not seem to have the possibility to bury his maternal grandfather once and for all, founder of the company, nor his father who passed away when he was sixteen. Later we come to know how much this grandfather represented, and still represents, for Mr B—the founding ancestor; a figure invested in a very ambivalent way, because he was the one who "crushed" Mr B's father by relegating him to a subordinate role— even before his daughter—but he was also the person who made Mr B the real heir, the privileged son, and repository of all the best family aspects. We also heard about a complicated fraternal affair. Mr B thought his older brother was the only one responsible for the wreckage of the family's assets and the one who wiped out his, Mr B's, life: "It's his fault, that bungler and imbecile, and I'm still paying my dues." The younger brother, by moving to another city, got out of the family's grasp, in particular that of his mother: "At least he saved himself," said Mr B, in a somewhat resentful tone.

Mrs B is the daughter of a rich lawyer, a greatly idealised father whose footsteps she followed in. The parents' situation was already represented and described as a relationship-non-relationship. They have never been married and have been living separately in the same house for ages. The mother had been bound to stay home for a long time, due to her mother-in-law's connivance, because she had once cheated on her husband. About her father, Mrs B said that he had had two or maybe three families.

This led us to Mrs B's complicated fraternal situation. Indeed, she spoke about a young lawyer, a partner in his father's company, who had turned out to be her brother a few years earlier, and who was very much loved by his father's second family. Her younger sister, on the other hand, is believed to be the fruit of her mother's infidelity: "Still today, I look at her and can't believe it … to me she's my sister, but my father has always made her feel different from me, sometimes almost a stranger." She added that, from the time when she was still a child, an aunt of hers had been telling her about the existence of another sister she had never met, who could have been either a fancied or a real figure, maybe a member of her father's third family: "I've never known, I've never understood whether she was real or was only my aunt's fantasy."

The partners talked about themselves, portraying themselves as the elected members, the dearest children, the heirs of familiar tasks which slowly appeared to us as if they were inviolable. Mr B had not been working for years, caught up in the dream of rebuilding the family's industry together with a related sense of degradation, but against which he seemed to be unable or unwilling to react. It should have been that job, or nothing: "I'm waiting for the outcome of a lawsuit which has been going on for ten years … if everything turns out all right, I'll be able to recover, to save the company's name … it's my family's name! And in any case, I should be able to collect more than 800,000 euros …"

Mrs B wondered if she had chosen to be a lawyer only to follow in her father's footsteps, a figure with whom she seemed to completely identify, to carry on a successful task that has come down from her grandfather's generation, another strongly idealised founder ancestor, and at the same time, a person to be afraid of: "I'm not sure any more … if I had to do it all again today, I'm not sure I would take the same decisions … all those years studying hard even the subjects I didn't like at all … and then today the price I pay is the fact that I can't stay with my child as long as I would like to."

In such situations, "the ancestor as a model" becomes what rules the framing of the couple's link which will conform to that fantasy. This will create confusion between the partners and the fraternal link and will also produce a "generation foreclosure" (Jaitin, 2008).

It was after they had accepted our proposal for a twice weekly psychotherapy that some elements seemed to emerge, which allowed us to understand some founding aspects of this couple, starting from what we called a partner "choice-non-choice", in the light of what we have just understood. From that moment on, their problems as a parental couple against their child began to emerge; he was almost one year old at the time and threw his parents into a crisis, unveiling their deep sense of inadequacy. Mrs B expressed her incapability to treat her child as a baby: "I realise he wears me out … I always rush in the morning …

I must take him to the day care and then run to the consulting room, otherwise no one would earn a living … and he doesn't want do get dressed, so I waste time … he doesn't listen to me … then I tick him off, sometimes I spank him too … I don't even have time to go to the toilet because he [addressing her husband] will keep on sleeping and won't wake up when the alarm clock rings, never!" Mr B replied: "It's you who can't manage your time, you just waste it … and to be clear, I wake up, sometimes I get up only ten minutes later than you … and you must stop treating me that way before my child … How will he judge me when he grows up? If you keep on treating me that way, as a logical consequence he won't have any respect for me and he won't do anything I ask him to do, he won't listen to me."

We arrived together at formulating a question which seemed to char-acterise well their situation: how can people build themselves as par-ents when they are caught up in a fraternal resentment in the presence of parents who are completely absorbed by themselves? In the presence of a mother always depressed and a father so caught up in worrying about his professional success?

During the first period of psychotherapy, we came to understand how the fact that she was a career woman following in her father's foot-steps, and that he was constantly looking for a professional identity, but above all, a male and subjective identity, affected their relationship. Their dynamics were made of debasements of each other, attacks, com-plaints, and violence which did not allow them to recognise each other as adult partners, or to be aware of each other's reality. They saw each other respectively as an other who seemed to represent, from time to time, the hated and debased brother, or the rival brother or sister before us therapists who had been called on to act as parents and judges in a never-ending struggle of fraternal resentment (Kancyper, 2004), never completely re-signified. But more than this, the fraternal other is felt here as a partial object, perfectly complementary on the one hand, and highly threatening[3] on the other, in a situation where the desire to kill that fraternal other, in the jealousy drama (Lacan, 1938) before the paren-tal object, is also to be interpreted as the desire to destroy the potential rivals who are the results of the parental coitus and of the desire that has sustained them and has been the origin of their own existence since their intrauterine life (Rosolato, 1978).

During the first year of treatment we tried to understand how the fraternal links of each partner had penetrated the amorous choice, gen-erating both the rare emotional rushes between them and their conflicts.

We also tried to follow the "destiny of these traumatic fraternal links" (de Butler, 2000, p. 69) and the way they had unconsciously invaded the present relationship.

As our work went on, we became more and more aware of the reactivation and re-signification in this couple's dynamics, as much in the oedipal struggle as in the unsolved fraternal complexes of both partners who, "feeling each other as a brother/sister, reproach, punish, and can't forgive the other's primary double wicked" (Kancyper, 2004, p. 89).

During that period we could talk about their sexual troubles, but it would be only after reaching the third year of psychotherapy that we could get back to this subject. It seemed, however, that the power dynamics, so severely present in their world as a couple, violently penetrated their intimate relationship. With her usual rage, Mrs B said to her husband: "How could I desire you when you're always depressed? You don't do anything all day! How can you manage not to feel a man without balls? You can't believe you don't have to work hard for it … It's useless to wait for the money, we need it now! How will you support your child?" Mr B, humiliated and furious, replied: "And me? What should I say? What should I do? Approach you to be bitten? You always grind your teeth … you scream!"

In situations like these, the primal scene, which was either fantasised about at an individual level and inter-fantasised about at a couple level, or else was suppressed, evoked a mortal and sadomasochistic scenery, well represented in the couple's stories to which they sometimes got back. They were related to each partner's parents. As the couple's sexuality "is cut by the [structuring] primal phantasies" (Conrath, de Butler, Lagrand, & Lemaire, 1991, p. 105), it is often inhibited.

In fact, as described in Bocquet (2010), if the passionate link with the fraternal object can represent a sort of alleviation of the oedipal struggle, at the same time it may "mark the unconscious imagery" of the couple, penetrating the partner choice and disturbing its sexual relationships: "These psychic parts encysted in the brother or in the sister are found again in the married couple, creating some indissoluble links, a role opposition, a sexual inhibition, rivalry and power struggles" (p. 68).

In the relationship with the child, all that has been described so far finds its expression in the constant mutual debasement between the partners and in the constant attacks at each other's parental authority which, indeed, impoverishes them, feeding their respective insecurities regarding their parental role still needing to be built.

Mr B, addressing us: "Can you believe that she curses at furniture? What is she teaching my child? If she bumps into a piece of furniture she starts to nag about it and it will go on for hours ... You're absent-minded and these things may be harmful for my child!" Mrs B immediately returned the accusation: "And what about you? You lost him in the park, you let him run away and he could have been run over by a car!"

The parental function seemed to be delegated to the grandparents: the paternal grandmother, who was considered unsatisfactory because she was caught up in her depression; the maternal grandmother, unsatisfactory as well because she clearly preferred her younger daughter's children.

The partner choice and the transference–countertransference dynamics

The partner choice—the choice of the love object—may be defined as one of the couple's unconscious organisers (Eiguer, 1998), based on a strongly organised and defensive unconscious collusion, within which it is necessary for the subject to assure himself of a protection against an unconscious tendency. It is its defensive value which establishes a relationship with the class of unconscious alliances; as Kaës asserts (2009), these alliances appear as psychic intersubjective formations which are in a privileged position within the psychic framing of the couple's link, in their function both as the organisers of the bond and in the preservation of the link, through the suppression of a common content at a meta-defensive level.

Remembering that in Freud's opinion (1905d), the discovery of the object is actually a "rediscovery" of the infant love object, we can assert that in the actual couple's link the love object is a heterogeneous representation which condenses some traces of many past experiences, partly removed, referable to by both the parental and the fraternal dimensions.

Indeed, it is Freud (1916–17) who reminds us that a boy "may take his sister as a love-object by way of substitute for his faithless mother", as well as a girl "may find in her elder brother a substitute for her father" (p. 491).

So it is possible, in the partner choice, that in addition to the parental imago, the ones of the brother and/or sister come to play, bringing with them the question of how the destiny of the fraternal complex might unconsciously penetrate amorous relationships in adulthood (Conrath, de Butler, Lagrand, & Lemaire, 1991).

Concerning this, clinical research has been able to highlight how in a couple's link the stakes in a game of the old fraternal couples may make themselves currently relevant again, prompting again, for instance, fraternal "boxing" (de Butler, 2000) for which partners feel nostalgia and which holds a reassuring or a narcissistically vital defence role. In addition, the couple may search again for—and recreate—the isomorphic condition of the fraternal psychic assemblage (Kaës, 1974) in an illusion of a perfect identity, with dynamics in which every brother or sister can be given a featureless place in the group.

This fraternal group, caught in group illusion (Anzieu, 1971), cannot here play the anaclitic function for a future separation and an opening to diversity, reproducing a scene that may be the basis for an unconscious alliance or an identification model; the latter two may steer, determine, and sometimes make deviant the affiliative future choices, above all the one that will be the couple's link foundation (Sommantico, 2008).

As to my definition of a partner "choice-non-choice", referring to that of the B.s, here we consider the game of psychic bisexuality and bisexual identifications as strongly active (David, 1992). I believe I may assert that Mrs B, strongly identifying with her father, found a partner-mother, a couple that has never been legalised and from which one may run away in every moment, and in her partner a victim who can be repeatedly sacrificed, a feminised man to dominate. Mr B also identified with his father, and seems to have prompted again and again a situation in which the man is knocked out, where it is the other one who dominates the relation, the other one who debases, attacks, and subdues. But at the same time and on top of it, in an unresolved conjunction of the most thanatic fraternal and oedipal aspects, Mrs B is repeating, from time to time, the impossible competition with the fraternal other, with her brother or sister, illegitimate but always preferred, and Mr B, in a mirrored movement goes back to the condition of the brother who is ousted and destroyed by a more powerful and dominating brother-partner.

The figures of these narcissistic bisexual doubles are exactly those as in the described case, explaining the game played by some of the perverse components of the fraternal complex that describes a defensive struggle against sex and generation differences and against the castration phantasy (Kaës, 2009). Following Green (1973), the bisexuality fantasy sustaining the illusion of self-sufficiency is related to the destruction of the other and of what represents it, of every sign of difference and otherness, accompanied by an erotic impoverishment. Therefore, what is missing here is the developmental component of the psychic bisexuality, the one which integrates the sex differences in the introjective post-oedipal male and female identifications, in a reconciliation of conflictual identifications and a resumption of the introjection of differences.

As far as couples like the one I have been describing are concerned, I believe that Morley's hypothesis is valid (2006): a person will make an unconscious choice of such a partner "who seems in some sense to share a similar emotional and familial background, with similar emotional 'tasks' … but has found a different 'niche', often an opposite way of dealing with the shared world" (p. 205).

Our subjects see in each other the revival of the most archaic fraternal imago of all: the fraternal other which ousts them, the fraternal other with which they struggle, the other as rival. What dominates the couple relationship here is the fear of one's own and the other's destructiveness; the other is the enemy to be faced and to defend oneself from: both partners are always belligerently ready to highlight imperfections in the other and make use of the other's faults, to draw their weapons. With Mitchell (2003), I wonder therefore whether the hate and the violence that characterise some unions, although founded on mutual and contemporaneous love, could come from the fact that these unions represent a new version of the hate and love dynamics that are typical of the infant relations between peers.

There is no desire to separate, to end this massacre game; on the rare occasions when the idea surfaced, the atmosphere immediately changed and seemed more relaxed, but the following time it seemed more exacerbated again. During one session Mrs B said: "Sometimes I believe I can't cope … sooner or later I'll go away with my son! It's not right to go on like that, it's not right for me, nor for my son." Mr B replied: "Where do you want to go? You can't stay on your own. How could you take care of yourself? And you know what? Go if you want, but forget my son!"

Suddenly, as if they were relaxed after venting their violence at one another, they started speaking about how they felt during the past days, much closer to one another; but inevitably, the following week their relation exacerbated further.

The other seems unbearable and yet indispensable at the same time. On the contrary, in the presence of the growing difficulties they face as a couple and a family, the idea of having another child seems to emerge: another action characterised by an absence of reflection and masked by the rational excuse to give their child a little brother. But this fantasy also slowly becomes the object of debates and struggles. This aspect recalls the famous statement by Caillot and Decherf (1982) concerning the paradoxical narcissistic position: "Living together may kill us, separating is deadly."

Dynamics recalling the "impossibility to listen to one another" (de Butler, 2008) and for which "during the session, each partner tries to win the therapist's attention as if the other were not there" (p. 67), are now reactivated: a configuration that in the couple's current situation displays the imprint of the deep complicity which has shaped the partners' fraternal links, within which hate and love constantly interact. So we believe that this case gives a good account of a couple's life that is set up on the model of precocious fraternal links (Conrath, de Butler, Lagrand, & Lemaire, 1991).

Finally, as to the transference–countertransference dynamics recalled from the beginning, we often found ourselves in the position of parents-judges, called on to solve an unrestrainable fraternal struggle: "Who's the cleverer?", "Who's the best?", "Who's the most disappointing?" These are the questions they wanted us to answer. Yet they seemed to deeply invest in the therapy: the couple never missed a session, though they often arrived early or late, or tried to postpone a session. And caught up in envy and jealous fraternal dynamics, they often asked us to come to another couple that they had met once and that was, in their imagination, perfect and preferable, the one that came before, our "favourite son".

Situations like these place the therapist, or the therapists, in the position of parents who must settle a fratricidal struggle represented in the session through words that have the power and violence of knives (Freymann, 2003; Trapanese, 2007); a struggle characterised by the impossible sharing of the parental object (Pontalis, 2006). In these cases, the therapist is feeling as if watching two children fighting (Conrath, de Butler, Lagrand, & Lemaire, 1991) rather than a couple, where the scene is dominated exactly by those fraternal elements that also characterised the individuals' story: a link that—though painful—looks to be indissoluble, a marked opposition of roles in the dynamics of the link, difficulty—if not impossibility—to identify with the different other, marked inhibition of genital sexuality, in favour of an unconscious organisation of the link in which power and rivalry dominate.

It is in the countertransference, then, that the aspects emerged that were most complicated to manage, those related to the hatred felt towards the couple or to the feelings of intolerance towards the couple; feelings which were the echo of those experienced by the couple within itself. The more the couple kept on telling that they couldn't stand one another in their inseparability, in their impossibility to live without the partner, the more the therapist in turn allowed to emerge, in the countertransference, both his intolerance of them and his desire to separate them, eventually reinforcing them in "their resistance to this therapist who *doesn't love them*" (de Butler, 2008, pp. 66–67, emphasis in original), just as they did not feel loved enough by their parental objects.

In the light of what has been portrayed, the therapeutic group work will be focusing on the analysis of both the intrapsychic and intersubjective movements, with the aim of reactivating the infantile past within which the partners seem to be blocked, to "… let it take again its place in each one's story … Progressively there will be made room to receive today's marital reality" (ibid., p. 67), in order to start the necessary process of mourning for the childhood.

Interpretative hypothesis and conclusions

In the light of the clinical case of which I have tried to give an account, I am led to wonder if such phantasmal, or, better said, interphantasmal functioning may draw an accurate picture of a real change in the modern couple's psychic dynamics, where, indeed, the fraternal dimension seems to prevail (Jaitin, 2008; Kaës, 2008; Trapanese & Sommantico, 2008)—the "horizontal axis" of the psychic apparatus structure, with its role in the formation of the ego and of narcissism, and of the identifications with the similar-different other that the brother represents—to the detriment of the structure-giving oedipal one which would constitute the "vertical" axis. In this sense I would talk about a prevalence, because as Kaës reminds us (2008), these two axes come constantly in contact with one another, fertilising each other—though often in a conflictual way—and they cannot fully exist without one another.

In more detail, I wonder if it is possible to hypothesise about a prevalence of the fraternal archaic aspect where, as Kaës reminds us (2008), with the "brother or the sister" (and we would add: with their imago and their substitutes), some relations are established "which have the psychic consistence of a partial object, an appendix of the imaginary maternal body or of one's own imaginary body" (p. 13); a prevalence that would be to the detriment of both the rivalry form (Laplanche, 1970), which is pre-oedipal (Lacan, 1938) and more differentiated than the fraternal itself, and the oedipal in the strict sense of the word, which would fail here to transform the archaic fraternal. The prevalence of the archaic fraternal, its main role on the scene, would testify to the fact that the Oedipus encountered an obstacle and failed in making certain of both the overcoming of a mirror-like relationship, with the narcissistic figure of the double, and the advent of a sexed identity. In fact, Kaës (2008) asserts:

> The oedipal realization of the fraternal complex demands a twofold movement of the identifications: the identification with the similar got out of the same imaginary or symbolic real origin: it's the narcissistic component of the identification; and the identification with the parent of the same sex which preserves at the same time the bisexual component of the identifications with the father and the mother … While the Oedipus complex has incest and patricide (and matricide) as an edge and castration anxiety as affect, the fraternal complex collides with fratricide and with weaning and abandonment anxieties. The fraternal complex, the pre-oedipal triangle and the rivalries triangle aren't completely overcome with the passing of the Oedipus complex. The fraternal complex changes when parents die, it reactivates at the birth of children and during every big transformation of life which takes us back to contact with the infantile. (pp. 263–264)

In brief, in the light of what has been said so far, I wonder if today we are confronted more and more with couple situations where the individual members are shut up in a world of dyadic conflictual relationships (Morley, 2006), from time to time with a parent or the other, with a brother, with a sister, with a child, all of them always felt like partial objects; we are confronted with cases where the partners cannot successfully negotiate the "next vertical step" (ibid.) of their relation, that would lead them to be parents, having found someone with whom they share these "horizontal" aspects during the formation of the sexual couple. But to say more, we are confronted with situations where the couple link "comes up parasitized by blood relationships", so the "places of husband/wife-father/mother will remain reserved to the original families, leaving the new family to be converted into a group of siblings fed at the expense of an inexhaustible consanguinity cost" (Gomel, 1997, p. 79). So in this sense the ideal of likeness would prevail over every form of structuring and oedipal difference—above all the one that recalls the castration and therefore the sex difference— as well as a sort of disjunction, within the family, among the paternal, maternal, marital, and fraternal bonds. I think I can say that we face some situations where it is the unconscious alliance itself (Kaës, 2009) of the couple that supports such a closure and does not allow the one to approach the recognition of the other of the link, the only course to the world of triadic relations, to set up an adult parenthood.

All this leads us to the last point I want to stress, one related to the present transformation of parental functions, specifically the paternal one. We can see that there is no reference to the third, meant as the necessary interrogation point and the engine of the psychic activity (Green, 2008), but for a fault in its function which, as Winnicott says (1964), consists in watching over the mother's *greed*: usurpation by the omnipotent mother of the paternal function, absence of the intermediary function of the father in the mother–child relationship which becomes, in this way, a direct and immediate one.

But while the paternal function—"organizer of the alliances on which the filiation and the sexed identities stand" (Kaës, 2009, p. 189)—and the maternal function are both necessary, on the other hand they are not symmetric, and in this sense Roussillon (2003) asserts that "There is no maternal symbolizing function without any reference to the father and his place in the mother's sexuality [nor a] symbolic paternal function without any reference to the mother and the place which the woman has in his desire" (p. 187). Furthermore, the two functions are represented and expressed in different logical times; indeed, if the original alliance is with the mother, both for the son and the daughter, the paternal alliance will intervene to frame it and introduce the logical time of separation and oedipal structuring—that is to say, the time of sex and generation difference (Kaës, 2009). In other words, the paternal function has a paradoxical position: if, on the one hand, the father comes second, interposing between the mother and the child and intervening in their link which otherwise would be narcissistic and confusional without any solutions, on the other hand paternity lays the foundation for maternity and filiation exactly because the father is the fundamental character of the primal scene and occupies an important place in the mother's conscious and unconscious thoughts and phantasies (Gaddini, 1974; Guillaumin, 2003).

These changes in the paternal function bring his protective function up for discussion again: offering an economic alternative to the totally absorbing investment of the first love object, a prelude to the possibility for the subject to find a place in the succession of generations and to accept the sex difference. Furthermore, we can see that within present families there is more and more confusion and lack of integration between the maternal and paternal function, and this brings on some real changes in the processes of resolution of the Oedipus complex, bound to the multiplication of the identifying models (Sommantico, 2010).

In the light of the aforesaid, I wonder what the nature of the interplay between the oedipal and the fraternal is that shows itself to us in what I proposed to define as fraternisation, but which we might also call *horizontalisation of the links*, in the contemporary clinical situations which increasingly present themselves to us.

Notes

1. In this sense, Matus (2003) highlights as a frequent fact to be observed in the contemporary clinic the presence of couple problems in which the relation between the partners is characterised more like a fraternal link than like a marital alliance capable of representing a real exogamic discharge.
2. My thanks to Dr Boscaino for consenting to the use of the clinical material.
3. In Kaës's interpretation (2008), these fraternal others, meant as partial objects, are represented as "devouring mouths, mother's body parts or an undifferentiated organs magma" (p. 132).

References

Abend, S. M. (1984). Sibling love and object choice. *Psychoanalytic Quarterly,* 53: 425–430.

Anzieu, D. (1971). L'illusion groupale. *Nouvelle Revue de Psychanalyse,* 4: 73–93.

Bocquet, F. (2010). Les incidences de la relation fraternelle dans le couple. *Dialogue, 189*: 67–77.

Caillot, J. -P., & Decherf, G. (1982). La position narcissique paradoxale: "vivre ensemble nous tue, nous séparer est mortel". *Dialogue, 78*: 98–103.

Coles, P. (Ed.) (2006). *Sibling Relationships.* London: Karnac.

Conrath, Y., de Butler, A., Legrand, B., & Lemaire, J. (1991). Quand le fraternel et le conjugal se mélangent. *Dialogue, 114*: 102–110.

David, C. (1992). *La Bisexualité Psychique.* Paris: Payot.

de Butler, A. (2000). L'écho du lien fraternel dans la séduction et la conflictualité conjugales. *Dialogue, 149*: 67–76.

de Butler, A. (2008). *Le Couple et l'Épreuve du Temps. L'Odyssée du Couple.* Ramonville Saint-Agne, France: Érès.

Eiguer, A. (1998). *Clinique Psychanalytique du Couple.* Paris: Dunod.

Eiguer, A. (2000). L'échafaudage narcissique du lien fraternel. *Journal de la Psychanalyse de l'Enfant, 27*: 261–277.

Freud, S. (1905d). *Three Essays on the Theory of Sexuality. S. E., 7.* London: Hogarth.

Freud, S. (1916–17). *Introductory Lectures on Psycho-Analysis. S. E., 15–16.* London: Hogarth.

Freymann, J. -R. (2003). *Frères Humains qui ... Essai sur la Frérocité.* Ramonville Saint-Agne, France: Érès.

Gaddini, E. (1974). Formation of the father and the primal scene. In: A. Limentani (Ed.), *A Psychoanalytic Theory of Infantile Experience* (pp. 61–82). London: Routledge.

Gomel, S. (1997). *La Transmisión Generacional, Familia y Subjetividad.* Buenos Aires, Argentina: Lugar Editorial.

Green, A. (1973). The neuter gender. In: *Life Narcissism/Death Narcissism.* London: Free Association, 2001.

Green, A. (2008). La construction du père perdu. In: D. Cupa (Ed.), *Images du Père dans la Culture Contemporaine. Hommages à André Green* (pp. 11–49). Paris: PUF.

Guillaumin, J. (2003). Archéologie du père, entre l'angoisse d'une présence et la métaphore d'une absence, le "père de la préhistoire personnelle". In: J. Guillaumin & G. Roger (Eds.), *Le Père. Figures et Réalité* (pp. 57–72). Paris: L'Esprit du Temps.

Jaitin, R. (2008). Violence dans les liens fraternels et conjugaux. La chaise vide. *Revue Internationale de Psychanalyse du Couple et de la Famille, 2*: 67–81.

Kaës, R. (1974). *L'Appareil Psychique Groupal.* Paris: Dunod, 1976.

Kaës, R. (2008). *Le Complexe Fraternel.* Paris: Dunod.

Kaës, R. (2009). *Les Alliances Inconscientes*. Paris: Dunod.

Kancyper, L. (1991). *Resentimiento y Remordimiento. Estudio Psicanalítico*. Buenos Aires, Argentina: Paidos.

Kancyper, L. (2004). *El Complejo Fraterno*. Buenos Aires, Argentina: Lumen.

Lacan, J. (1938). *Family Complexes in the Formation of the Individual*. London: Karnac, 2003.

Laplanche, J. (1970). *Life and Death in Psychoanalysis*. Baltimore, MD: John Hopkins University Press, 1976.

Matus, S. (2003). Vínculo fraterno: de la legalidad paterna a la multiplicidad de las legalidades. In: E. Czernikowski, R. Gaspari, S. Matus, & S. Moscona (Eds.), *Entre Hermanos. Sentido y Effectos del Vínculo Fraterno* (pp. 9–45). Buenos Aires, Argentina: Lugar Editorial.

Mitchell, J. (2003). *Siblings. Sex and Violence*. Cambridge: Polity Press.

Morley, E. (2006). The influence of sibling relationships on couple choice and development. In: P. Coles (Ed.), *Sibling Relationships* (pp. 197–224). London: Karnac.

Nicolò, A. M., & Imparato, G. (2000). La relation à la fratrie chez le patient adolescent. *Journal de la Psychanalyse de l'Enfant*, 27: 179–193.

Pontalis, J. -B. (2006). *Frère du Précédent*. Paris: Gallimard.

Rosolato, G. (1978). *La Relation d'Inconnu*. Paris: Gallimard.

Roussillon, R. (2003). Figures du père: le plaisir de la différence. In: J. Guillaumin & G. Roger (Eds.), *Le Père. Figures et Réalité* (pp. 185–203). Paris: L'Esprit du Temps.

Sommantico, M. (2008). Ritorni del fraterno in una consultazione psicoanalitica di coppia. In: G. Trapanese & M. Sommantico (Eds.), *La Dimensione Fraterna in Psicoanalisi* (pp. 203–221). Rome: Borla.

Sommantico, M. (2009). Prefazione. L'apporto di René Kaës alla comprensione del fraterno in psicoanalisi. In: R. Kaës, *Il Complesso Fraterno* (pp. 5–11). Rome: Borla.

Sommantico, M. (2010). Il disagio familiare. Un possibile operatore di lettura dell'attuale disagio della civiltà. In: M. Ciambelli & S. Marino (Eds.), *Per un'Etica del Disagio. Materiali per una Riflessione sulle Forme del Disagio nella Civiltà Contemporanea* (pp. 51–73). Naples, Italy: Filema.

Trapanese, G. (2007). Il destino dell'odio tra complesso fraterno e complesso materno. *Quaderni di Psicoterapia Infantile*, 53: 85–102.

Trapanese, G., & Sommantico, M. (Eds.) (2008). *La Dimensione Fraterna in Psicoanalisi*. Rome: Borla.

Winnicott, D. W. (1964). *The Child, the Family, and the Outside World*. London: Pelican.

PART III

CLINICAL WORK WITH FAMILIES AND COUPLES

CHAPTER TEN

Couples and the perverse link*

Anna Maria Nicolò

The pathology I want to discuss in this paper is mainly one I found in a few married couples undergoing psychoanalytically oriented treatment once a week.

As Freud also noticed, we should remember that perverse patients would never come to treatment for that reason, but that they come to be treated for the consequences caused by perversion in their life or when for some reason the unconscious perverse deal is broken.

---

*Masud Kahn (1979, p. 21 of the 1989 reprint) talks of "intimacy technique" for the special kind of relation established by a pervert with his object, for which the experience of intimacy becomes a solitary game because there is no relation and therefore no nourishment. According to Khan, for a pervert the object is essentially a transitional object because "through its readiness to comply, it lends itself to be invented, manipulated, used and abused, ravaged and discarded, cherished and idealized" (p. 26 of the 1989 reprint). In my opinion, in a perverse couple, a partner does not assume the value of a transitional object, which is at the same time me and not me, and is located in an intermediate area that requires a third space between subject and object, inside and outside. This transitional space, supported by the object's illusion and creation, does not seem easily referred to by a perverse couple, where space becomes flat and the other is forced into a relation while at the same time being willing to respond to this coercion by letting her/himself be exploited and abused.

In such cases we face a double problem: on one side, we need to focus on some features of perverse relationships and on the other we have to understand how they intertwine and how they are located in the couple's organisation.

Some comments on the term "perverse"

Before discussing the functioning of perverse couples, we should remember the psychoanalytic debate of the past few years over the term "perverse".

Glasser and many other authors have fixed the age limit of perversion, stating that in adolescence we cannot talk of a proper perversion due to the possibility for adolescents to experience perverse polymorph actings (Glasser, 1979; Nicolò, 2009).

With the term perverse we mean a fixed and organised pathology, while regression in childhood and adolescence assumes the continuation of development before the sexual body image is defined and fixed with the gender differentiation between male and female.

Meltzer, for example, distinguishes: 1) perversion proper, i.e., "those erotic phantasies or activities in which the inflicting of mental or physical suffering or injury is central to the excitement" (1973, p. 107); 2) perverse polymorph experiences in subjects with specific mental organisations such as borderline and psychotic persons; 3) a peculiar type of mental functioning characterised by impingement on and destruction of mental life, splitting, and inadequate primary idealisation accompanied with difficulties in distinguishing good from bad.

For the last Meltzer employed the term perversity. It is quite frequent in analytical rooms also because "anybody"—as Meltzer writes—"has an element of perversity in his mental life" (1979, p. 102). Perversity is therefore something different from a perverse sexual behaviour.

Kernberg (1989) thinks that elements of perversion are compatible with normal sexuality and sees a kind of continuity in functioning with behaviours ranging from normal with a certain degree of integrated aggression, domination, and masochism, via perverse polymorph in borderline or narcissistic personality, to psychopathic, psychotic, or antisocial behaviours with openly perverse structures.

Acknowledging an element of perversion in the mental life of any of us is quite useful to dispel the halo of viciousness and loathing elicited by this kind of pathologies. It is, however, advisable to keep in mind the specific nature of this pathology which is still unclear, despite the many discoveries made, since what is also still unclear is the area of sexual life, which is additionally subject to cultural and social changes.

It is clear that in a normal couple to see and to be seen, exhibition, are important elements of sexuality and there is no doubt that sexual intercourse is enriched by the possibility of enjoying one's homosexual aspects through the other. Identifying with oneself and with one's partner during intercourse allows the subject to enjoy two contemporaneous and complementary fusion experiences, in addition to overcoming the barriers separating the sexes. Aggression, the fight for dominance and power are also present in all couples, and sexual passion integrates love and hate that in a sense represent the oscillation from fusion to separation and back in healthy couples.

The unconscious integration of love and hate, the playful use of "mutual exploitation" of the partner's body (ibid.) are commonplace in a couple, so much so that the sexual use of an object "reflects a split of the sexual object or rather a doubling of the same where the reality of the object relation is maintained while a fantastic and regressive reality is playfully represented as an element of sexual desire and excitation" (Kernberg, 1989, p. 270).

Obviously various elements merge in erotic desire, from the wish to take over the other to the wish to surrender to the other. The limits of these complex processes will then be determined by the superego with the function to contain aggression and the tendency to dominate and control the other and the aspects projected onto the other.

In these love relations, at the climax of pleasure one fuses with the other and repeats the primal relations with the parental object. Kernberg neatly distinguishes "erotic desire" from passion and mature love. For him, these three aspects are elements of a healthy love relationship.

Just as acknowledging that there are psychotic aspects in personality does not mean that we are all psychotic, to see perverse aspects in sexual relations should make us reflect on what exactly is perverse functioning.

In my work as couple analyst I think I have seen in many couples and many men polymorph aspects in their fantasies and sex lives, but I think it is useful to distinguish these aspects from true perversion. While polymorph aspects refer to the possibility of integrating infantile elements seen as unconscious fantasies on oedipal and pre-oedipal objects, in adult sexuality the perverse quality of excitement and behaviour is in my opinion something completely different.

These statements reintroduce the concept of polymorphism (not perversion) into normal sexual relations and create clear-cut delimitations: first of all, is this behaviour felt as egosyntonic or not, and more important, is it compulsive and indispensable for reaching sexual pleasure?

The latter element, referring to sexual pleasure, is also extremely important today, when the concept of perversion is easily applied also to other areas.

The perverse link in the couple

Freud states that the pervert loves himself in the child representing him and chosen as a sexual object. Freud adds that through narcissistic identification with the mother, the pervert seeks a sexual object that will be for him the ideal child he had been for his mother (1905d, 1910c).

Masud Khan adds that a true relationship or reciprocity is not possible in a pervert because "… the pervert seeks to make the reparation to his own idolized self … through projective identification with another who represents his idolized internal self" (1979, p. 16). He also states that in perversions, the mother treated her child in infancy as something that she created, idolising some personal aspects of the child, in general those corresponding to aspects of herself.

Various authors agree in thinking that all perverse sexual organisations make narcissistic use of the other.

Working with these patients in the couple setting, can we add any other comments?

In married couples organising a true perversion we see, however, special features. I think that the perverse solution is used by both partners to support and/or define a damaged and confused identity. In these situations a partner embodies the idealised image of the subject that projects onto him/her not only what is lacking in her/himself but also those parts that are felt as dangerous and in this way are repaired, recovered, or controlled in the other and in the couple. Magically, the perverse solution allows them to turn an internal conflict outwards.

However much one partner may say he/she is against perversion, or scared by it, or even horrified by it, a deep and strange fascination will seal the couple's unity and prevent separation. I noticed (often in the same session in which I had noticed this phenomenon, and even in the same process) a couple's paradoxical oscillation from feeling deeply different to acting in a deeply similar way, from expressing diversity to behaving under a surprising unconscious complicity, so that I can say that in these couples, each partner is functional for the other.

However narcissistic a relationship is, it always requires the other partner to be an accomplice (Khan, 1979), to be treated like a fetish object, like a thing object, the outcome of the pervert's imagination, an object playing the role assigned to it by the pervert's fantasy, not only in terms of behaviour but also of emotions.

The perverse partner requires the other not only to do what he/she wants, but also to enjoy, suffer, feel emotions, humiliation, or triumph exactly as requested.

The irony is that the partner must feel what the other commands or requests. This is why a pervert recreates in reality scenarios that he/she imagined in detail. Sometimes the other knows these scripts and must play the role assigned to him/her. In other cases a pervert creates a detailed preliminary script until something is suddenly introduced into the relation and causes surprise, bewilderment, or a sudden change in emotions, and the partner will have to decide whether he/she wants to be part of the scenario and continue enacting it.

In this sense, the sadomasochistic relationship, more than other forms of perversion, is the prototype of a complementary relation, a sort of *folie-à-deux* that concerns a split level of couple functioning.

In this shared insanity represented by the perverse moment in a couple, the existence of a functioning level characterised by a mutual fetishist use of the other seems to be quite relevant.

The peculiar quality of the relationship and the use of the other in perverse relationships

With the help of a clinical case, I will now outline the peculiar quality of the relationship and the use of the other in a couple with perverse issues.

Even though some classical descriptions of perversion were applicable to my patients, for other aspects there were significant differences. In fact, the link between partners was not temporary, like in an affair, where they knew that separation and loss were inevitable and therefore traumatic (as Kahn says of close relationships in perverse patients).

On the contrary, my patients shared a stable marriage link and, as I mentioned, would not have come for treatment if something had not threatened their balance. In the case of the patients I was seeing, couples requested treatment because the perverse link they had been sharing was collapsing. For example, in one case the situation became critical when one partner in the couple had fallen in love with a third person and could establish a non-perverse relation with that person. In another case a problem with the couple's son threatened the collapse of the couple.

The request they made was paradoxically to help them get back to the previous situation.

Rather than on perversion as a nosographic category or personality disorder, I intend to focus on the peculiar quality of functioning of the couple link in a couple where one partner or both request the implementation of "perverse" rituals for reaching satisfaction or sexual potency.

In my experience, the very fact of accepting treatment shows the egodystonic quality of the couple's disorder: the couple requests a change and expresses distress (even if one partner might partially or totally disagree).

In addition, asking for couple treatment means that their link is important for both partners.

The issue of the possibility of a true relationship or reciprocity in these patients is very important, as we tend to think of a perverse personality as one where a person is in a narcissistic relationship only with her/himself.

Marco and Francesca

Marco and Francesca have been coming to therapy, for treatment provided by me and Bachisio Carau, once a week for nearly four years.

He is the last born of four siblings and says his mother was a religious woman and important to him, but distanced from him.

From the very beginning, wife and children had been exposed to the oddities of a father who, for example when angry, would shut wife and children out of the flat.

More than once, Marco mentioned the shame he felt for his father's behaviour, while he himself tried to be seen, as his mother suggested, like a true gentleman.

Francesca is the second of three children. One of them is vaguely described as dominated by the mother. The mother is described as intrusive and strict, jealous of her husband. She used to take Francesca, then aged two, with her when she went around town looking for her husband, while he was supposedly seeing his lovers, the truth of which however was never confirmed later. Because of this Francesca says she soon stopped looking for her father.

Her relation to her brother became important in her development and they even played sexual games. At a certain point the sister too was drawn into these games. Francesca had a deep mirroring relationship with her sister whom she admired.

Crisis

The reason why they come to see me is a period of crisis that caused distress for the husband.

The contingent reason is that Marco discovers that Francesca is having an affair with a friend of the couple.

From the beginning of their relationship, they have come to a partially conscious agreement to act like an open couple in the cultural climate of the late Sixties.

Marco elaborates a theory that Francesca puts into practice. She looks among friends and acquaintances for people to include in sexual relations, in groups of three or more participants.

In most cases when actual sex takes place, Marco just looks on.

In any case, these encounters form a prelude for their intercourse. In other cases Marco makes Francesca tell him her experiences with others as a prelude to their making love.

He says that he often identified with his rivals.

At times, one character in these verbalised fantasies was Francesca's sister. What was typical of their relationship was the constant fantastic reference to acting outside the couple.

So their first relation as a couple is with Marco's best friend.

Marco has premature ejaculations, but Francesca accepts it without anxiety, and with reference to this, Marco suggests two hypotheses to explain why he enjoyed her sexual stories. At times he felt like Tarzan who had captured a much coveted kill, at other times he just enjoyed listening to the story of the kill.

But one day Francesca falls in love with a colleague and the external and internal organisation of the couple collapses.

She discovers she needs secrecy and her emotional cathexis makes Marco feel "betrayed and abandoned" for the first time.

And this is the peculiar aspect that makes them come to ask for help: Marco cannot tolerate that she lived for two years nurturing feelings and emotions that he could not control and that he thought belonged only in their couple. In addition, the intellectual superiority that they had defensively built with their theories collapses, and he feels weak and potentially at the mercy of his feelings.

After the initial impact, the couple establishes a climate of apparent intense cooperation. On one side this showed their motivation, on the other it seemed like a couple seduction.

In time Marco realises that he is unable to access his own or his wife's internal world. On the other hand, he feels a growing aggression against his wife's affair that she cannot give up, as well as against their daughter's upbringing, and this then becomes their battlefield and area of misunderstanding.

Aggression continues to underlie Marco's attitude to therapy and his behaviour at home for about a year, and it seems to represent a screen over the therapeutic work that from the very beginning allowed us to catch a glimpse of primitive and distressing contents.

As an example I present one of the first dreams brought by Francesca and one of the first rare dreams brought by Marco.

Marco says: "I am standing in a group of men near a rock outcrop on a beach.

Suddenly one of these men who looks like me takes his trunks off and starts running around naked crying happily: 'Bugger me, fast, before the other comes.'"

With this dream he associates the idea of breaking cover before being discovered by someone. He also adds that southerners come in two types: the floppy, depressed ones, like the playwright De Filippo, and the exhibitionists, letting us glimpse his oscillation between these positions. In my interpretation I highlight how the patient is willing to show his real face in the setting, but I also highlight the dialectics existing between two versions of oneself, one passive and accepting to be sodomised, the other still unknown. I consider this to be an exploratory intervention also because I think that the other that should arrive in the dream does not only represent another version of the patient's self, but also his wife.

Francesca recounts the following dream. She is in the street close to a cardboard box that contains dead violets. She hears a cry for help coming from a room of her flat so she moves to the street door and finds out that she has become a child wearing a toy rifle, so she marches like a guard patrolling the gate with her rifle.

The only thing the dream suggests to her is to remember when she was small and her mother told her that no man would be able to love her, in reference to her experience with her brother. I interpret that the patient in her life has lost a phallic defensive position and has armed herself with a penetrating masculine aspect to defend herself from the traumatic patterns characterising her family. I also highlight how each one of them defensively plays an inverted gender role: Francesca with her gun plays a male role, while Marco plays a passive one. I also point out to them that in their marriage they have each found in their partner a mutual complementary defence that protects them from both old and recent traumas.

As the therapeutic work proceeds, the couple's acting lessens and the confusion of identity moves aside, leaving room for very painful issues.

The body that used to be seductively dressed up and exhibited to receive admiration is now in dreams and in reality it is a wounded body that needs to be repaired. For example, the presence of a fibroma in the uterus that led them to avoid pregnancies is now a serious worry for Francesca. And Marco often complains of somatic disorders and headache. This coincides with their individual search for gender identity.

In a dream during this period, Francesca goes to the gynaecologist. At the end of the examination the doctor tells her she needs to undergo surgery. The operation is performed by the same doctor who applies a net to the womb to cure a prolapse of the uterus (an illness she does not have, but which her mother has). Her husband is present at the operation which proves to be bearable because the doctor explains it step by step.

As the perverse solution is discarded, or at least blocked, and collusion on this aspect vanishes, what emerges is the question of a devalued and helpless self. Marco feels he cannot satisfy his wife; she is afraid of his aggression and violent excitement, which, she feels, is coloured with sadism.

Marco dreams to see another self of his as a poor blind beggar wearing earphones, lost on a road and helped by the firemen. The sessions are filled with talk of death, madness, and illnesses along with dreams taking place close to the breaks in therapy. Marco dreams of the death of his best friend, of his recently recovered father, and Francesca dreams of miscarriages and abortion. Clinging to a sick body is a sign of the emergence of a more differentiated self in search of a new foundation.

Main issues

I will now summarise the main issues in the relationship of this couple.

1. Each partner held for the other the special attribute of being a "thing-person", as Khan (1979, p. 15) called it, a sort of fetish used by each for his/her own pleasure.

   For example, Marco wanted Francesca to dress as he dictated in detail, he criticised her when he saw her tired and with bags under her eyes, letting herself go. In the "open couple" period she would dress very provocatively and go around looking for people to seduce while he admired her exhibitions. Posing as objects to be admired, they both felt superior and despised others.

2. They shared a request for idolisation of themselves and their couple that mimicked in their marital relation the attitude displayed by their mothers. Marco, for example, said his mother was warm and reverential and considered him an example for his siblings because of his alleged gentlemanly manners.

3. The perverse solution is used to support or define an identity that is perceived as confused, uncertain, or damaged. The partner concretely embodies the subject's idealised image; onto the partner one projects what is lacking and those parts of oneself felt as dangerous, parts which in this way can be repaired, recovered, or controlled in the other and in the couple.

4. In the split-off area that is the perverse core of the couple, the partner does not have an independent existence, nor can he/she be placed outside an omnipotent control, but, as Freud and later many others, such as Greenacre, have taught us, this gives the other the features of a fetish, an object with bisexual characteristics (Freud, 1905d, 1927e; Greenacre, 1971).

5. In a perverse couple the identity confusion of one partner becomes a total omnipotent fusion, bisexuality in action, due to projective identification. The attempt to leave the perverse solution leads to

abandoning the omnipotent bisexuality and fusion fantasies. It becomes a brave and painful search for a new foundation for the self, primarily experienced as an unacceptable, devalued, unhealthy bodily self, full of death anxiety.

6. Enactment in a perverse relationship allows the couple to cope with a painful intrapsychic situation, to avoid one's frozen internal world, externalising conflicts in the partner. The resolution of the perverse link highlights shared issues of devaluation and death of the self that can be re-enacted in front of the analyst. This allows the partners to avoid signal anxiety and, in this way, the couple can remain in a state of suspension, waiting to see if it can start a new elaboration.

7. The very status of a married couple sees the body as an object of exchange. In this double coincidence the couple plays a therapeutic and/or reparative function because it includes the issues of each partner and can change them into a perverse solution. The use of the body (of each partner) is part of a split functioning that corresponds to perversion. While sexual intercourse in a mature relationship of intimacy and mutuality is based on the acknowledgment of differences (gender, role, etc.), on the ability to stay in touch with one's inner world as with the internal parental couples, and through the mechanism of primary identification, to fuse in the act with the other, a perverse relationship tends to support the denial of otherness, and of the differentiation of self and other. This denial, supported by splitting, can lead to the annihilation of the bodily and sexual dimensions or to a poor eroticisation and the massive and instrumental use of the other's body. In some couples the complete absence of sexuality can hide a massive defence against perversion, just like in other couples this role is played by massive eroticisation. The partner must be converted to the other's fantasies, becomes inanimate, and deprived of his/her features, used, exploited, and therefore parasitised.[1] This means that in the pervert, by means of a vertical splitting, there ensues a dissociation of the fantastic and the real world that must never be allowed to come in contact. The partner needs to support this splitting and the related fantasy of adjustment and normality that are in reality pseudo-adjustment and pseudo-normality.

In these cases we can see a sort of autoerotism performed with the partner's body. By autoerotism in perversion I mean an activity that does not see the object as other from oneself, in a separate existence, unlike what happens in the regressive phases of normal development and in moments of fusion in couples.

This aspect provides a confirmation of the acceptance of a body that would otherwise be experienced as devalued, unacceptable, or used, and in any case split-off from the mind and from possible fantastic elaborations.

Comments

Work with a couple allows us to grasp the confused and hard core of perverse partners, while also highlighting the healthy parts of their personality. The extraordinary swiftness of change is surprising if we think of their pathology and probably it is the couple setting itself that gathers all the elements that are externalised, drawing them onto the partner who would remain split-off and dissociated in an individual treatment.

Some pathological couple relationships derive from a shared pathology, more evident in one partner than in the other and built up in time with the contribution of both partners. The very relationship tends to press the partners to make pathological enactments. Thus the link imprisons them and makes evident pathologies that would otherwise remain hidden. We must therefore consider the fact that in the couple there is not only a collusive process based on a sort of unconscious complementarity organised on mutual projective identification, as described by many authors (Dicks, 1967; Giannakoulas, 1992; Norsa & Zavattini, 1997; Willi, 1975), but that there is a new structure co-constructed by the partners. After many years of experience in this field, I am convinced that this link, as a third element, is so strong as to influence the life of the couple and of each of the partners. And I believe that because of this link each partner can activate a complementary version of himself that in extreme conditions can overwhelm the identity that up to then had been known to all others.

What I have seen in these couples has convinced me that in such situations all strategies, including the choice of a partner, are directed at reaching a defensive pseudo-adjustment for fear of breaking down.

It is a very complex defence that implies death anxiety and self-inconsistence in addition to a defence from the confusion in gender identity.

References

Dicks, H. V. (1967). *Marital Tensions*. London: Routledge [reprinted London: Karnac, 1993].

Freud, S. (1905d). *Three Essays on the Theory of Sexuality. S. E.*, 7: 125–243. London: Hogarth.

Freud, S. (1910c). *Leonardo da Vinci and a Memory of his Childhood. S. E.*, 11: 57–138. London: Hogarth.

Freud, S. (1927e). Fetishism. *S. E.*, 21: 147–158. London: Hogarth.

Giannakoulas, A. (1992). La membrana diadica. *Interazioni, 0*: 129–132.

Glasser, M. (1979). Some aspects of the role of aggression in the perversions. In: I. Rosen (Ed.), *Sexual Deviation* (pp. 278–305). Oxford: Oxford University Press.

Greenacre, P. (1971). *Psychoanalytic Studies of the Gifted and a Great Variety of Other Individuals*. New York: International Universities Press.

Kernberg, O. F. (1989). A theoretical frame for the study of sexual perversions. In: *Aggression in Personality Disorders and Perversions*. New Haven, CT: Yale University Press, 1993.

Khan, M. M. R. (1979). *Alienation in Perversions*. London: Karnac, 1989.

Meltzer, D. (1973). *Sexual States of Mind*. Strathtay, UK: Clunie Press [reprinted London: Karnac, 2008].

Meltzer, D. (1979). Perversità. *Quaderni di Psicoterpia Infantile, 1*: 101–121.

Nicolò, A. M. (2009). *Break-down et Solutions Défensives chez l'Adolescent*. Unpublished paper given at the Conference of Société Européenne pour la Psychanalyse de l'Enfant et de l'Adolescent (SEPEA) Paris, September.

Norsa, D., & Zavattini, G. C. (1997). *Intimità e Collusione*. Milan, Italy: Cortina.

Willi, J. (1975). *Couples in Collusion*. Northvale, NJ: Jason Aronson, 1982.

Couple and family psychoanalytic psychotherapy's contribution to current psychoanalysis

Jean-George Lemaire

Couple and family psychoanalytic psychotherapies are specific applications of psychoanalysis, just like group therapy and psychodrama. Their contribution to psychoanalysis however has not been discussed so far both as regards their therapeutic and practical as well as their conceptual dimensions with their cultural implications.

Family therapy in fact, like psychodrama, does not directly stem from psychoanalysis. Although different at the beginning, these therapeutic approaches were later revisited by psychoanalysts. Nonetheless, even though some true analysts participated in their creation, their practices were rejected or made fun of by some practitioners of a psychoanalytic treatment conceived a little earlier and as strictly individual. Even today, this anathema has not completely disappeared in certain "fundamentalist" circles of individual psychotherapy. There has been conflict for a long time, with the controversies being linked to many factors, more particularly to the need for public and cultural recognition both for the classic analytic practice and its new applications, with each treatment claiming its place in the sun and dreading, like Diogenes, that its sun could be hidden by Alexander's shadow …

Luckily, thanks to other psychoanalysts with broader views, and notwithstanding the critical looks of some colleagues, the spirit of psychoanalysis, its understanding of the unconscious processes, of the defences and the transference, has permeated all these methods which little by little have acquired an official place among the different psychoanalytic practices: the psychodramatist, the group analyst, the psychoanalyst practising relaxation body therapies, etc. All are currently recognised as likely to provide some contribution to the theoretical clinical corpus of psychoanalysis. The same thing is happening currently, although with some delay, with couple and family psychoanalytic psychotherapy.

A significant evolution of the practices and their theoretical understanding has become manifest in family therapy as well as traditional individual psychoanalysis. Although since the beginning of his work, Freud greatly emphasised the notion of the group, and even more so the relevance of the mother–child, father–child, and family structures, the area in which such discoveries were used by him remained strictly individual and centred on the adult, even when he set his heart on treating other family members, as in the renowned case of Little Hans (Freud, 1909b). This first attempt would be rejected nowadays by both the "cure-type" (treatment) supporters and those of the family therapies. On the one hand, the early family system approaches, even carried out by psychoanalysts, sometimes were considered to be at the limits of a psychoanalytic model, or they were confused with certain "systemic" therapies whose accentuated deviances from their own methods have vexed analysts. On the other hand, individual psychoanalytic practice developed considerably, sometimes also presenting some deviances, for instance, when the patient-analyst relationship was reduced for some only to its language dimension and the analysis to a dehumanised subject and a theoretical "desire": deviances which made it hard to understand the group and family approaches which other psychoanalysts were developing further.

Needless to say, the social and cultural context also changed a lot in the course of half a century and it entailed a great evolution regarding the kind of requests for treatment. They were strictly individual "requests" at first, which allowed for the Freudian creation. It was only much later that the "patient" request concerned the issue of family relations, the patient-child and then the couple relationships. This development followed many socio-political factors, such as social upheavals, wars, and displacements of people; it also underwent a practical and theoretical progress, especially in the area of child psychiatry where the therapists realised that many individual therapies for children were hindered or prevented by pathogenic family contexts.

Family therapists also observed the repetition of different symptoms or reactions across many successive generations, thus questioning the phenomenon of their transmission. This joined forces with the criticism made by Balint (1960) about a psychoanalytic practice too often reduced by some to a "one body psychology". Moreover, the attachment theories have moved closer to psychoanalysis and have been accepted by many analysts. Winnicott's and Bion's paediatric and psychoanalytic approach to children and groups allowed the development of group therapies already attempted by Foulkes, Ezriel, and others. A new epistemology of psychoanalysis developed, one whose recent development is remarkable, passing from the search for the "content of the unconscious" to its "container" which is its psychic functioning, and also from the person or from the subject-object relation to the *transitional space*, in order to link the processes of *subjectivisation* and *mastery*.

In these developmental social and cultural conditions, what did family psychoanalytic treatments and their analysis bring forth, or what can they still contribute to, invalidate, or confirm in the overall psychoanalytic corpus?

The work I am proposing is first of all the result of stepping back and viewing a broader picture supported by a parallel analysis of several kinds of psychoanalytic treatments I personally performed. This has led me to a sort of meta-analysis starting from:

- rigorously classical individual psychoanalytic treatments, "cure-type" style as well as vis-à-vis, with adults, children, and adolescents;
- body psychoanalytic therapies, once called relaxation treatments (at the time when the use of the term psychotherapy was dreaded by those patients with somatic symptoms), based on the progressive expression by the patient of bodily sensations and memories experienced about bodily perceptions:
  - group therapies with initially unconnected individuals
  - bigenerational family psychoanalytic therapies
  - couple psychoanalytic therapies.

Overall, it has been shown and confirmed nowadays by many experienced and versatile analysts that the ubiquitous unconscious processes not only are translated differently in the various therapies performed, but also, and above all, that they correspond to the different unconscious layers which often do not seem to communicate with one another, as if they were independent. Let us take as an example an analysand who previously started a true "cure-type" treatment with a very competent colleague, and later on discovered, during a couple analysis, a whole series of aspects of his internal functioning that he never thought he had during his previous analysis. He realised that some of his unconscious phenomena whose specific meaning he had grasped during his individual therapy currently became something to be worked through, having acquired a completely different sense in the framework of a narcissistic problem which was reactivated by the analysis of his couple bond, etc. These examples show a superposition of different unconscious problems manifesting themselves during equally different psychoanalytic approaches.

On the basis of some of the original observations here, this concerns particularly some phenomena emerging during the couple analysis, within those patients who had previously undergone deep individual psychoanalytic therapy, often due to their professional activity in the field of psychoanalysis. For this reason or for other personal or family reasons, they experienced intense events and emotions aroused in them by their couple relationship, ones which upset the equilibrium of their object relations. During their couple analysis, usually unexpected problems emerge, ones which are absent from their ordinary social life or which are at times observed in some diseases (phenomena which sometimes correspond to what the juries of the great trials or even their expert witnesses themselves often have a hard time understanding!). Here we can find again the kindred relation evoked by Freud between psychosis and loving passion. Thus, phenomena of surprising influence, almost possessiveness, or splitting appear within the couple, ones which can be analysed during the session through the couple transference.

In this chapter, we shall be able to deal only with some conceptual aspects.

First conceptual aspect

The first one concerns the central concept of the unconscious or rather that of the "non-conscious", whose general character shall be underlined, but we will not reproduce what Freud dealt with at length during the years of his first argument, when psychic dynamism was understood as a consequence of the dialectic conflict between the agencies of the unconscious and of the consciousness. Basically we will not reexamine the issue he dealt with during his second argument either, between the agencies of the "*Es*", the ego, and the superego, since the unconscious processes can be fully found in each one of the three agencies.

Both the conceptualised practice of group and family analysis and especially couple therapy compel us to take into account a "non-conscious space", where sometimes images or other sensory perceptions emerge, ones which are not conscious but presumably also not repressed, and simply cohabit with other phenomena of neuropsychological origin.

"Original", one may call them, as they originate in the early stages of the neuropsychic development and since it is possible to understand them thanks to a better knowledge of the neurosensory development of the baby and the foetus, at a time when the different sensory systems are still undifferentiated. Images of this type can sometimes emerge during the body psychotherapies (so called relaxational) in psychosomatic patients: multisensory images, or even "sensory convergences", but not real ghosts or scenarios with their well-known psychic character. *Non-conscious*, perhaps, rather than *unconscious*?

Second conceptual aspect

A second conceptual problem is focusing on *identity* and the threat to it by an intense and long-term loving passion. The depth of the conflict within couple psychoanalytic therapy compels us to greatly emphasise the narcissistic or identity dimensions of it. Of course, the libidinal dimensions are always present, particularly in their pregenital regressive forms. But the phenomena of psychic differentiation between the psyches of the partners, or, better said, between the *ego* and the *alter ego* emphasise certain individual processes of identity defence in each partner, thus generating obscure conflicts between the lovers, within the archaic fusion of love. These are phenomena which often translate into a kind of acting or into behavioural disorders that make us think about a sort of "behavioural howl" such as, "Who am I?" and "Am I still?" or a sometimes inaudible cry of alarm, since they are deprived of a clear verbal form, followed by abandonment.

The difficulty in constructing and keeping the feeling of being oneself above all is located in the conflict between the individual ego and the "we" that represent the couple-group, itself a reliving of the early identity perceptions built in the individual prehistory, preceding the construction of the ego and even the perception of the self.

During the couple analysis, each analysand can perhaps discover many strange and archaic impressions which, in the still unconscious depths of the love life, interact with the ones of the partner. Together, they discover more or less mutual affects which they have somehow wedged one inside the other, within the special bond that the couple has created together: desires, fears, or even defences. They realise then that they "act them out" in the intimacy of their current conjugal relation, through various sentimental, verbal, and above all sexual compromises or expressions which are restricted to that couple. In general, during other amourous adventures, neither of them had the occasion of experiencing the same specific interactive phenomena.

A specific "we" has been established and is very narcissistically invested. On what sensory or mnestic basis? The feeling of being oneself, the basis of one's identity can be shaken. How can one maintain it or restore it and how does the individual survive it?

The evoked unconscious psychic phenomena are often associated with affects of invasion, impingement, intrusion, encompassing the sense of belonging, and even total appropriation that the partners had ignored until then, accompanied sometimes by fusional desires of differentiation which they had fully prohibited each other until then. The partners are now surprised at finding themselves experiencing these desires, for instance in specific forms of enjoyment at times accompanied by a specific anxiety, or else through behaviours actually set up for escaping them.

During the couple psychoanalytic work they evoke simultaneously perhaps very blurred yet repetitive images, as if taken from sensory experiences from a long time ago.

They are not like true memories, rather perceptions or superimpositions of multisensory perceptions whose meaning they did not grasp then: something about a confused "atmosphere". For instance, a smell associated with a sort of melody or with an image, with an envelope or simply its colour, or else with a "speechless voice" or with other "atmospheres" in general experienced within a sensation of estrangement. What is striking is that the partner of the couple often discovers close links with something that he himself had "forgotten"! In fact, the verbal associations that end up emerging often evoke a general atmosphere of a fusional and undifferentiated nature.

Customary language does not have sufficient vocabulary to distinctively define these experiences. But contributions from neuroscience suggest something about the early ways prior to the development of the human psyche and ultimately of consciousness. They are close to certain insights present in the contemporary development of psychoanalytic thinking.

Thus, let us go back to the construction of a feeling of identity, with a different basis of identity. The identity construction is an essential problem, now more so than ever, for the narcissistic balance of every human being, particularly of children and adolescents, during this time of fast cultural change. On the one hand, the models for identification are unstable, contradicting, and confused. On the other, the idea that being oneself is a mistake is given publicity in the media, a sort of morbid and defeatist acceptance of time and ageing accompanying it.

All clinicians confront the clinical, psychic, and social faces of the dialectic movement between the two main sources of the processes of identification: identification by difference (becoming oneself by separating and distinguishing oneself), and, before, identification by belonging (one exists as one is part of something or of an enveloping matrix, child of …, member of …, or worth being a member of such an ideal, group, or worth more being the loved object of such a good and powerful character, etc.). Of course, these two identity bases do not exclude but rather support one another and they even mix up, especially in any love relation. Thus, what are these identity construction and identification processes based on?

They use above all very archaic means that are emotional rather than verbal, thanks to a pre- or ante-language material, prepared or supplied since birth by sensory rather than by verbal "atmospheres", which are nonetheless loaded with meaning, although ambiguous.

These first "incorporates" do not proceed through culturally invested ideals, but through certain perceptions, images, or sounds whose global meaning is accessible only in a certain context rather than through verbal content: images therefore, rather than strictly defined signifiers (or even these "uncoded" or "enigmatic" "strange signifiers" of recent authors). Perhaps we are getting close to an aspect of both Freud's and the early authors' insight, although it has never been explored, through the quite vague concept of the "primary unconscious".

The understanding of identity disorders gained from the clinical work on narcissism and the love relation then obliges us to return to the original, almost pre-individual steps of the construction of a feeling of identity and leads on to give value to some key notions, such as the one of belonging and of possessiveness and those of transmission by the environment, even before the introduction of the negative.

In fact, the most important transgenerational transmissions go through something linked to emotion, through a sort of "group emotionality" (Avron, 2001), or through a sort of biologically primitive mimicry (almost pre-human?) (Girard, 1990), namely through some very archaic relational modes, general phenomena which can be seen everywhere, yet deprived of negation and sometimes of temporality. That is where everything starts. That is also what is maintained in the most enduring fashion, notwithstanding the additional repressive, conscious, and unconscious modifications which are going to form the matrix of speech, rationality, and the belated components of personality. These modifications will demand access to a new ability, that is, negation, which the early emotional phenomena that passed on the early perceptions establishing early identifications did not have.

Let us compare then these archaic or very early phenomena to the traditional psychopathological and psychoanalytic concepts concerning identification and identity itself. All our psychoanalytic concepts following Freud are linked (like the Oedipus complex, etc.) to differentiated representations of people. During that rationalist time, trusting that reason was present within each individual, Freud did not show much interest in the theme of identity, which is barely a psychoanalytic concept. For him, there was a sort of first evidence of the identity feeling, as something that goes by itself almost as a fact, even a rock in the sense formulated elsewhere when speaking about the "biological rock". Thus, each adult was supposed to have his identity almost naturally. It is also necessary to take into account the fact of a very progressive anthropological evolution, brought on by history, which for thousands of years has been enhancing individual development, at the risk of opposing it to the defence or the survival of the group, even up to the point of sometimes causing trouble to the construction of identity itself.

What is more, at the beginning of psychoanalysis, the treatment was designed only for structured adults with psychopathological symptoms, who were essentially neurotics.

Psychoanalysis was only later extended to individuals under development (very young children and then infants), or to individuals affected by serious pathologies (autism, infantile psychosis) that entail profound disorders of identity or of the feeling of identity. Thus, the identity question was mainly dealt with only after Freud. Nowadays, the identification processes are usually referred to via classical identification models between individuals.

Nonetheless, during the most profound family analysis (and especially couple psychoanalytic therapies), it seems as if identities get organised well before the recognition of the individual as such. These facts concur with an important course of contemporary psychoanalytic thinking which, since the analysis of children and psychotics, has emphasised the early bonds with the family circle, a current of thought that is particularly developed in the Winnicottian concept of "transitional" (1957) and more recently the concept of mastery. In couple psychoanalytic therapies, where the love bond is worked on together, in other words, the most archaic and one of the most complex affects, it is possible to observe that the individual in love, under certain circumstances, "con-fuses" his ego not so much with that of his partner, but rather with the shared "we" that ties them strongly. In a close intimacy, each partner feels that his bond to the other partner builds a very narcissistically invested "we", holder of a specific identity, namely the couple-group's identity which is closely connected to each one and belongs to each partner and *is even part of* each one of them.

Now, a psychic agency of "we" was indeed at the origin of the ego in each partner: it is and was the early origin and matrix which fed and wrapped up the future developing ego of each partner. Narcissism, which is self-love and necessary love for the image of one's Self finds its first support in it. This we stays in each human being as a *pre-form integrated within narcissism*, a pre-form which is going to be projected in further group psychic organisations. It is necessary to refer to the mysterious sentence by Freud (1914c), in "On Narcissism: An Introduction", about the "double existence". "The individual actually leads a double life: as long as his own end depends on him, and as long as he is a link of a chain against his will or at least without wanting it. (He himself [the individual] keeps sexuality as one of his ends, while another perspective shows us that he is a simple extension of his germinative plasma, to which he offers his strength in exchange of a prize of pleasure, and he is the mortal carrier of a perhaps immortal substance ...)" (p. 78).

Thus, when within a couple in love, the affective load and its emotional and drive support are important, a new we is built, one which is very much invested in and which maintains the traces of the early we of each partner, and at the same time, it "represents" a pre-form by now inscribed in the love bonds. This love bond binds a "me" to a "you", which is profoundly invested in within both an object and a narcissistic mode; since this "you", at first "object", becomes more or less an alter ego and sometimes even risks taking the place of the ego. Thus, identity conflicts that had been unconscious for a long time emerge between the individual I and the we. The I sometimes merges or even disappears in a certain manner within the we that wraps it up, by reproducing during the passion the issue of the early existence, when the psychic borders were barely established. This leads to a conflict on a narcissistic level between the me and the us, an us preceding this me from which it stems from.

A sort of incestuous aspect is sometimes experienced in certain lovers, which nonetheless then is not biologically natural any more than during the early moments of shared life between mother and foetus or baby. A sexual (male or female) inhibition in the adult can express something about this last defence of the individual ego, as the clinical work shows at times (it should not be confused with a form of masochism, a term exaggeratedly used in the media which popular use has extended excessively). On some occasions, one of the partners fears a distressing fusional annihilation, whereas he was previously experiencing with delight the orgasm of the "small death". On other occasions, always when the relationship is dense, different types of mastery develop within the couple as part of a common identity. From then on, it is not even aggression which is dangerous or deadly, paradoxically it is the unifying depth of love, invasive and enthralling in the strong sense of the term. This phenomenon is exhibited by some love couples who become aggressive and even dangerously violent to each other and even notice it without understanding that they are simply looking for a protective psychic distance.

Thus, the classical model of the oedipal identification, as much as it is pertinent elsewhere, is not enough to grasp the frequent revival of images linked to very archaic and most probably group type identification phenomena in the clinical work. The psychoanalytic clinical work with couples and families compels us to go beyond the early concepts of identification, without disowning them.

Perhaps is it necessary to speak about "proto-identities" rather than processes or forms of identification? After all, an "identification" does not refer to precise objects or individuals, but rather to an "environment" marked by its own archaism—or even better, by the revival of the love passion of the initial *transitional* atmosphere?

In fact, before recognising a psychic *object* like an *individual* as being *one self*, one is not yet a *subject* and one is not yet distinct from the whole, or one cannot feel oneself as a figure in the sense of a distinct Gestalt. It is a matter of *becoming* before *being*, of feeling oneself *within* a whole, within something *being part of* ... This emphasises that the first mode of identification goes through belonging: belonging to a group or being part of a certain badly defined environment. At the beginning of the existence, *one is not* yet, one gets ready to be and *one is within* an envelope, a matrix, a transitional universe.

One is part of, one belongs to *"Ich bin dein, du bist mein ..."* says the poet.

In addition to the psychopathological observations of childhood, one can also refer to the progressive construction of the body scheme, which is a neurological rather than a psychological concept. It is not a sensation, rather a neurological and structural organisation, which manages to reach the consciousness, but it is also essential for the organism and without it the body cannot use its motor functions. This construction is a progressive integration of the whole neurological sensitivity. It is also equally distinct from the psychic process, this time called "body image", which is also a progressive construction of the perceptions, also before the actual consciousness, which shall appear only later: a *body image* underlying an early *self-image*, which comes before the image that one shall discover later in the mirror, one that shall precede a more authentic yet belated *self-consciousness*.

This makes us think about the perception or the sensation of a first differentiation of the *self-world* during foetal life. The biological and neurological data show that the body's perception becomes possible only after a certain development, that of the myelination of the axonal sheaths, and that the different sensory systems remain more or less confused before that, with probably a priority for the sense of touch, before the sense of taste of the future orality. Thus, the first experience of the existence of a *non-self* passes probably through one of the foetal envelopes. The foetus registers them probably during its early experiences thanks to a primitive sense of touch. It is something indistinct, but beyond the Self, *something which is not the Self* and soon something that will exist outside the Self, different from the Self later, whose premises are still being established.

This is what probably helps to grasp the ambiguities and the identity conflicts which our experience of couple and family psychoanalytic psychotherapy brings to us every day.

First of all, "identity" is the perception or feeling of being, before becoming a "representation". It is a construction starting from previous impressions, experienced well before any consciousness, before any distinction between non-conscious and conscious, before the integration of the "time" phenomenon. At this occasion, one understands that the process of individuation is a progressive construction, never completely finished. Paradoxically, the first distinction of the *Self-world* seems to precede the creation of a rudimentary *Self*. The limits of the *Self* are still not clear or perceivable, but a first "pre-identification" process has started from badly defined, evidently unconscious atmospheres. The impression of being the Self starts and continues, probably relying on the bodily perception of a limit and of something which is "something else", perhaps enveloping, even impossible to represent, which the family psychoanalysts bring closer to a "family we", which in contrast is more or less clearly defined, especially in recomposed families.

Third conceptual aspect

I shall briefly illustrate a third outline about what psychoanalysis practised within the area of couple and family therapy can contribute, in terms of understanding and conceptualisation, to the whole of the theoretical body of psychoanalysis. It is the notion of "link".

Although the "link" is not part of the original psychoanalytic concepts, it is used increasingly by psychoanalysts, not only those dealing with family therapies, but also by those who practise only individual psychotherapy. What is more, an evolution of the semantic content of this concept emerges, one which for a long time was close to the concept of object relations coming from individual psychoanalysis (de Brusset,

1988, after Green, 1988) and from the ego-object relationship, a pillar of Freudian meta-psychology. The concept of "link" was not necessary for them, whereas it is very important for those psychoanalysts providing family and couple therapies. Its frequent use by us "falls back" on the concepts of individual analysis.

With the evolution of this concept, we go beyond the traditional individual or individualistic concept of psychoanalysis: the notion of object relation is not enough for us anymore, even if it happens to help us help partners to realise or to share the self-analysis of their object relations. Yet, if we are still speaking about an object in our specific discipline, this means mainly thinking about a "group psychic object". In the entire movement of contemporary group psychoanalysis, we are concerned with this concept, and we are even a lot more concerned with it than the analysts of artificial groups, since our family work obliges us to be worried about the meaning and the origin of the "we", a term universally used without definition, rigorously so by our consultants, who call by this name something which has to do with a "group object".

Our consultants, children, adolescents, adults, spouses, or parents, who say "me", "I", "us", and above all "they", need to distinguish their personal identities from the ones of the family-group, without confusing these two main forms of their identity and of the narcissism which is linked to it. Needless to mention here, the alter ego, sometimes the superego, the ego ideal, the "toilet-ego", the bad object or the spokesperson of a social we are often confused with the we of the origins. Thus, a link, or rather a multitude of present and past links are intertwined within any couple and family. Each ego has an ambivalent and archaic relationship to this link.

It is this archaic dimension which deserves our thoughts and imagination efforts for representing its origins and by doing so, a part of its meaning. As was previously mentioned, before speaking in the first person singular and on behalf of an individual identity, the human being remains dependent on a vague primary perception of what the *Self* is, in contrast with a *Non-Self-envelope of Self*. From a Self and a world, confused at the beginning, the Self is distinguished little by little in its envelope, while still staying inside it, since the perception of existing cannot be acquired without participating in this envelope, which shall become a sort of a badly defined "they" and then a "we" (Lemaire, 2005).

In the more recent vocabulary of contemporary analysis, the notions of transitional space, of envelope, and of Self-skin express what we hear or feel at the heart of our transference–countertransference clinical work. Out of the initial chaos of this global confusion emerges the first perception of a transitional space between the developing ego and its envelope, this "we" which precedes the additional ego. But the traces of this transitional space between *ego* and *non-ego* definitely persist, not on a sensory-perceptive level, but rather on a psychic one and "subjectivisation" shall be defined as a step towards allowing the perception to become representation.

The "link" is in fact the avatar of this evolution, an avatar which is distant from the original sensory perception, an avatar then of the transitional space which performs the primary "we" (Lemaire, 2007).

The notion of "link" and "us" can thus be understood in the framework of deep couple and family psychoanalytic therapies. Nowadays our couple and family psychoanalytic psychotherapy allows us to introduce it into the psychoanalytic thought and movement, something which is sometimes criticised. We bring into it another perspective which does not aim to suppress the device of couch or armchair, with their identification modes, yet it understands the construction of identity as prior to these psychic processes, as a perception. Perceived at a sensory level, a sort of "environment", it allows us to build a first transitional space, at the origin of the primary bond, matrix of the ego.

Just like at first the sensory and then the psychic envelope, which come before it, the link will serve as a matrix. Some will experience it painfully, sometimes like a place of seclusion.

In the best cases, this avatar of the archaic processes will blossom into loving feelings.

And even to being in love, an indescribable phenomenon.

Conclusion

Couple and family psychoanalytic therapies allow us to explore very archaic psychic processes which left projective traces in the creation of "group-objects". An essential narcissistic aspect is represented by the universally recognised "we" without being nonetheless clearly defined. These phenomena suggest a new conceptualisation of any psychoanalytic practice, in any setting: particularly, the one of the "unconscious" or of the "non-conscious", the one of "identity" or of "pre-identification process", and the one of "link".

References

Avron, O. (2001). Une forme d'organisation du Nous: l'émotionnalité groupale. *Dialogue, 154*: 27–36.

Balint, M. (1960). *Le Défaut Fondamental*. Paris: Payot, 2003.

Brusset, B. (1988). *Psychanalyse du Lien*. Paris: Centurion.

Freud, S. (1909b). Analysis of a phobia in a five-year-old boy. *S. E., 10*: 1–150. London: Hogarth.

Freud, S. (1914c). On narcissism: An introduction. *S. E., 14*: 67–102. London: Hogarth.

Girard, R. (1990). *Shakespeare, les Feux de l'Envie*. Paris: Grasset.

Green, A. (1988). Preface. In: B. Brusset, *Psychanalyse du Lien* (pp. i–8). Paris: Centurion.

Lemaire, J. -G. (2005). *Comment faire avec la passion*. Paris: Payot et Rivages.

Lemaire, J. -G. (2007). *L'Inconscient dans la Famille*. Paris: Dunod.

Winnicott, D. W. (1957). On the contribution of direct child observation to psycho-analysis. In: *The Maturational Processes and the Facilitating Environment* (pp. 109–114). London: Hogarth and the Institute of Psychoanalysis.

CHAPTER TWELVE

Fraternal incest: fraternal links*

Rosa Jaitin

Presentation

Questions concerning the fraternal link and incest are complicated topics. Imagos and complexes, such as they have been studied by psychoanalysis, permeate them.

Until now, research has focused on the weaning complex (Klein, 1932), the intrusion complex (Lacan, 1938), the complex of the death of the father that enables the construction of the social group, as described by Freud in *Totem and Taboo* (1912–13) and in *Group Psychology and the Analysis of the Ego* (1921c), and finally the complex of small differences as Freud described it in *Civilization and Its Discontents* (1930a).

As for me, I will work on the question of incest starting from the fraternal complex but with the perspective of a dead parenthood. Hence, incest would be a form of expression of the parental void.

I will consider different configurations of fraternal incest characterised according to the family's fantasmatic structure and the way it is inscribed in inter- and transgenerational links of filiation. That is to say, I am going to look at direct, indirect, primary, and secondary incest.

---

*Translated from French to English by Thekla Kausch.

Subsequently we will analyse how the transformations of the shapes of the fraternal link will push for a differentiation between eroticism and sexuality and will operate as a transformation apparatus of the family.

The fraternal link is necessarily incestuous

The fraternal link is necessarily incestuous. On the one hand, because the maternal body is necessarily a space of sharing and a passageway for being born. The physical relationships between the mother and the children make the fraternal link an incestuous one. One cannot get away from it. On the other hand, it is an incestuous link since the body of the brother or the sister is an object of seduction and exploration.

No one can do without the exploration of the other's body, brother or sister, as one cannot do without exploring one's own body.

This means that the fantasy of fraternal incest is normally a major driving force in our social imagery, as we can observe in myths and literature.

How can we define what is and what is not incestuous? Today, the anthropological research of Héritier (1994) gives us the possibility to define incest as having the double characteristic of being direct and indirect. It concerns direct sexual relations between same-sex partners (brother–brother or sister–sister) or partners of different sexes (brother–sister), whether blood-related or not. For example, in a recomposed family, sexual relations between stepbrothers and stepsisters are considered incest. But at the same time, fraternal incest is considered indirect since there is always a third party mediator: the mother.

Fraternal incest is not forbidden in all cultures. This is an aspect I have emphasised in my work on pseudo-myths, as it was the case for the Incas of Peru, the Pharaohs in Egypt, as well as in Greek mythology.

But if the fraternal link has the potential to be incestuous, how come that some siblings go through these situations differently?

This leads me to take a detour to outline the question of the fraternal link and to analyse with you its different possible developments.

Functions of the internal fraternal group

I would like to precisely define how I situate the question of the fraternal link within psychoanalytic theory. In this sense, I speak of the subject of the fraternal link because we are all brothers and sisters, meaning that we are subjects to ourselves and our generational link. This means every subject is subjected to his unconscious, his family, his social group, his culture, his political system, and the socio-historical reality through which the subject of the fraternal link is transiting. In this way, he is at the same time a node, an identification model, and a transformative driving force in the family.

The fraternal link corresponds to an organisational mode of psychic groupality that is built as a heritage and as a psychic construction specific to the members of a group of the same generation, whether blood-related or not. Its characteristic would be to make sure of the mediation and exchange of the transmission of links (of intra-, inter-, and trans-subjective nature) in their social, cultural, and political aspects.

The small child not only leans upon the mother, but also on the collective self of his peer group, in particular the fraternal group that is a mediator between the familial (Eiguer, 1986), the social, the cultural (Kaës, 1993), and the political selves.

The internal fraternal group constitutes a passageway between the inside and the outside links. In this sense, the internal fraternal group accomplishes a binding function between intersubjective and transsubjective reality. It facilitates the construction of a matrix of relations that articulates the psychic and the cultural representation of the link. The fraternal link would be a representational matrix of the relationship between the intrapsychic, the micro-context (family), and the macro-context (society-culture).

The social, cultural, and political elaboration of fraternal representations produces models of groupality that inscribe themselves in the family and organise it. The political organisers of the fraternal group representation also work as backgrounds; they are models that relate to the organisation and the exercise of power among siblings. In particular they designate a way of governing relations within the fraternal link. These representations are of the following type: power-oppositions that rest on the concordance or discordance of the siblings with regard to the exercise of power in the family. These representations are identificatory models that translate the ways in which power is articulated within the fraternal and parental link, as if "politics were made out of phantasies". They would be ways through which the siblings could or could not identify themselves with the power-models of the family within the society.

Hence, we can observe that in their mediation or "interchange" function, the siblings constitute an internal group because they function as an operator through which reciprocal formations and processes of the intrapsychic reality, and of the psychic apparatus of the inter- and transgenerational groupings can be linked.

The internal fraternal group can be seen as accomplishing individual narcissistic purposes (the brother as *adelphos*, as same-blooded), but it also fulfils the function of being a psychic organiser in the process of assembling and setting up the grouping (the brother as *frater*, as a partner in a symbolic generational link).

The brother has a double function: he helps to recognise oneself in the resemblance of the familiar and in the difference of the unknown.

Moreover, the fraternal group also has an appropriation function that enables the transmission of the transgenerational primary internal group (internal parents and family). Just as the mother is the first intermediate object between the child and the world (between ego and non-ego), the brother and the sister, as real subjects, represent the first toys, the first instruments of appropriation or use. The fraternal link is the first object of play, either in the way it constitutes a support for the drive for knowledge, or in the way it provides a backing for the epistemological obstacle and prevents thinking about oneself and the social and cultural reality (Jaitin, 2000a, 2000b, 2000c).

Furthermore, the fraternal psychic apparatus would be like a transformation apparatus that enables the structure of the fraternal link to change. Narcissistic links (structured either as a syncretic sociability or as a homoerotic fantasy) could give way to object links (structured either as a mutual representation, or as bisexual fantasies).

Consequently, the fraternal link is the prototype for the transformation of a set of links.

The fraternal link allows us to analyse the morphogenesis of the internal group. I use this word to designate the transformation of shapes in the organisation of the fraternal psychic apparatus.

The question of morphopsychology brings up psychological shapes that have been studied by Freud (1905d) in the infant, and which he defines as those of the polymorphous pervert and of "metamorphosis" in puberty.

It is in this sense of "metamorphing itself" that the fraternal link takes its shape. It is based on the myth of Proteus, a sea deity that had the capacity to change shapes.

The shape of the fraternal psychic apparatus seems to be bi-shaped (girl and boy). But at the beginning of the fraternal subject's life, it is shapeless in the way that it is incomplete and unfinished; and since it is unfinished, it is obliged to metamorphose itself into feminine and masculine components. This is different from a snail that seems to have only one exterior shape, but two shapes inside (it is hermaphroditic). In contrast, the fraternal link appears to be bi-shaped (boy and girl) on the outside, but it is shapeless inside at the beginning of the construction of the fraternal psychic apparatus (Jaitin, 2006, 2010).

The fraternal psychic apparatus will adopt two main forms to take on its transmission task: imagos and complexes.

I—Imagos are forms of transgenerational transmission, collective representations, views held by ancestors, on the identificatory project of being brothers and sisters in the family; complexes on the other hand are forms of intergenerational transmission.

II—Complexes are forms of the unconscious representations of inter-subjective links that manifest themselves through the real or fantasised place that the subject occupies in his family.

The fraternal link will build itself through multiple imagos and complexes, because the fraternal link bears flexibility, and it is easier transformed than others since it is most mouldable, the "youngest" one in the family. It will undergo transformations all through life, following the different avatars of family configurations. And in this sense it is the transformational motor of the family as a whole: it transforms itself, and through this, it transforms the family, which will in turn and reciprocally transform it.

I have just presented the central issue of the fraternal link as a transformation apparatus. Now I will move on to the question of incest.

Configurations of fraternal incest

In order to move on, the subject of a fraternal link has to overcome the obstacles that prevent him from getting out of the maternal and fraternal incestuosity.

The first obstacle lies within the family itself. The family's first problem is to differentiate whether it belongs to the category of the living or not. One comes across this problem when working with families that have children with defective psychoses or severe physical malformations, because in the countertransference of the work teams they bring about the feeling of being dehumanised.

The family's second problem is to differentiate whether it represents itself as being out in nature or inside the house. This is a spatial representation in family groups that suffer from having a psychotic member (Berenstein, 1991).

I have elsewhere introduced this problematic of non-differentiation between the inside and outside of the family's body through a clinical case, the Simonet family, whose grandparents were at the same time husband and wife and brother and sister. In this family, I put the transgenerational aspect into perspective (Jaitin, 2006). In my clinical experience, I have often found fraternal incests in the current generation that were repetitions of fraternal incests of ancestors.

The third problem that the family encounters is situated within itself. It is about everyone being able to discern who are the adults and who are the children. In our clinical experience of the fraternal link, we observe this well through primary or secondary fraternal incests.

Secondary incest would be an incest perpetrated in a peer group that symbolically represents brothers and sisters, as in the case of recomposed families or of children placed in institutions. It is different from primary incest, which is a sexual union between blood relations from the same generation, in effect brother and sister, who can have the same mother and the same father, or have just one common parent. Here the problem is that the family and the siblings in the family have difficulties in building the category "big-small" that will allow them to access the generational difference.

I have undertaken some research on this question of fraternal groupality in the context of a foster home, where children were transgressing the prohibition of incest.

Eroticism and sexuality

The family's fourth problem comes about when after a firstborn there comes a second child. The mother sees herself as being in-between the two: between the first (very special for the mother because their link of filiation is the foundation of the family) and the second one that has to make its place in the family which in turn must also leave it a space.

And here we are, this is the scene where the mother is feeding the little one. At this moment, a feeling of envy (in the Kleinian sense of the word) overcomes the fraternal subject. The older one watches the scene of his mum with his little brother and feels an impossible desire of killing him. But since he cannot kill him, he will tell himself, I am him, in an identification with the brother—and thus we are in the presence of Lacan's (1938) metaphor of the mirror stage. Also, it is in this scene that the subject of the fraternal link discovers that he has a mum, and that the other, brother or sister, that exists in the desire of his mother, is stealing his mum. The mum is often represented by toys: children always want the same toy at the same time (Jaitin, 2000a).

The drama of jealousy helps to discover the third. The notion of the third allows us to build another category: parents are different than children, because they are big and being big, in a child's mind, corresponds to being strong.

The story continues, because once the siblings recognise themselves as being different from the parents, the children mutually explore the resemblance of their bodies and they touch each other, beginning to wonder about the problem of being man or woman, a question that children consider not in terms of being, but in terms of having—a question that will stay with them during their whole life until death (it is a difficult mystery to solve). The problem is having a differentiated exterior shape but an undifferentiated internal one.

These different shapes of girls and boys make us "conform" differently as subjects, depending on whether there is or is not a successful coherence between them.

The issue is that in the history of psychoanalysis, Freud was obsessed with seeing castrated men in women. It is true that we have different exterior shapes as men and women. Nonetheless a physical shape is not a psychic shape. And although the body may be a representational support, the material body is not the psychic body.

The phallus is a psychic representation of the discovery of sexuality. The phallus can be represented for the man as a penis and for the woman as a child. But, if the representational supports are different, the question of the phallus raises the same problem of having or being, for the man as for the woman. There are phallic women and phallic men. But Freud as a man only saw phallic women.

The problem that we have in our psychic construction is to differentiate between having (a penis, a child, a woman, a man, a car, prestige) and being a man or a woman. Being is a radical negativity, whereas having is a relative negativity. This is the problem faced in transsexualism, where men who mutate their body to have womanly shapes do not succeed in eroticising their womanly body because the external change is not sufficient.

Ferenczi (1914) worked on the intermediate homoerotic stage, seen as an intermediary between autoeroticism and heteroeroticism. He developed the question of homoeroticism from his experience with homosexual patients. He did not use the word homosexual because he was one of the first ones to emphasise that what is at stake is not yet a sexual matter, since it is an issue of psychic hermaphroditism.

A first example will give us some understanding of how homoeroticism evolves to an adelphic (fraternal) bisexuality that may or may not lead to a secondary identification problem with one's own or the opposite sex, to resolve the question of the recognition of having or being a man or woman.

Adelphic bisexuality concerns first of all the bisexual fantasy which is androgynous in relation to an original bisexual almighty maternal imago that is dangerous and corresponds to a phallic intrusion anxiety.

Furthermore, adelphic bisexuality gives access to discerning the difference between sexes, to the attraction for another, to complementarity, which is what prefigures the Oedipus complex (Kaës, 2008).

Let us look at a scene from Almodóvar's *Talk to Her*: in a hospital room a woman is in a coma. She is looked after by a male nurse, Benigno. To care for her, he massages, washes, and dresses her. In another sequence, both are sitting outside on a balcony; she is dressed in a very erotic way and wears sunglasses. And as part of his care, he talks to her, comments on the latest news, and imagines projects of how they would be well together.

Benigno had noticed the young girl who is now in a coma because his window is situated opposite from where she used to take dance lessons. To meet her he decided to see her father, a psychiatrist. Rapidly this colleague came up with a diagnosis: the subject is homosexual. On these grounds he will later leave his daughter in Benigno's care, after the accident that puts her in a coma.

Coming back to the question of eroticism, the end of the film reveals that it is not about a homosexual problem, but a homoerotic one. Each person has their own erotic sexual development. But sexuality can at the same time awaken vital eroticism.

In this sense, René Kaës, agreeing with other researchers, addresses the issue of adelphic (fraternal) bisexuality. Adelphic bisexuality or narcissistic homoeroticism is seen as the cornerstone of the fraternal complex, the foundation stone, and the backbone of the construction of the differentiation between the sexes.

However, I would like to take the issue one step further by working on the modalities of passing from eroticism to sexuality. This passage will mobilise other manifestations. These manifestations belong to what André Green (1983) described as the white series, with regard to what he called the work of the void or the work of the negative.

I would like to present a short clinical vignette to understand this question. It is about a homosexual man in treatment. The follow-up on this homosexual patient in analysis allowed me to discern that homosexuality, under certain conditions, could be a way of resolving an incestuous desire between sister and brother, as a solution for the economy of the link.

Joaquin is thirty-five years old. As the second sibling he is placed between two sisters. The youngest sister has undergone regular psychiatric hospitalisations. During one of them she confesses to her brother that she is in love with him. This revelation triggers associative chains in which his own desire for his sister is brought to light. His difficulty to give up the double position of his homoerotic and heteroerotic desires becomes important when faced with his sister as a source of arousal. She is his double as a subject that is overwhelmed by madness (an overwhelming amount of arousal).

Madness and homosexuality are ways of staying together in front of the parents. He is facing a delirious, depressed mother, a living-dead mother; facing the absence of a father who died young, when Joaquin was fourteen years old, and also facing the death of a maternal uncle. He mentions his parents' wedding: the day when his mother's only brother committed suicide.

Making a choice for homosexuality allows him to keep his sister safe from a mortal danger.

The fantasy of fraternal incest in this case can be read as a homoerotic incest, without differentiation between the sexes, as an overinvestment of the phallic sexual complement: the sister for the brother, the brother for the sister. It enables the siblings to awake the dead mother and at the same time pass from homoeroticism to bisexuality. The fantasy of fraternal incest for Joaquin and his sister is an acknowledgment, an acknowledgment of the mother's, the father's, and the maternal uncle's absence. This modality of resolution of the fraternal complex allows us to notice its defensive value, as a form of protection from dead parenthood.

The incest fantasy is a way to awake dead parents. In the case of my patient, killing the parents was the necessary passage to differentiating between mum and dad, which allowed him to elaborate the problem raised by adelphic bisexuality of having or not having, to take on the problem of being a subject that identifies itself as such, an active homosexual subject, to use Ferenczi's terms.

Finally, fraternal incest is a way to awake dead parenthood, but we know that there are different ways of waking or killing it off.

This can be illustrated by a geological metaphor: the Dead Sea. Like the Aral and the Caspian Sea, it is a remnant of the Tethys Ocean, an archaic form of the original sea. Like the Aral Sea, it is about to disappear. Its survival depends on the water supply from its tributaries that in the present are channelled away for industrial and war purposes. We could ask ourselves if the fratricidal war between Israelis and Palestinians could not be a way of awakening dead parents.

Hence, fraternal incest is not the only way to finish destroying or helping a dead mother or father to live. The parental function will eventually disappear when in the filiation there are no ancestors able to transmit and to guarantee that the major law prohibiting fraternal murder is respected.

Conclusions

Three levels of analysis of fraternal incest can be distinguished:

1. *The transsubjective level that refers to the undifferentiated transgenerational aspect.*
To clarify this I presented the case of two grandchildren whose grandparents are brother and sister. I analysed the situation of primary fraternal incest with the help of anthropology, in particular the family's relation to the maternal uncle. Here the filiation of the descendants inscribes itself in a non-differentiation between the filiation and affiliation. This temporal collapse defines fraternal incest in a non-differentiation between inside and outside.
2. *The intersubjective or intergenerational level.*
In this sense, fraternal incest reflects a failure in the familial envelope (container of the negative). Fraternal incest is always an expression of

the transformation of an affect into its contrary: transforming love into hate, displaced from the maternal to the fraternal link. It is a way of destroying a link that would be the equivalent of a fratricidal struggle in biblical and mythical tales.

I have worked on this issue on two occasions.

The first one relates to fraternal groupality, which is more easily observed in situations of family break-ups. For children placed in foster homes, the experience of losing the paternal home brings back the depression triggered by the birth of siblings. Confronted with this experience the siblings will organise themselves as a "proto-group" that takes the form of a syncretic fraternal link. In this syncretic fraternal link there is no paradoxical representation between the resemblance and the generational difference, marked by the taboo of incest. Consequently, we observe "secondary incests".

In the second example, dead parenthood corresponds to a massive disinvestment of the child, characterised by the disappearance and reappearance of the parents. I examined this hypothesis with the help of a case of siblings placed in a foster-home. The parents, political refugees from Thailand, uprooted and victims of genocide, were estranged from their parental function, and delegated their frozen grief to their children (Jaitin, 1999).

3. *The intrasubjective level, worked on in this article, looks at incest fantasy as a universal fantasy.*

The fraternal incest fantasy is a universal fantasy that we carry with us and that allows us to elaborate a living-dead parenthood. It is a psychic process of differentiation between real and imaginary death.

If the fraternal subject does not undergo this psychic process of killing the mother (a mother that also features the father present in the maternal body's shape), he cannot get over the representation of phallic parents. It is in this sense that we encounter direct, indirect, primary, or secondary incests in our clinical experience, inscribed at inter- or transgenerational levels.

Fraternal incest is a homoerotic incest, without differentiation between the sexes, as an overinvestment of the phallic sexual complement in which the siblings have difficulties in building a non-mother category that gives access to the representation of the brother as a third. This level of analysis is designated to understand the acting-out of incest. It is not necessarily death or maternal failure that leads to the acting-out of incest. It is only when the siblings cannot elaborate their psychic hermaphroditism and the dead parenthood that the universal fantasy of incest is acted upon.

References

Berenstein, I. (1991). *Familia y Enfermedad Mental*. Buenos Aires, Argentina: Paidos, 1995.

Eiguer, E. (1986). *Un Divan pour la Famille. Du Modèle Groupal à la Thérapie Familiale Psychanalytique*. Paris: Centurion.

Ferenczi, S. (1914). The nosology of male homosexuality (homoerotism). In: S. Ferenczi, *First Contributions to Psycho-Analysis* (pp. 296–318). London: Karnac, 1994.

Freud, S. (1905d). *Three Essays on the Theory of Sexuality. S. E.*, 7: 123–246. London: Hogarth.

Freud, S. (1912–1913). *Totem and Taboo. S. E.*, 13: vii–162. London: Hogarth.

Freud, S. (1921c). *Group Psychology and the Analysis of the Ego. S. E.*, 18: 65–144. London: Hogarth.

Freud, S. (1930a). *Civilization and its Discontents. S. E.*, 21: 57–146. London: Hogarth.

Green, A. (1983). *Life Narcissism/Death Narcissism*. London: Free Association, 2001.

Héritier, F. (1994). *Les deux soeurs et leur mère. Antropologie de l'inceste*. Paris: Odile Jacob.

Jaitin, R. (1999). Parentalité morte et lien fraternel. Le déracinement. *Le divan familial*, 2: 123–132.

Jaitin, R. (2000a). Mon frère et ma soeur: mes premiers jouets. *Journal de la psychanalyse de l'enfant*, 27: 279–296.

Jaitin, R. (2000b). L'inceste fraternel: mythes et pseudo-mythes. *Le divan familial*, 4: 143–155.

Jaitin, R. (2000c). Le lien fraternel. Transmission et créativité: les frères Lumière. *Journal des Psychologues*, 183: 44–49.

Jaitin, R. (2006). *Clinique de l'Inceste Fraternel*. Paris: Dunod.

Jaitin, R. (2010). *Clínica del Incesto Fraterno*. Buenos Aires, Argentina: Editorial Lugar.

Kaës, R. (1993). *Le Groupe et le Sujet du Groupe*. Paris: Dunod.

Kaës, R. (2008). *Le Complexe Fraternel*. Paris: Dunod.

Klein, M. (1932). The psycho-analysis of children. In: R. Money-Kyrle (Ed.), *The Writings of Melanie Klein, Vol. 2*. New York: Free Press, 1984.

Lacan, J. (1938). *Family Complexes in the Formation of the Individual*. London: Karnac, 2003.

CHAPTER THIRTEEN

Anamorphosis, sloughing of containers, and family psychical transformations

Pierre Benghozi

Introduction

In our daily practice, we are constantly confronted with clinical manifestations that seem to get bogged down in chaotic family and social situations. For example, a suicidal teenager in an adoptive family fraught with disavowal; a pregnant anorexic mother in an incestuous family; the aggressiveness of a youth whose immigrant family disclaims its own birth-roots. Or what about a psychotic child born from artificial fertilisation with the semen of an anonymous donor, and about whom the homosexual mother has an auto-procreation fantasy?

What about family configurations in extreme situations with numerous problems like addictions, actings out, serious somatic problems, situations that are legal and social dead ends, involving several members of the same family? In all these clinical situations, transformations of the individual psychical containers promote the vulnerability of family links and the social link.

What family transformations are we speaking of? Transformations of containers?

On the one hand, there are transformations in the individual and family life cycle, which I call the genealogical psychical anamorphosis, and which I would like to represent with the notion of "sloughing of containers"; and on the other hand, what we call the "containers in transformation" (Benghozi, 2009b) of new family configurations.

In the two cases that follow, we will be interested in a psychoanalytic metapsychology of containers in transformation. We envisage this in analogy with José Bleger's work on "The Psychoanalysis of the Psychoanalytic Setting" (1979), within a psychoanalytic approach to links.

Questions:

- If these sloughings of genealogical containers concern new family configurations, is there also an emergence of a new clinical practice?
- What about transformations of the "family-making" process?

For instance, in a patchwork or mosaic family, unlike in the traditional family, we are going to have several parental figures with homosexual types or hetero-types, and a mosaic of uncombined siblings, composed of children who are the outcome of plural filiations. Children can live simultaneously or successively in sequences of links with numerous parentalities and siblings. Nowadays, the child becomes the organiser of "family-making". These new mosaic families "make a family" by uniting pieces of families. What is characteristic of contemporary "family-making" is the acceleration and type of transformations of the family configurations. The horizontal link of affiliation seems more and more to be taking the place of the filial link.

From a psychoanalytic perspective of links, all these family modifications correspond to the new configurations of what I call "genealogical meshing".

The meshing of genealogical containers

The constant psychical work of meshing, de-meshing, and re-meshing of links of filiation and affiliation constructs a kind of net, the genealogical container.

It provides the family psychical apparatus with a containing function of psychical transformation, in Bion's sense (1963).

To clarify the transformation issues, I propose two aphorisms: "*The link is not relation*" and "*Parenthood is not parentality*".

Parenthood is to the link what parentality is to the relation. There can be, for instance, conflictual relations between a father and his son without there being any doubt about either's inscription in the genealogical link of father–son filiation. There can be gaps of links that do not appear in the parentality as relational problems, but which are transmitted into the unconscious of the "ghosts-carrying" heirs.

Transmission is to the link what communication is to the relation

Transformations question the types of change depending on whether they concern the organisation of the links (Kaës, 1995) or only the refittings of the relation, and therefore the parentality. What about invariables, psychical universals and types of change?

Links are to the container what relations are to the content

It is necessary to differentiate the transformations of the containers which involve the de-meshing and re-meshing of psychical links from the transformations of contents which concern the processes of binding (liaison).

The psychical issue of modifications in the configuration of links that come with new family identities is therefore the issue of the capacities for psychical transformation when the genealogical meshing-container, itself in transformation, is put under tension.

It is a history in the form of Russian dolls.

From this perspective, the transformations of the psychical container involve the meshing of links, the dead ends of psychical transmission, and the foundations of kinship.

Psychical anamorphosis, the sloughing of containers

I speak of psychical anamorphosis to indicate all the phenomena, processes, and psychical productions that are at stake when the container is itself in transformation, distorted, changeable, transitional, or when it is disorganised, disrupted, broken, and failing.

Anamorphoses are gestalts of transformations of container/contents. I relate this to Didier Anzieu's (Anzieu et al., 1993) notion of "formal signifier".

To quote him: "These are mainly representations of the psychical containers. 'Formal signifiers' are easily metaphorisable".

"They enable the location of psychical envelopes and their impairments ... They constitute images ..."

The notion of anamorphosis is a metaphoric concept. This model is conceived according to a logic of complexity (Morin, 1990).

I define "psychical anamorphosis" as a perspective on psychical transformations analogous to the description of anamorphic pictures given by the art critic Baltrusaïtis (1984), in his book *Anamorphoses ou Thaumaturgusopticus*. In an anamorphic picture, the picture appears distorted, resembling a distortion of the object depicted projected onto a curved mirror. It is likened to the *trompe l'œil style* (Benghozi, 1999a, 1999b).

1. Psychical anamorphosis corresponds therefore to the stages of transformation of the psychical containers.
2. Whatever the family configuration is, there is one invariable: the family genealogical container is put under tension by the occurrence of an anamorphic event.
3. *An event* is characterised by a radical fork in a curve of development. It can be:

   – either a genealogical event inscribed in the individual, conjugal, family, or social life cycle, like a village feast at a change of season;
   – or what I call an event-accident, that is to say an exogenous or endogenous event, which happens in an unpredictable manner and breaks into the genealogical containers, such as a cancer, or a major trauma.

The genealogical anamorphosis in the individual and family life cycle is a complex phased process.

• in which the individual level and the genealogical group level are involved at the same time,
• and which brings into play modifications at the somatic and the psychical level and at the level of the social link.

It is at the same time: continuity, in comparison with a process of growth, and a fork in the path, that is, radical discontinuity.

Pregnancy, birth, adolescence, the climacteric are all genealogical events that are sources of anamorphosis.

"Perinatality" is to the event natality what "peri-adolescence" is to the event adolescence, and the "peri-climacteric" to the climacteric.

Perinatality, peri-adolescence, the peri-climacteric are, in the individual and genealogical cycle of life, configurations of anamorphosis.

The chrysalis families: sloughing of container and the unconscious body image

I describe anamorphosis as a sloughing of a psychical container (Benghozi, 2009b). Sloughing or moulting is a partial or complete change that the skin of snakes, the carapace of crustaceans, and the coats of some animals go through at precise times of their life. Analogous to *The Skin Ego* by Didier Anzieu (1989), it is a change of skin, and therefore of psychical envelopes, like the envelope of a teenage boy's tone when his voice is changing.

It is translated at the individual level of the *unconscious* body image by what the psychoanalyst Françoise Dolto (Dolto & Dolto-Tolitch, 1989), referring to adolescence, has called "the lobster complex". During its growth process, the lobster loses its carapace before rebuilding a new one. It is a new psychical skin, a new "self skin", as Anzieu would say. In the passage from one container to another lies a psychical vulnerability.

I have temporarily described this, with reference to peri-adolescence, as a particular singularity, the "identity chrysalis" (Benghozi, 1999b).

The process of anamorphosis is characterised as one of sloughing, not only of individual containers, but also of family genealogical containers, community containers, and social containers. The sloughing of containers is fundamentally not only an individual identity-defining narcissistic crisis but also one of the family. The anamorphosis of the genealogical container corresponds to the chrysalis family.

Among the chrysalis families, I distinguish between pregnant family, teenager family …

How are the individual and the family group interconnected? A psychical architecture trans-containing

How are the container and the unconscious images of the individual and the family body co-constructed? Taking a transversal trans-containing approach, we can represent these levels of capacity as fitting within each other like Russian dolls, so that there is a mutual shoring between the individual container, the family genealogical group container and the social psychical container.

I use the kaleidoscope as a metaphor. As in a kaleidoscope, a new figurability is created from the kinetic movement of every cylinder until a stable enough picture is formed. In this metaphor, every cylinder represents the psychical container and body image.

This metaphor aims to show that the co-building of the body's individual image and of the family image's genealogical body (Benghozi, 2009a) is a process of a mutual dynamic trans-containing support.

The notion of anamorphic identity-defining is specific to the transformative processes of a phased passage. However, there really is an identity-defining feeling of specific belonging during this interim period in the development. This identity is registered in an ephemeral dynamic.

The intimate, the private, and the public

From a topological point of view, these psychical objects correspond to three psychical territories. And each territory corresponds to a capacity for mutual and reciprocal support between the containers of the intimate, the private, and the public.

These topological areas concern, simultaneously and transversely, the social, the individual, the couple, the family, the community, and the social.

Thus, as one family member undergoes a transformation, the whole family group is affected by the process of the crisis.

"Crisis", "in crisis", or "catastrophe"?

Let us envisage the meshing of a family container affected by an anamorphic event. There are three possible situations: "crisis", "in crisis", and "catastrophe" (Benghozi, 2007a, 2007b, 2007c).

When the meshing holds, this is a "crisis".

When there is a break-in, with the partial breaking open of a stitch, it is "in crisis". This is expressed by a container with holes in it. The production of symptoms is a form of re-meshing the holes in the family container.

The re-meshing makes certain that the holes are patched up, avoiding their enlargement.

The group application of psychoanalytic family therapy is a good indication.

When there is a true tear in the container, this is what I call a catastrophic de-meshing.

The void (vacuum, empty) as a narcissistic depression is the expression of problems concerning a container, torn or full of holes.

In these catastrophic families, narcissistic haemorrhages relating to a torn container are found with symptoms of family dis-containment borne by several members of the family, without anyone appearing to be able to re-mesh the gaping tear of the genealogical container.

In this type of catastrophic clinical case, the de-meshing consists of trans-containing with an unmaking of the mutual supports between the containers of the intimate, the private, and the public.

These can be expressed at the psychical level and at the somatic level, but also at the level of the disintegration of a social link.

There we find families with numerous problems who call upon physicians, psychiatric professionals and, very often, social workers.

This necessitates the application of a multidisciplinary medico-psycho-social meta-setting to ensure the support of the torn container by a meshing network.

- In each of these families, the fragility of the family containers' mesh in transformation is manifested in a peculiar way, in vulnerabilities of the links in touch with the dead ends in the metabolisation processes and psychical symbolisation (Abraham & Torok, 1978).
- I formulated the aphorism: "Shame is to the container what guilt is to the content."

The shame-carrying patient (Benghozi, 1994) is the symptom-carrier, heir to, and ventriloquist of the family's unconscious shame.

Is not the transmission of the "un-avowable" what is at stake in the upsetting of the containing function, in the confusion of boundaries between the inside and the outside, in the containers' drift? At the unconscious level, we are in a treatment of ideality, the ideal of the grouped ego; at the conscious and the preconscious level, we are at the level of the organising myth of group belonging through values, beliefs, and identity. Here, I cannot develop the importance of ritualising work in the processes of the anamorphic transformation of genealogical containers.

It is not possible not to transmit, even if it is in the form of an indented print left by a container.

In this sense, symptoms can be considered to be one expression of the genealogical container's pathologies.

For instance, adoption constructs a new family configuration, re-meshing the genealogical containers of the adoptive parents' birth-families. During the anamorphosis of adolescence, there is an elaboration of a family neo-romance and the psychical stakes of the genealogy of the adoption will be renewed. If there is a denial of the filiation's link in the child's birth-family, "crisis" can evolve towards "in crisis", or even towards a catastrophic de-meshing of the new adopting family configuration.

Unconscious denial can exist even if there is no secret about the adoption. With respect to the alliance that differentiates the filiating link with the birth-family from the affiliating link to the adopting family, there exists a mythical substitution for a unique link of filiation of the adopted child in the adoptive family during disavowal. So, instead of a "double link" psychically associating, for the adopted child, the meshing of a filiating link to the birth-family with the affiliating link's meshing to the adopting family, there will be a double link, or "double bind" that is a source of an identity collapse (Benghozi, 2004).

Is not one of the advantages of psychoanalytic family therapy that it can be receptive to the containing conditions of an alternative creativity?

Example of psychoanalytic family therapy—teenager family: "cheat the void"

I will present an example of "cheat the void" (cheat the vacuum) symptoms in a teenager family "in crisis" and in a psychoanalytic family therapy.

We meet the family at the request of the psychiatrist who looked after Johann during a hospitalisation of eight days in the adolescent crisis centre, following a new suicide attempt. We meet Johann and his mother, with whom he seems to have a serious conflict. Johann will present an addiction to video games. His school grades are poor, despite his obvious intellectual capacities. My co-therapist and I are impressed by the contrast between the presentation of this big fourteen-year-old boy, well-dressed, well-combed, sitting crisp on his seat, and that of his mother, who has rosy cheeks possibly due to alcoholism and is dressed in a bohemian style with rather long and neglected hair.

Johann says: "Since the beginning of the school year, I've thought of only one thing: how to kill myself." His depression would appear to have followed a first disappointment in love. He spends hours alone, trying to build up his muscular chest through bodybuilding. He seems to have an insatiable hunger. What does his withdrawal tell us, in which he bombards himself with the exciting visual and sound effects of video games, while he is overcome by suicidal impulses that scare him? He is unable to say what is happening to him.

The biggest absence in the session is that of his father. Johann's parents separated when he was four years old.

Johann's difficulties could be heard as just a way of expressing individual manifestations of his adolescence at a time when his body is changing.

We receive him in family therapy, as the expression of a genealogical group scenario in which we are actively involved. How are the problems that Johann presents set up at the individual level, at the level of the parental couple's alliance ("pact of alliance"), and in the family economy?

All of that played out again in session, in the transferential-countertransferential dialectical movement, by putting under tension the therapeutic setting itself.

(The family is dis-contained … Issues of the separated parental couple's pact of alliance are revisited. There is a confusion of the generational boundaries.)

During the holidays, Johann is going to see his father, a guitarist in a somewhat precarious situation, alone with his mates. Johann says: "He is like a friend."

His father immigrated to France when he was a teenager, together with his mother who was seeking treatment for his handicapped brother. His brother's illness will remain mysterious, like a shameful and cryptic defect.

Johann's mother experienced a difficult pregnancy, during which she was terrified by the fantasy that the baby could inherit a defect from the father's family. After the death of her own father, whose "precious little girl" she had been, she left her companion, her son Johann's father, and came to live in the south of France with her depressed and lonely mother.

Johann accuses his mother "of doing everything backwards". She is continuously disqualified.

According to Johann: "She is an alcoholic, who spends her time with alcoholics … She is a hysteric. She doesn't care for anything." She does not even give him enough to eat! He must go to his maternal grandmother's home to be fed. He says "everything would be fine" if he could go and be alone at boarding school! But after trying out a boarding school for three days, he comes back to live at home again … The impasses in the mother–teenager link are symptoms of the problems in the mesh of the family genealogical container.

In this type of de-composed family, the closeness of the mother and the son's incestuous link is facilitated by the absence of the paternal third. The parental conjugal link does not provide a sufficiently containing intergenerational border that would ensure that the territories of the intimate and of the private of each one are clearly delimited and protected. In the absence of this envelope, Johann reacts hypersensitively, bad-tempered, and aggressively towards his mother; he is in danger of psychical death agony, an anxiety of breakdown that he expresses by his suicidal impulses. The mother feels guilty not to have been able to break away earlier from her baby. She breastfed him for an extended period.

Johann, like his mother who struggles to defend herself, seems very dependent on his maternal grandmother.

At weekends, when he feels exasperated by his mother, he goes to live at his grandmother's home; she lives nearby and is part of the family's daily life.

We are interested in continuing the talks by including the grandmother, and inviting the father.

The grandmother is eighty-two years old. Unlike her daughter, she appears to be an energetic and ordered woman. She speaks for a long time, on her life as a sickly child, which was fraught with dramas and frights. She had chosen to live with her husband, Johann's grandfather, who is presented as a hero. He bore the scars of eight months of torture and humiliation in the prison camps during the war in Indochina. "He is a survivor!" The family myth is "By force of will we can hang on!"

My co-therapist and I feel ourselves invested in as protective guarantors against invasion, bearers of a big paternal imago. We will also have to hang on! This counter-transferential affiliative position is going to perform a third party function in the new therapeutic scene, providing a hold for the narrative neo-container in the session. Johann seems to have been the depressive grandmother's child-medicine after her husband's death. Johann and his mother are her two children. This confusion resonates in the session with the infanti-lisation of Johann's silent mother in the presence of the grandmother. How about Johann's room? Is it not also a metaphor for the teen-ager's identity crisis? I invite them to represent it by drawing their home.

I call a *spaciogram* (Benghozi, 1996, 2006b), the complete representa-tion of "the lived space" in the sense of Gisela Pankow. Each person is invited to co-draw it and to formulate verbal associations. Introduced in this way, it is used like a group dream.

Johann begins to draw their flat on a paperboard present in the therapy room. Areas are badly delimited and confused; for example, there is a confusion between the lower floor and the upper floor. The common areas—the dining room and the living room—are loaded with miscellaneous objects picked up by the mother who plans to sell them at the flea markets where she trades in "mishmash". The mother picks up objects and collects them. In the kitchen there is a large refrig-erator and in the bathroom a washing machine that came from the maternal grandmother's house. But where is Johann's room? It is non-distinctively located in the extension of a hall. It has no real door, just a simple curtain.

A small bed is positioned in an office where only the place for the computer has been drawn. Clothes are folded in a corner, next to the comic book collection. My co-therapist and I had difficulty imagining how one moves about in this place and how to find the parental room. It is the mother who gets up and helps Johann to complete the spa-ciogram. "In fact I was able to get another room from the flat upstairs. It can be reached by a small staircase in the back of Johann's room." My co-therapist and I are perplexed. The mother, and perhaps her boy-friend, must therefore cross the end of the hall which is used as Johann's room to go to their own room or to come back to the bathroom. In this spaciogram no doors are drawn. There are not any windows either. A space at the bottom of the drawing paper is allocated to a small court-yard, itself filled with old objects waiting to be restored before possibly being sold.

"My house is really packed, a bit like a flea market," says the mother. "I am not good at throwing things away, parting from them. There is no empty space."

In this house blocked up by "mishmash", the inside is filled by objects belonging to the grandmother, and by objects that come from the street. The outside overflows to come indoors.

Parting from an object is like an amputation. Loss is narcissistic, mourning is melancholy. Depression is anaclitic.

Accumulation of objects, "encumbrances", blockage, and muddle in the spaciogram are the expressions of the mechanisms of a family group defence; they are fillers trying to hide the void, the horror of the void, and to ensure a protection from breakdown anxiety in the face of the body image's gaping holes. This fuzziness, this confusion, this absence of any clear distinction between the territories of the intimate, the private, and the public is found at every level, not only at the level of space, but also at the level of time.

To the lived space corresponds psychical spatiality and temporality. Johann says: "We are completely unorganised: we have no timetable!" Through his disturbed behaviour and depressive mood, the teenager Johann speaks about the psychical vulnerabilities of the family group container. The individual symptoms are manifestations of a teenager's family "in crisis". They can perpetuate throughout a catastrophic adolescence in a sequence of other shared symptoms, diffracted onto different members of the family ... The unconscious body refers to the family container, riddled with holes, and thus unable to support an individual container in mutation.

The drawing of the "flea market home" is a projection to give an image to "cheating the void".

During the last session of this ongoing therapy

It is exciting to notice how all this was present at the level of a countertransferential "daydream" and expressed through a feeling of a strange familiarity, manifested as a revelation of the unconscious conjugal and family "pact of alliance" with Johann's parents, centred upon cryptic religious conversions and calling out to a disavowal of origins and an attack against the filiation.

The grandmother, in session, wonders about some hidden Jewish origins on Johann's mother's side. Why did the family speak of her (the grandmother's) grandfather with a certain fuzziness, claiming that he had been circumcised when he was supposed to be from a Catholic family, and that he rushed away almost secretly with his baby son (Johann's great-grandfather) wrapped in a blanket to get him circumcised a few days after his birth? And on the paternal family side one learns that Johann's father disowned his Islamic and north African roots and has converted to Catholicism, which in Muslim culture is an attack on filiation. He rejected his father, whom he considered as having left his family. And all this family is there with Johann, with the assumption that everyone should be Catholic. The family and conjugal alliance is an affiliating, collusive re-meshing, in reverse, of the perforated containers of the two parental families. The transmission of the family prints in the two families echoes, in session, the mythical importance ascribed to the family transmission of music, on both sides of the two families.

On the mother's side, the "fiddler on the roof" pertaining to the Ashkenazi culture of central European Jews, and on the guitarist father's side, the "oud", a kind of guitar in traditional oriental music. Johann is a very gifted musician, and his grandmother had passionately wished to make a violinist of him, something that she herself had dreamed of becoming. When Johann abruptly stopped learning the guitar a few months ago, she says that she felt "killed"; then, with a lot of emotion, she starts to cry. Johann and his mother discuss the possibility of getting a passport, because Johann wishes to meet his father's father, who is said to be a powerful man, a man of independent means in the Maghreb. By registering himself as grandson of his grandfather, he re-meshes the filiating link disowned by his father, the link between the father and his own father. The grandfather assumes a place in the genealogical fresco, in therapy, as an ancestral mythical figure.

The session provides an opportunity for a narrative deconstruction of the family myths, and of the family-conjugal "pact of alliance".

Spaciogram A1: *Confusion*

The new spaciogram

Our surprise grows when the mother proudly explains that her "home has changed a lot since our last talks!" The new spaciogram impresses us. It speaks only about openings, about windows, about doors which

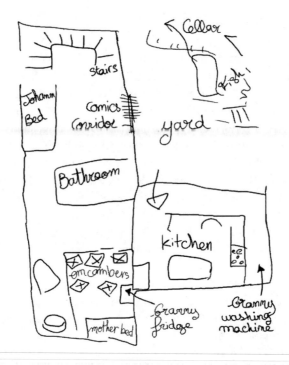

used to be sealed off and which they plan to reopen so that they can move around while respecting each other's space, and about Johann having a room of his own upstairs, while his mother would make the living room into a room for herself! In the next spaciogram, they draw two different levels, one for each generation, one for the parents and one for the children.

Spaciogram A2: *Differentiation of the spaces*

But of course this is work in progress, in trans/formation. While the construction is going on, Johann during the week lives at a friend's home, where he meets others teenagers and is no longer alone with his mother. But with a well-justified perplexity, he wonders how long the work will go on, how long this "stage" of construction will last. In the meantime Johann continues strengthening his muscular outer shell.

This is what makes us certain about the gradualness of the anamorphic sloughing of the familial adolescence being "under construction"!

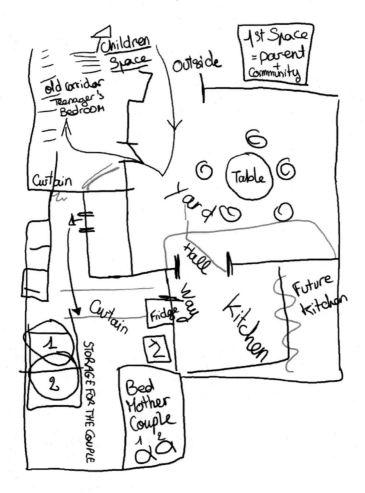

Genogram and spaciogram (Benghozi, 1996, 2006b) are forms of mediation which allow one to represent in temporality and genealogical space, within the family preconscious, the projections of the unconscious image of the perforated family body. Like the drawing of a human figure in child psychotherapy, the spaciogram is a projection of the unconscious body image. Better than many verbal utterances, the spaciogram shows the interlacing between the family genealogical group body and the individual unconscious psychical body of each person. It represents encroachments, fusions of the common psychical bodies, of the non-separated Siamese bodies, confusion, attachments, and intrusions between the psychical areas.

It is interesting to indicate that the chaotic *spaciogram of the room* of the teenager illustrates the chaos of the individual unconscious image of the teenager's body. Family psychical spatiality and temporality are configurations of the family myth. The spaciogram is a mnesic organising mediator and a support for daydreams.

It is an invitation to travel in the stories and legends of the genealogical family epic that is deconstructed in therapy.

It is an illustration of the family anamorphosis crisis (Benghozi, 1999a).

The de-meshing of the links corresponds therefore to a perforated container and a hole in the image of the unconscious body. The body in transformation is the theatre of the inter- and transgenerational genealogical transmission.

Narrative deconstruction of the myth and the genealogical family fresco

How is the psychical transmission of what is non-elaborated ensured? The psychical materials (equipment) are not introjected, but are incorporated and diffracted in the family group psychical apparatus. They do not give access to a production of the fantasy. De-linking attacks are manifested at the level of repression by a stupefaction through inter-fantasising, an attack of the fantastic production capacity. They are an attack against fantasy poiesis.

Narrative figurability: spaciogram, deconstruction of the genealogical myth, narrative neo-container, and family genealogical fresco.

The work of transforming feelings and what is non-representably incorporated is ensured by the therapist's capacity for containing receptiveness.

During anamorphosis, there are dead ends in the work of figurability. It makes me think, in a sense, of the notion of "psychical transparence" in peri-natality, during the woman's pregnancy, as it is described by Monique Bydlowski (1971). The work of reception is principally in a position of containing-listening and of group daydreaming, in the Bionian sense. The work of representing the family psychical body in narrative is illustrated by the use of mediations such as the spaciogram and the co-construction of a narrative neo-container.

The group process in psychoanalytic family therapy engages with our own fractures in our individual and family stories, a narrative deconstruction of the family genealogical myth, and makes the familial "unthinkable" depictable, which comes from the narrative "daydreams" in therapy (Benghozi, 1994).

Transfer on the frame as container (Benghozi, 2006a)

There is a correspondence between the therapeutic frame, the family group container, and the psychical apparatus. I described the existence of an isomorphy, that is to say, an analogy of form, between the therapeutic setting, the modifications of the unconscious image of the family body, and the configuration of psychical containers, the modelling of the spaciogram and of the genogram, and the metaphorisation of the genealogical meshing object. These images are definite signifiers of the containers in transformation.

The therapeutic space becomes a transitional play-space. It is a real work of the co-creation of group neo-daydreaming (Benghozi, 1994).

It has a fundamental supporting function. The containing function of the family therapists who are analysts is essential for ensuring the guarantee of a "holding" and of a therapeutic "handling" in the Winnicottian sense (Winnicott, 1971).

The therapeutic work of mythical narrative figuration of the genealogical family fresco emerging in therapy allows for the elaboration of a narrative neo-container which can give rise to a scenario that is an alternative to the repetition of the family genealogical scenario. The topological space affected by these anamorphoses of containers is the subconscious.

Failures of the familial group capacity are transferentially projected by the family group, onto the therapeutic setting as container.

The "fillers" in the "flea market home" may show that the psychical apparatus is a sieve and bear witness, in resonance with the investment of the therapeutic setting, to a family container filled with holes (Benghozi, 1995).

The ritualisation of a family neo-container enables a gradual elaboration of separation, individuation, and the subjectivisation of each member.

Conclusion: an incestuous society?

Generally speaking, the family and social transformations towards an affiliative mode make one wonder whether there is a feeling of discomfort in filiation, with the emergence of what I call an incestuous society.

"Individual psychology presents itself at the start as, at the same time, *a social psychology*" (Freud, 1921c, emphasis added).

We can observe changes on the anthropological and sociological side. "Families in transformation" are not those of others, they also are those of the therapists. Institutional containers and care structures are also in transformation.

Can we think of the anamorphosis of the family and of the social links while Jean Furtos (2009) tells us that a "melancholisation of the social link" seems to affect the clinicians themselves?

References

Abraham, A., & Torok, M. (1978). *The Shell and the Kernel: Renewals of Psychoanalysis*. Chicago, IL: University of Chicago Press, 1994.

Anzieu, D. (1989). *The Skin Ego*. New Haven, CT: Yale University Press.

Anzieu, D., Haag, G., Tisseron, S., Lavalle, G., Boubli, M., & Lassegue, J. (1993). *Les Contenants de Pensée*. Paris: Dunod.

Baltrusaïtis, J. (1984). *Anamorphoses ou Thaumaturgusopticus*. Paris: Flammarion.

Benghozi, P. (1994). Porte la honte et maillage des contenants généalogiques familiaux et communautaires en thérapie familiale. *Revue de Psychothérapie Psychanalytique de Groupe, 22*: 81–94.

Benghozi, P. (1995). Effraction des contenants généalogiques familiaux, transfert catastrophique, rêveries et néosecrets. *Revue de Psychothérapie Psychanalytique de Groupe, 24*: 91–99.

Benghozi, P. (1996). L'image du corps généalogique et le géno-spaciogramme. In: *Image du corps. Du groupe à la famille*. Besançon, France: Actes du colloque AFPC.

Benghozi, P. (1999a). *Adolescence et Sexualité—Liens et Maillage-Réseau*. Paris: L'Harmattan.

Benghozi, P. (1999b). *L'Adolescence, Identité Chrysalide*. Paris: L'Harmattan.

Benghozi, P. (2004). Esthétique de la figurabilité et néocontenants narratifs groupaux, médiations d'expression. *Revue de Psychothérapie Psychanalytique de Groupe, 41*: 7–12.

Benghozi, P. (2006a). Pré-contre-transfert, cadre et dispositif. *Revue de Psychothérapie Psychanalytique de Groupe, 47*: 25–29.

Benghozi, P. (2006b). Le spaciogramme en thérapie psychanalytique de couple et de famille. *Dialogue, 172*: 5–24.

Benghozi, P. (2007a). Le leurre comme symptôme des contenants généalogiques troués, dans la psychothérapie familiale à l'épreuve de l'adolescent. *Le Journal des psychologues, 245*: 35–40.

Benghozi, P. (2007b). La transmission généalogique de la trace et de l'empreinte: temps mythique en thérapie familiale psychanalytique. *Cahiers critiques de thérapie familiale et de pratiques de réseaux, 38*: 43–60.

Benghozi, P. (2007c). La trace et l'empreinte: L'adolescent héritier porte— l'empreinte de la transmission généalogique. *Adolescence, 62*: 755–777.

Benghozi, P. (2009a). Image du corps individuel, corps psychique familial et anorexie mentale, les thérapies familiales. *Revue Psychiatrie Française, 1*: 179–193.

Benghozi, P. (2009b). Une approche transcontenante groupale des anamorphoses de l'adolescence, *Revue de Psychothérapie Psychanalytique de Groupe, 53*: 41–55.

Bion, W. R. (1963). *Elements of Psycho-Analysis*. London: William Heinemann Medical.

Bleger, J. (1979). Psychanalyse du cadre psychanalytique. In: R. Kaës (Ed.), *Crise, Rupture et Dépassement* (pp. 255–285). Paris: Dunod.

Bydlowski, M. (1971). *La Dette de Vie. Itinéraire Psychanalytique de la Maternité*. Paris: PUF.

Dolto, F., & Dolto-Tolitch, C. (1989). *Paroles pour Adolescents, le Complexe du Homard*. Paris: Hatier.

Freud, S. (1921c). *Group Psychology and the Analysis of the Ego. S. E., 18*: 65–144. London: Hogarth.

Furtos, J. (2009). Does the clinic change? *Rhizome, 35*: 2–3.

Kaës, R. (1995). *Le Groupe et le Sujet du Groupe*. Paris: Dunod.

Morin, E. (1990). *Introduction à la Pensée Complexe*. Paris: Le Seuil.

Winnicott, D. W. (1971). *Playing and Reality*. London: Tavistock.

CHAPTER FOURTEEN

Infidelity in the couple relationship: one form of relationship suffering*

Carles Pérez-Testor, Montse Davins, Inés Aramburu, Berta Aznar-Martínez, and Manel Salamero

Introduction

Infidelity has been and remains one of the main reasons for crises in couples due to the repercussions it has on the relationship. It is regarded as one of the most frequent reasons for visits to clinical practices and the main cause of divorce worldwide (Romero, Rivera, & Díaz, 2007). In the United States, more than 50 per cent of marriages end in divorce, and the infidelity of one or both members is the cause of the rupture in the majority of cases (Amato & Previti, 2003; Ortman, 2005). Due to the presence of infidelity among couples in our society and the impact it has on both individuals and their relationship, it is a phenomenon that is drawing more and more research attention.

In the past twenty years, there has been a surge in studies on extramarital relationships, which mainly focus on studying the prevalence and risk factors via comparisons between faithful and unfaithful members

*Acknowledgement: The authors wish to acknowledge and thank the Institut Universitari de Salut Mental Vidal i Barraquer for making it possible to write this chapter through the Research Support Grant of the Universitat Ramon Llull.

219

of couples. There are also broader studies such as the one conducted by Allen and colleagues (2005) which more deeply examine not only the characteristics of the unfaithful person but also the couple to which they belong, the marital relationship, and the context in which the infidelity takes place. Likewise, there are also many studies that specifically focus more on the consequences and therapeutic treatment of infidelity than on describing it and the factors that come into play. For example, we have recently performed a study on the phenomenon of infidelity and how it has been dealt with in films (Aramburu, Pérez-Testor, Davins, Cabré, & Salamero, 2011).

Regarding the definitions used by different authors when studying infidelity, we can find three basic types: *sexual infidelity*, as described by some authors, denotes a purely sexual relationship with a third person outside the primary relationship (Choi, Catania, & Dolcini, 1994; Forste & Tanfer, 1996; Whisman, Gordon, & Chatav, 2007); *emotional infidelity*, which implies spending time and mental space on a person other than one's partner, whereby an amorous relationship, a desire, or a sexual fantasy may arise yet is never consummated in a sexual relationship (Shackelford, Leblanc, & Drass, 2000); and *combined infidelity*, meaning a sexual and emotional relationship conducted outside the primary relationship, which entails a violation and rupture (either openly or cloaked) of the agreements reached in the couple by one or both of its members (Allen & Baucom, 2004; Blow & Hartnett, 2005; Glass & Wright, 1985).

This classification enables us to more deeply examine relationship dynamics and helps us to distinguish the different kinds of infidelity.

Psychoanalytic perspective on infidelity

When we discuss couple infidelity, we tend to think about a certain kind of infidelity, namely sexual action; however, this is merely a reductionism. We instead suggest that infidelity should be understood as the rupture of the implicit or explicit agreements that underpin the couple's relationship. We have based this on Dicks's theories on the concept of the *dyad* and the concept of *membrane* or dyadic boundary.

According to Dicks (1967), we can understand "dyad" to mean a unit made up of both members of the couple who share an interpersonal common space. Much has been written about this space. Sami-Ali (1974) has described it as a "psychological space of reciprocal inclusion". According to Balint (Family Discussion Bureau, 1962), we could say that within the dyad, the internal life made up of the desires, hopes, disillusions, and fears of one partner interacts with the same elements from the other partner's inner world. Theories about married life can be formulated based on this interaction, as Dicks (1967) did with his "theory of collusion", Guillermo Teruel (1974) did with his "dominant internal object" and Anna Maria Nicolò Corigliano (1995) did with her concept of "conjugality".

Infidelity entails breaking the intra-dyadic agreement. In the sphere of sexual exclusivity, Dicks (1967) believes that infidelity represents a sexual action, an acting-out against the agreements made by both members of the couple. To Kernberg (1995), infidelity is a kind of triangulation that can either destroy the couple, or, in the best-case scenario, strengthen it. Kernberg distinguishes between direct triangulations and inverse triangulations.

To Kernberg, direct triangulation is "the unconscious fantasy of both partners with an excluded third person, an idealised member of the subject's gender: the feared rival who duplicates the oedipal rival" (ibid., p. 87). All men and women either consciously or unconsciously fear the presence of someone who would be more satisfactory to their partner, and this third person is at the root of emotional insecurity in sexual intimacy and of jealousy as an alarm signal that protects the integrity of the relationship.

Inverse triangulation is the "compensating, vengeful fantasy of commitment with a person other than one's partner, an idealised member of the other gender who represents the desired oedipal object" (ibid., p. 87), which establishes a triangular relationship in which the subject is courted by two members of the opposite gender instead of having to compete with the oedipal rival of the same gender for the idealised oedipal object of the opposite gender.

Kernberg (1995) suggests that in couple relationships, the bed is always shared by six people: the couple, their respective unconscious oedipal rivals, and their respective unconscious oedipal ideals.

In a survey of the purpose of the oedipal conflict, Lawrence (2010) further develops the theory held by numerous evolutionary psychologists who state that the oedipal conflict might have evolved with the purpose of selective sexual adaptation ensuring the reproductive function. The oedipal conflict facilitates the monogamous resolution which ensures biparental care of the offspring, creating intense anxiety regarding sexual infidelity and the appearance of a third person who endangers the relationship. Likewise, the oedipal conflict in humans may trigger deceitfulness regarding our real sexual intentions both before others and even ourselves.

Kernberg (1995) believes that one form that aggression related to oedipal conflicts often takes is the unconscious collusion of both members of the couple to truly find a third person who represents the ideal of one and the rival of the other in a condensed form. In accordance with the contributions by Armant (1994), Dicks (1967), and Willi (1982), by "collusion" (from co-ludere, or play between two) we mean the unconscious agreement that determines a complementary relationship in which each member of the couple develops the parts of themselves that the other needs and gives up the parts that they project onto the partner (Font & Pérez-Testor, 2006). The most common scenario is that marital infidelity, in both brief and lasting triangular relationships, reflects unconscious collusions in the couple, such as the temptation to act out their deepest fears and desires.

Kernberg (1995) picks up an idea developed thirty years earlier by Dicks (1967):

> The unconscious rival is also a sexually desired object in the negative oedipal conflict: the victim of infidelity often unconsciously identifies with the partner who has betrayed through sexual fantasies about the latter's relationship with the jealously hated rival. (p. 88)

In the same work, the author posits another provocative idea:

> When the severe narcissistic pathology in one or both members of the couple makes it impossible for there to be a capacity for normal jealousy—a capacity that implies achieving a certain tolerance for the oedipal rivalry—it is easy for these triangulations to be acted out. (p. 88)

Partners in a couple capable of keeping their sexual intimacy and protecting themselves from invasions by third persons not only keep their obvious conventional boundaries but also reaffirm their "couplehood" in their struggle against rivals. The unconscious gratification of the fantasy of the excluded third person represents an oedipal triumph and simultaneously a subtle oedipal rebellion. Fantasies about the excluded third person are typical components of normal relations.

In his book *Marital Tensions*, Dicks (1967) distinguishes between benign infidelity and malignant infidelity.

Benign infidelity is characterised by the existence of a dyadic agreement to ignore the casual sexual transgressions that do not harm the feeling of mutual belonging. The unfaithful spouse "distinguishes between trivial and significant acts" (ibid., p. 167). Trivial acts are experienced as minor battles with no importance, relationships with partial bonds which do not compromise the dyadic boundaries, unlike a significant relationship, which could open up a breach in the membrane or dyadic boundary. "This boundary is always unconsciously recognised by marital dyads, though it varies greatly in its elasticity and in what it includes" (ibid., p. 167). In Dicks's opinion, "culture and norms differences may draw the boundary in rather inconsistent shapes for the two partners, not recognized until a crisis, or covered by denial" (ibid., p. 167).

The breach in the dyadic boundary can have unexpected results. In this kind of so-called benign infidelity, the partner's response to the breach is to release a considerable proportion of hatred and jealousy along with an advanced thawing of the anti-libidinous coldness, which deepens the partner's recognition of the necessary libidinous object along with the recognition of one's own latent sexual powers. The subordinate, complacent, silent partner finds him/herself facing an identifiable rival and feels that his/her strength grows to the point where they react aggressively to the intrusion and reveal him/herself to be a new partner with a great deal of pleasure for the other partner, for whom this was the last, desperate, unconscious attempt to spur on a result.

Both members of the couple confess that they now feel much closer to each other after that "horrible stage". In these cases, the "third person" plays the role of "transitional object" used for the dyad's purposes and often disappears without a trace. However, the invasion of the dyadic boundary has in theory fostered the eruption of libidinous inversion and idealisations regarding this third person, which vanish in view of the injured partner's reaction.

Many times the third person comes from the "best friend" sector of the injured partner. We can find everything from the innocent partner's ambivalent projective identification with the rival, who provides the missing link in the dyadic sexual relationship, to the manipulation of the situation in order to put an end to a marriage, which is practically destroyed anyhow. In Dicks's opinion (ibid.), the unconscious manipulation within the dyad that merits the most attention is the one in which one partner virtually pushes the other towards infidelity. There are many variations: from the husband who uses an envious male friend on whom he projects his absent libidinous power, to the variation of the unconscious relationship with the homosexual "best friend", through projective identification with the satisfaction of the wife who has relations with this friend. From this perspective, the transitional object can not only benefit the frustrated partner but also embody the repressed sexuality of the offended partner.

The following quote illustrates how in some cases, infidelity seems to be the outcome of unconscious incitement by one of the members of the couple:

> It's the worst thing that could happen to me. I had never questioned my husband, or especially my best friend. I was so stupid. I can't understand it. How was I unable to imagine it? You know what they say: that the wife is always the last to know. That's for sure! I was so trusting that if my husband brought home theatre tickets and I had a work engagement I told him, "Call Laura, I'm sure she could go". I felt bad that he couldn't go to a party just because I couldn't ... "Call Laura and see if she can go with you" ... And I was grateful to Laura! She was my best friend ... I don't know how I'm going to survive this betrayal ... my husband and my best friend ... it seems like a horror movie.

In contrast, *malignant infidelity* is a destructive phenomenon that permanently ends the couple relationship. In this situation, the partner is later rejected or destroyed as a libidinous object, while the rival is exalted and attributed far superior sexual qualities. Instead of feelings of guilt and attitudes of repair after the dyadic boundaries have been transgressed, there is insensitivity and indifference to the consequences which the offended partner might now suffer. In these cases, infidelity can be used to hurt, to demean, or to drive the partner mad, depending on what was previously established in a sadomasochistic, cruel collusion.

The conduct of the offended partner is supported by the social system, which tends to protect them. Hatred in larger or smaller degrees and fantasies of revenge may appear as a kind of law of retaliation which demands "justice" and punishment for the unfaithful partner. There is no possible repair, nor can any act of contrition be accepted; the wound is too deep and cannot form scar tissue. In these situations, a paranoid structure in its active phase responding to an unbearable wound can act violently and cause the death of the partner and/or the intermediate object. Countless cases of this appear in the newspapers, and it has often been the inspiration for literary works, films, and songs.

External conduct towards infidelity can be highly varied, ranging from what are called "Othello"-style reactions based on Shakespeare's play, in which the injured partner kills the unfaithful partner, to the "Gabriela"-style reactions, based on Jorge Amado's 1958 work *Gabriela, Clove and Cinnamon*, in which despite the social pressure that requires the injured partner to seek vengeance by killing the unfaithful woman, he instead reacts by forgiving her and reconciling with his partner.

From this standpoint, the clinic should very carefully evaluate whether the couple who comes in for consultation may benefit from a couple treatment or whether it would be better to address the issues individually. Our experience with this kind of problem tells us that when the couple comes in together, this means there is a good chance that they can be treated together.

However, this is not always true. Therefore, if there are indications that there may be violent acts that endanger the physical integrity of either member of the couple, the indication should be individual treatment.

Clinical case study: Johan and Marianne

The clinical story recounted below is that of an intake interview with a middle-aged couple who came in after the shocking discovery that the husband had been unfaithful. Given that the situation was highly reminiscent of some of the scenes from director Ingmar Bergman's film *Scenes from a Marriage*, we used the names Johan and Marianne for the members of the consulted couple.

The couple came to the office at the wife's request. Marianne, a forty-eight year old, was disconcerted by what had happened. She had discovered her fifty-year-old husband's infidelity, which had totally turned her world upside down. She had never suspected that her husband could be unfaithful to her. If she thought carefully about it, he must have had reasons. Their sexual relations had cooled off to such an extent that they had not had sex for six or seven months; she could not recall it exactly. She put it down to menopause and her job at an NGO, which absorbed too much of her time, and she thought that her husband was too stressed from work to even think about sexual relations. He always came home late from work and exhausted.

They had a twenty-two-year-old son and a twenty-year-old daughter who were studying at university while living with them. Marianne described Johan as a good father and good husband, although he rarely showed signs of affection. However, he had always been like this and she had accepted him the way he was.

Johan recounted the situation as "a moment of mental alienation or something like that". He was overwhelmed by work, family routines, problems: "Maybe it was my midlife crisis …". He fell madly in love with Paula, a thirty-two-year-old colleague who was recently separated and had a four-year-old daughter. He felt like a new man with her. She listened carefully to him, understood him, encouraged him, and admired him, while things were cold with his wife.

Marianne interrupted him several times to tell him that he was wrong. She admitted that there were things that were not working properly, but she had not been aware of them at the time. She claimed that they had been having good times and that they had had fun on their most recent vacation, despite the fact that he was already going out with his new girlfriend at that time, even though his wife did not know it. According to Marianne, he had behaved very badly: he had cheated on her and was a coward. He could have been up front about it so they could have talked about it and given her a chance. Instead, she had to be the one who put two and two together after reading a text message on his phone. She had never been nosy about his phone or email until Johan began to behave strangely: "He would take his mobile phone to the bathroom with him."

This is a case of combined infidelity, since there is not only a sexual relationship but also an emotional tie with Paula, to whom Johan dedicated time and mental space outside his primary relationship.

J: I told you clearly what was going on.
M: Right, but only after I discovered it. You told me horrible things, that you didn't love me, and that you had never loved me.

J: That's how I felt; I was daft.

M: My friends told me to kick you out of the house and keep every-thing for myself, but I felt bad, it made me feel sad ... we had been married for twenty-five years ... a curious milestone.

J: I was the one who left home. I rented a flat. I went to live with Paula. I think I left after twenty-four or forty-eight hours; I saw clearly that I had made a mistake. I wanted to come back. After ten days I asked her [Marianne] to forgive me; I told her that I only loved her.

M: I still hadn't gotten over my shock. He had left me after twenty-five years of marriage. I had never even looked at anyone besides him ... and suddenly I found myself alone, with nobody by my side. I still hadn't gotten over the shock that he told me he wanted to come back. It was too much for me. I didn't know what to do. Some friends told me to come here.

J: I immediately told her we could. We could do whatever she wanted.

M: I feel sorry for Paula. Her husband left her and now she's alone again. But Johan is my husband. I love him. I have always loved him, even though right now I'm not sure what I should do.

J: We spoke last week. I went home because the kids weren't there. They were angry with me.

M: That's normal. Their father abandoned me.

J: We made love like we hadn't for many years.

M: I've always loved you. But I'm not sure what I should do. I don't know whether I can trust you or whether it's going to happen again.

J: No, it's never going to happen again. You can trust me.

This story shows quite a frequent situation. A high percentage of couples cannot tolerate infidelity, and hatred and anger invade their entire bond, while in other couples there is a reaction similar to that of Johan and Marianne. The predominant collusion in this case is the collusion due to dependency, in which Johan acts as a naughty child under the watchful eye of Marianne, who serves as a maternal figure tolerating Johan's mischief. Indeed, the infidelity is treated as a case of mischief. The basic behaviour of this collusion between the caregiver and the cared-for is similar to the relationship between a child and his mother, but an eager child full of fear that the mother is bad or may abandon him, and a mother who is the victim of her child, subjugated to him and required to satisfy him in every way due to his helplessness.

Johan wants to be cared for and is characterised by the need for immediate gratification and his yearning to devour anything that is possible for him. This eagerness leads him to insatiably seek satisfaction, which can become a bottomless pit. He seeks a partner who is willing to care for him maternally with no limitations. At the same time, he is afraid of actually depending on his partner and cannot deal with frustration. Concealed infidelity soothes him since he feels like he depends less on Marianne. Johan is somewhat charming, with an air of ingenuousness; he is a bit of a flatterer with a perennially youthful appearance. He seems like an idealistic person who shows infantile desires and seeks unreal elements in his marriage, since he is only in partial contact with reality. His way of attracting his partner is by showing a certain lack of confidence which stimulates the other to care for him.

Marianne takes on the role of caregiver, as an apparently protective, warm person, yet one who is rigid in her principles, in which she passionately believes. She is a competent, active person who is self-sacrificing in her profession. She does everything without expecting any kind of compensation, and she deliberately gives generously to the neediest or weakest. However, when they no longer need her, she breaks off the good relationship they had and places herself in the role of the needy one who aggressively demands. As long as she acts as the caregiver she has plenty of positive energy, and if she can participate in care-oriented psychosocial activities, she feels rewarded and they help her to avoid the failures of her own psychopathological defences. She prefers to give rather than to receive care, as if she was playing the role of mother, and she thus avoids the anxiety she feels when she experiences the need to be cared for.

When she believes that she has not fulfilled a role well, she seeks to invalidate her partner, sometimes even to destructive extremes. Afterwards she experiences feelings of both guilt and inferiority. In order to recover her violated narcissistic self-esteem, she has to become altruistic with others once again.

Marianne can feel like a bad mother and even become one. Johan finds an alternative in Paula. It seems that Paula may become a new caregiver. Marianne has no other choice but to accept the failure with "shame and humiliation" (Benghozi, 2006). The result is that the caregiver does not care, and the person being cared for is not appreciative; the conflict is vivid and becomes impossible for either one to resolve.

If they both act as the person being cared for they will need someone to care for them, a role which is transferentially projected onto the therapist. If they are both caregivers, they need someone to care for.

We can note that this is a predominantly oral relationship, like the breastfeeding infant with his mother. If the infant is excessively anxious, he can feel destructive fears at his mother's breast and respond to the mother with aggression; she becomes a bad mother and the infant feels vulnerable. The infant seeks a totally solicitous mother and lashes out if he does not feel her to be that way; by lashing out, he feels even more vulnerable when the mother withdraws.

We have witnessed a relational disturbance between Johan (the breastfeeding infant), who is disproportionately and mistrustfully demanding, and Marianne (the mother), who withdraws. Johan tries to bind her so she cannot escape, even by hurting her, but the more he binds her, the more she escapes. What Johan could have done to foster the relationship is to appreciate what he receives from the mother and feel that when the mother withdraws she does so lovingly.

Referring to Dicks's terminology (1967), Johan and Marianne experienced a situation of benign infidelity. Johan detracts importance and meaning from his affair with Paula; he shows his remorse and promises that it will not happen again, while Marianne's feelings of anger and shock at the injury come hand in hand with a thawing of the libidinous coldness and an acknowledgement of her own latent sexuality.

This means that in reality, the infidelity plays a secondary role in this situation. Many interpretations could be proffered, but we could surely agree that this was an acting-out that revitalised the relationship. In its Greek etymology, the word "crisis" can refer to this function of bringing a new opportunity. Johan's infidelity has managed to unblock the monotony and deterioration of his relationship with Marianne, so Paula played the role of transitional object in the situation.

In conclusion

In this chapter, we have viewed infidelity as a rupture of the implicit or explicit agreements that underpin a couple's bond. Often this conflict is what mobilises couples to seek professional help. In fact, infidelity is one of the main reasons couples come to seek help at our service.

Obviously, if both members of the couple come to the office it is a positive sign. Many of these couples come with the conscious desire to revive their relationship. Others, however, come to seek separation in the least painful way possible. In the clinical material examined here, the characters belong to the set of couples that come with the purpose of rescuing their relationship.

In our opinion, marital infidelity tends to reflect couples' collusions, such as the temptation to act out their deepest fears and desires. That is, behind an act of infidelity there is often a certain previous relational functioning, both conscious and unconscious, which determines the partners' lives and influences their vicissitudes. For example, some of the couple's unconscious dynamics can unwittingly promote infidelity by one or both members.

Therefore, attending to couple treatment can help the partners to understand the role that the infidelity plays in their relationship and identify what is happening emotionally between them. We try to prompt a therapeutic change in the relationship that enables the predominant collusion to be mobilised.

Our job as therapists is aimed at fostering the capacity of the pact between both partners and thus to help to demystify the fear of argument. The therapist's purpose is also to reveal to the patients what they do not know about themselves, from both the conceptual and operative standpoint. One of the most significant aspects is the patients' newfound awareness of the contradictions and frustrations either felt or triggered by the infidelity.

However, it is important to bear in mind that each couple has its own unique features; each infidelity is singular and therefore the way it should be addressed should be exclusive for that given couple. No two couples are alike; each couple constructs its own dyadic system through the pair's dominant internal object.

The wound caused by infidelity may not allow separation to be worked on, and a litigious war breaks out without any foreseeable end except the suffering of all the family members. Helping the partners to repair their bonds without legal aggression is a sound alternative to the permanent destruction of many couples.

References

Allen, E. S., & Baucom, D. H. (2004). Adult attachment and patterns of extradyadic involvement. *Family Process, 43*: 467–488.

Allen, E. S., Atkins, D. C., Baucom, D. H., Snyder, D. K., Gordon, K. C., & Glass, S. P. (2005). Intrapersonal, interpersonal and contextual factors in engaging in and responding to extramarital involvement. *Clinical Psychology: Science and Practice, 12*: 101–130.

Amato, R., & Previti, D. (2003). People's reasons for divorcing: Gender, social class, the life course and adjustment. *Journal of Family Issues, 24*: 602–626.

Aramburu, I., Pérez-Testor, C., Davins, M., Cabré, V., & Salamero, M. (2011). La infidelidad en las películas de Woody Allen (Infidelity in the films of Woody Allen). *Aloma, 29*: 309–324.

Armant, C. (1994). Fundamentos teóricos. In: A. Bobé & C. Pérez-Testor (Eds.), *Conflictos de Pareja: Diagnóstico y Tratamiento* (pp. 29–34). Barcelona, Spain: Paidós.

Benghozi, P. (2006). Le travail de ritualisation du pardon en TFP et la réparation transgénérationnelle des liens. In: *The Ancestors' Share: The Transgenerational in Psychoanalytical Couple and Family Therapies.* [Symposium conducted at the Second International Congress for Psychoanalytic Family Therapy, of the International Association of Couple and Family Psychoanalysis, Montreal, Canada.]

Blow, A. J., & Hartnett, K. (2005). Infidelity in committed relationships, I: a methodological review. *Journal of Marital and Family Therapy, 31*: 183–216.

Choi, K., Catania, J. A., & Dolcini, M. M. (1994). Extramarital sex and HIV risk behavior among US adults: Results from the national AIDS behavioral survey. *American Journal of Public Health, 84*: 2003–2007.

Dicks, H. V. (1967). *Marital Tensions.* London: Karnac.

Family Discussion Bureau (1962). *The Marital Relationship as a Focus for Casework.* London: Codicote Press.

Font, J., & Pérez-Testor, C. (2006). Psicopatología de la pareja. In: C. Pérez-Testor (Ed.), *Parejas en Conflicto* (pp. 81–115). Barcelona, Spain: Paidós.

Forste, R., & Tanfer, K. (1996). Sexual exclusivity among dating, cohabiting and married women. *Journal of Marriage & the Family, 58*: 33–47.

Glass, S. P., & Wright, T. L. (1985). Sex differences in type of extramarital involvements and marital dissatisfaction. *Sex Roles, 12*: 1101–1120.

Kernberg, O. F. (1995). *Love Relations: Normality and Pathology.* New Haven, CT: Yale University Press.

Lawrence, J. (2010). The evolved function of the oedipal conflict. *The International Journal of Psychoanalysis, 91*(4): 937–958.

Nicolò, A. M. (1995). Capacidad de reparación y parentalidad. In: M. Garrido & A. Espina (Eds.), *Terapia Familiar: Aportaciones Psicoanalíticas y Transgeneracionales* (pp. 83–91). Madrid: Fundamentos.

Ortman, D. (2005). Post-infidelity stress disorder. *Journal of Psychosocial Nursing, 43*: 46–54.

Romero, A., Rivera, S., & Díaz, R. (2007). Desarrollo del inventario multidimensional de infidelidad (IMIN). *Revista de la Asociación Iberoamericana de Diagnóstico y Evaluación Psicológica, 23*: 121–147.

Sami-Ali, M. (1974). *L'Espace Imaginaire*. París: Gallimard.

Shackelford, T. K., Leblanc, G. J., & Drass, E. (2000). Emotional reactions to infidelity. *Cognition and Emotion, 14*: 643–659.

Teruel, G. (1974). *Diagnóstico y Tratamiento de Parejas en Conflicto: Psicopatología del Proceso Matrimonial*. Buenos Aires, Argentina: Paidós.

Whisman, M., Gordon, K., & Chatav, Y. (2007). Predicting sexual infidelity in a population-based sample of married individuals. *Journal of Family Psychology, 21*: 320–324.

Willi, J. (1982). *Couples in Collusion*. New York: Jason Aronson.

CHAPTER FIFTEEN

The other, the stranger, the unconscious: psychoanalysis and multi-ethnic therapeutic relationships

Ludovica Grassi

"But you're the one," Avram smiled, "you're the one who showed me what I came up with." This quotation is from David Grossman's 2008 novel *To the End of the Land*, in which we meet two brothers: the elder does not take after either parent, although his facial features to a certain extent do recall their dear and unfortunate friend, whom they have not seen for many years and who has been the focus of much of their love and care. The second is the son of the mother and the couple's very same friend. However, his father has never wanted anything to do with him, while he was devotedly raised by the father of the elder child. Furthermore, his birth brought the couple back together again who, following the arrival of the firstborn, had gone through an extremely painful separation.

The drama of the main characters' story is heightened by being set in the socio-historical context of the Israeli-Palestinian conflict, while also compounded by inherent issues of integration and expulsion, as well as mutual non-acknowledgement. Against this background subjectivisation and historicisation processes force the protagonists to come to terms with either the representative void of full trauma or with an excess of events which an interminable war lasting generations prevents from being properly worked out and thought through. This non-definition of placement of the self or of the other, this entwinement of familiarity and strangeness running through the entire novel expresses the psychic process which has been called for, ever since the beginning of life when one individual first meets another. This psychic work takes on a special form when the "other" is from a culturally and experientially distant world that is unknown and difficult to communicate with.

Multi ethnic situations have been the subject of research in several academic fields specifically because each bid to obtain greater understanding demands the confrontation and integration of diversified and often apparently contrasting points of view. Particularly, when there are reasons to intervene clinically in situations of individual or group malaise, the transcultural approach requires especially flexible and comprehensive tools. The family, however it may be structured, should be understood to be both the terrain where intrapsychic, relational, transgenerational, and cultural suffering is rooted as well as the best path to use for an intervention with an aim at assigning meaning and direction to blocked or deflected subjectivisation processes in situations where even cultural identity is confused, uncertain, or damaged. Psychoanalytic theory, founded on the discovery of the unconscious and its inherent heterogeneity, aptly lends itself to a dialogue with transcultural clinical work: the latter, exactly as it happens in the psychoanalytical process, cannot but focus on anxieties aroused by the encounter with the stranger and related conflicts alternating between tendencies to integrate and to expel.

Psychoanalysis and the other

Psychoanalysis has always concerned itself with the other, the stranger, and the unknown that is at the same time what we are the most familiar with. Psychoanalysis has founded the concept of the unconscious which, since the very origins of psychoanalytic thought, has stopped being an object or a content to be either unveiled or discovered, as it used to be in earlier philosophy, but has been the very process of the discovery itself.

Christiane Lacôte (1998)[1] suggests that the unconscious is in itself an operational concept, in which there is no separation between method and object, adding that it simultaneously defines enunciation and implementation. And ever since his essay on the *Unconscious* (1915e), where Freud confronts our perception of it with the sensing of other individuals' consciousness, it has become a key factor in the representation of an other as distinct from the self, a reality which we moreover may only know of through the experience of relating to the other, including therefore transference.[2]

In *Group Psychology and the Analysis of the Ego* (1921c) Freud said that in the life of the individual the other is always present, therefore individual psychology has at the same time and always been a social psychology. Nevertheless he had already described in *A Project for a Scientific Psychology* (1950a) how the other human being's entity is made up of two components, the structure of the one standing out for its constancy as a coherent thing (*das Ding*) while the other may be understood through the subject's memory activity. The first is the neighbour *sensu strictu*, referred to as "the unnameable other, which is alien, strange, incomprehensible, radically other" (translated for this edition) (Balsamo, 2005). And, Balsamo adds, "This otherness in its incomprehensible, unattainable form leads to going 'beyond the pleasure principle', establishing itself as evil, deprivation, exclusion, enigma." And yet, while the process of identity-building demands complex labours of dis-alienation, rigidly calling for connections with others and the continual flow of identifications to be interrupted, this break preserves traces of what it would like to leave on the other side of the confines, thereby inevitably undermining our narcissism.[3]

More specifically, in the essay on "The Uncanny" (1919h), Freud dealt with the issue of the foreignness that trespasses into familiarity: the uncanny is that kind of "frightful" that goes back to what has been known to us for a long time, to what is familiar to us. The meaning of *Unheimlich*, the German term used by Freud, may in fact coincide with its opposite, *Heimlich*. According to Schelling (1842), *Unheimlich* is everything that should be kept secret, concealed, but has instead surfaced. In Freud's view, however, the uncanny element is really neither new nor foreign: it is, on the contrary, something that has been familiar to the psychic life since very early times, but perceived as foreign as a result of the process of repression.

The feeling of the uncanny is linked to the endless revisiting of sameness, and specifically speaking to the figure of the double: the other turns into a source of anxiety precisely because he is the same, far too much the same. And just like the double becomes uncanny also because we are dragged back to remote times, today superseded, when the borders between the ego and the outside world, and the ego and the other had not yet been clearly defined, the repetition mechanism is in turn uncanny because it confronts us with the radicalism of the drive itself.

The multi-ethnic therapeutic setting

The transcultural therapeutic relationship highlights these central aspects of psychoanalysis. Accordingly, the unconscious is a knowledge which is created starting from a new relationship with the other, and which therefore derives from the transference, as Lacôte herself maintains. The other, the unconscious, and the uncanny are themes that fruitfully intermingle in clinical work with migrant families, who evoke feelings of being outsiders, emotions felt to be all the more lacerating given that they are forever caught up in a melting pot of diverging and incomprehensible, although sometimes all too familiar, realities.

Hence a difficulty is encountered in appraising and adjusting to the exchange with the other, oscillating between rejection and withdrawal on the one extreme and a longing for an impossible annihilation of the difference on the other, this appearing even more threatening and marked by persecutory traits. A common example of this situation is the difficult choice that is facing families settled abroad, of whether they should fully adopt their new language and culture, which is often associated with the apparent cancellation of their original traditions and expressions, or a total rejection of them, leading to marginalisation within a tiny world with inflexible and oppressing boundaries.

I came across the first option when I met the family of Mohammed, who was not allowed to speak Arabic or, consequently, to spend time with children from his own ethnic background. Moreover, his mother used Arabic only in order to scold him.

Mohammed's story embraces the wealth of migratory experiences handed down through generations, reaffirming in various forms the need to face up to otherness, while identity-building and the working through of mourning by family members are made excessively complicated. His paternal grandparents had already left their homeland for a European capital, where Mohammed's grandfather held a high public office, following a coup d'état. Mohammed's father therefore lived for fifteen years abroad, while his parents adopted two young girls from their new country. On returning later to his home country, as a consequence of renewed political turmoil, Mohammed's father, who was twenty-four at the time, encountered serious difficulty in reintegrating, both as far as fitting in socially and finding a job were concerned. These very obstacles eventually prompted him to move to Italy, taking advantage of fresh immigration legislation.

The same discontinuity featuring in Mohammed's father's family life may also be found in the story of his mother, who had sought through education to offer her own peasant family an alternative way of life. However, marriage forced her to drop out of her university course. During her interviews, it also transpires how at many important moments of her life she had felt unprepared. She manages "through willpower" to get over a long spell of post-partum depression, but when Mohammed is four years old she arrives at the clinic enquiring about "the reasons" for the problems of her son, who does not speak or draw, while being erratic both in focusing his attention and in his behaviour. Furthermore, he is incapable of playing with his peers and also unable to bear being physically distanced from his mummy. His mother has given up speaking to him as she thinks Mohammed does not understand. She is incapable of even playing with him but instead strives to teach him to write, virtually as if hurling herself head first into this adopted culture, while casting aside emotions tying her to her native land. She is at first absolutely dumbfounded when Mohammed, during their first session at the clinic, starts drawing, especially when he sketches a human figure, something he had never previously done. It is an image of a girl, perhaps the girl his mother has yearned for ("it would have been so much easier altogether"), because boys are problematic (as her brothers are) or ill (like her husband's schizophrenic half-brother).

Between the absence of the father, away at work the whole day, and the absence of words, which is the "reason" prompting his mother to contact the clinic, Mohammed represents the other, unfathomable and unable to understand, filling every space with fragmented things, noises, and activities that beg for meaning, connections, and containment. He appears as one of the characters in search of an author described by Marie Rose Moro (2000), trapped between the verticality of conscious and unconscious transmission and the horizontality of the here and now, in the paradox of contradictory identifying utterances. The child is in fact expected to adopt the new culture (through language), just as the girls of the foreign country were adopted, but also to re-establish broken ties.

In this specific case it was thought the child should be offered a "soft" supporting treatment aimed at language development, carried out by a speech therapist, whereas the family underwent psychotherapy leading the parents to recognise and be recognised by Mohammed in their role of containment and as mediators of the external reality. Similarly, the role assumed by the child of bearer of an otherness, which nobody else appeared willing to take on, was also worked through. Some of the ties with their original worlds were re-established, both those points of support by now felt to have been forever lost, as well as those viewed to be negative which had been deliberately cast aside, but had nevertheless resurfaced in the form of unintelligible and therefore traumatic experiences.

As psychoanalyst, I was confronted with a countertransference which had been overcharged with idealisation as a consequence of the couple's and, I would go so far as to say, even the child's own demanding and overconfident attitude, as well as a result of the fluid untying of knots which gradually proceeded as our work made progress. All these developments led me to almost overlook the differences in culture and experience separating us. So I was taken by surprise when, a few months after concluding the family therapy, the parents suddenly withdrew the child in order to *elsewhere* seek a "stricter" speech therapy for him. However, they were only to return later to express their gratitude and to say how happy they were with the progress made by Mohammed, who had settled well into his primary school, was able to express himself without difficulty, and even studied Arabic.

In such instances, a risk, seen as threatening or even seductive, may arise, of the affiliation possibly becoming colonisation and obliteration of diversity (moreover an impossibility). In this context, Moro makes a distinction between *filiation*, meaning conscious or unconscious vertical transmission within the family and inscription into a genealogy, and *affiliation*, referring to external transmission achieved through "belonging groups" which everyone experiences at various stages of life; affiliation demands a deep and often painful psychic work aimed at redefining one's own desires and aspirations of resemblance, raising questions about belonging, identity, and creativity.

Discontinuity and integration difficulties in migratory experiences

It is therefore possible to observe how emigration enforces a deviation, a segmentation, or a definite interruption of the narcissistic contract, as defined by Piera Aulagnier (1975): a contract enabling the subject to place himself at the spot where the group's desire for permanence meets the individual's yearning for immortality. This contract is drawn up thanks to group pre-investment in the *infans* as a future voice, who will take up the place assigned to him. As a reward for his investment in the group and its values, the *infant* will demand the right to take up a position independent of exclusive parental verdict.[4] On broadening this concept to include various patterns of individual and group removals to outside their original environment, Kaës (2005) refers to "displacement of narcissistic contract", understood as the loss of a psychic place (the same as that described by Winnicott in 1971). The difficulty in establishing a place at which we are able to deposit what we find may go some way to providing an explanation for the problems of the world today. The importance of the psychic life's extrasubjective symbolising functions and extra-topic states enables its development, according to Kaës, only as a result of the demands made by the psychic work imposed on the psyche by its inscription on both primary intersubjective and social links. The condition and the very possibility of the unfolding of the subjectivisation processes, including the symbolic functions and sense of temporality involving the interplay between past, present, and future, depend on this fundamental articulation of social and psychic areas, that is between metasocial and metapsychic warrantors.[5]

The host community also suffers the consequences of the immigrant's arrival, which alters the group structure and destabilises the pre-existing organisation, while in various ways it poses a threat to its cultural, linguistic, institutional identity and, generally speaking, to the feeling of shared identity. On encountering the other, both parties are affected by traumatic potential and difficulties of integration in a process of mutual exchange between host and guest, trespasser and trespassed, as indeed has been so poetically described in Grossman's novel and also witnessed over the last sixty years of Palestinian history. The stranger nevertheless represents the otherness, the new (the new idea or the "mystic") which, from a Bionian point of view, provokes a catastrophic change in the container-contained relationship, whose outcome may be either destructive and pathological or evolutionary and creative, both as far as the individual and the group are concerned. According to Matte-Blanco (1988), the container-contained relationship may suffer a symmetrisation, where the result of tension between conflicting centrifugal and centripetal forces is explosive. If the container's elaborative function (*reverie*) were to fail and/or a violent process of mutual projective identification were to occur, the contained, owing to its destructive power, may determine the destruction, collapse, or disintegration of the container itself; the latter, in turn, when excessively rigid or apprehensive, may well suffocate the "contained", preventing it from evolving or causing its annihilation or evacuation. On the other hand, when the container and contained prove to be sufficiently flexible for the container to be able to accept the contained as it is not judged to be destructive, then integration and evolution will ensue, to the advantage of both parties (Bria & Lombardi, 2008).[6]

The family and the stranger

Since, therefore, the migrant represents the uncanny for the host, he, if a parent, has the task of gradually presenting to the child the new world, which is in his view felt to be strange and uncanny. In turn, the child, on assimilating this novel reality, is over time increasingly destined to turn into a stranger to and betray his family, thus representing a constant threat to its continuity: this complicated and tormented field of reciprocal influence may easily result in a kind of identity discontinuity of the child.

Maila, born in Italy and the only daughter of sympathetic and caring parents, has difficulties in correctly finding her own place in time and space. As her parents are telling me about their home towns, the two main cities in their country of origin, she butts in to proclaim "I am half of my father and half of my mother." While her teacher describes her as being immature, her paediatrician states she is "too smart". Furthermore, she has difficulties learning the days of the week and the months of the year and she especially has problems with the perception of the order of time. She "lost" her pacifier while on holiday with her grandparents, subsequently rejecting any other offered to her: since then this loss has been restaged every day through a release of a small amount of urine. She draws herself with blue eyes and blond hair; she hates her hair because it is curly and very thick and she is unable to grow it long. Consequently her mother strives to soothe her by flattening it as best she can and artificially lengthening it. Hence the girl appears to be expected to fulfil the impossible task she has been assigned by her parents, of concealing her origins (De Micco,

2008), which have at the same time been idealised and deposited in an incommensurable "elsewhere". One possible solution may be realised through a "phantasy of the reversal of generations" (E. Jones, 1950),[7] which I propose as an interpretation of a drawing of me as mother of two children, a girl and a boy, where the overflowing excitation appears to be directed towards the idea of both of us as parents of the parental couple. However, one of the children sucks a pacifier, while the other does not, as if the two also represent the two Mailas: one looking forward and the other back, in other words one more, the other less willing to welcome the "other".

The combination of losing self-aspects and objects, which is the mark of migratory experience, brings into play maniacal defences as well as splitting and negation processes. These, as we have already seen, are distributed and reverberate inside each family and are expressed in various ways qualitatively and quantitatively among the family members. Therefore mourning and working-through processes are extended to involve the entire family, who should always be kept in mind when taking a therapeutic path in order to sustain feasible integration processes, which, via regressive and progressive movements, lead to a new adjustment.

Children who either emigrate to or are born in the new country of their parents' adopted residence, are on the one hand protected by the shield provided by their family as well as by their own greater ability and pliability in absorbing and assimilating new languages and habits, while on the other hand, however, they are affected by the impact of the migration experience on their families. According to Leon and Rebeca Grinberg (1982), parents may have chosen or may have been forced to be emigrants, but children will always be "exiles" who have no choice in either leaving or staying.

A typical picture involves parents failing to function as guarantors of safety and as intermediaries in relation to external reality: the father because he is totally focused on meeting the family's material needs in this new context and the mother because she longs for her original world, a separation from which she experiences as an irreparable laceration. When they do manage to ask for help, the father is the only one capable of putting his request into words although he sounds as if he is really delegating it as a result of his inability to face up to unbearable, painful feelings, whereas the mother is trapped in a silent, hostile and paralysing depression, confining her to the regressive and claustrophobic few square metres of her living quarters.

Meeting the other between intrapsychic and relational

The Grinbergs have already succeeded in identifying the impact of eradication and loss on identity sentiments as well as the resulting crisis, often featuring a catastrophic change, as lying at the core of emigration psychopathology. Even in myths (Eden, Oedipus, Babel) migration frequently symbolises birth and is associated with the quest for knowledge, with guilt and the pain felt over the loss of the protective object. The availability of a link with a good, stable, and safe internal object helps putting up with and working out external and internal changes, enabling the migratory experience to assume the value of a *depressive birth*, paving the way towards growth and enrichment. In contrast, the phantasy of a *catastrophic birth* leads to this experience becoming marked by persecutory and destructive traits. Emigrants, the Grinbergs point out, are in need of a *potential space* to be used as a *transitional space* and *transitional time* between the maternal object-country and the new external world: potential space ensuring them a continuity of existence and therefore overcoming their post-traumatic disorganisational phase, resulting in increased personal creative potential.

In the foundation of ethno-psychoanalysis, George Devereux's research and clinical work was specifically focused on the encounter with the other, simultaneously from an intrapsychic, interpersonal, and intercultural perspective. From this standpoint, he underscored (1967) how the observer may observe the other only through observing himself, and how difficulties and anxiety inherent to the relationship between the observer and the observed should be seen as the main tools at our disposal in order to approach situations we strive to understand: anxiety becomes the method.[8]

This provides an explanation as to why in a transcultural therapeutic relationship, just as in a psychoanalytical one, countertransference becomes a crucial course to take in the passage between the search for common ground and the anxiety caused by the unknown and incomprehensible. Emphasis is also put on the mutuality pertaining to the encounter between strangers by Marie Rose Moro, who urges us to experience *decentralisation from within* in order to be able to embrace the other's knowledge, a reality which should arouse our curiosity in order to together create a totally new story.

All this can also become extremely complicated, as in the case of a six-year-old Chinese girl, isolated and unable to learn anything at school, who was brought to me by her mother, herself speaking just a few words of Italian. The eldest daughter, who was only present during the initial interview, angrily stated she no longer wished to have anything to do with family matters, solely because she was the only one capable of communicating with the outside world and, in any case, she had problems of her own which no one seemed to want to care about. The father was impossible to get hold of as he worked throughout the day and this apparently also kept him away from home at night. However, I was soon to discover further "mysteries" as, through an interview with the mother, I learnt how completely unknown her daughter was to her. Virtually from her birth onwards, the girl had been brought up by her grandmother in China, resulting in the mother's complete ignorance about her child's development and indeed any significant moments of her growth, as well as having no idea in whose care the baby used to be entrusted while the grandmother was at work. Mrs W came to the clinic only because she was under pressure from her daughter's teachers and had understood that their apprehension could perhaps be allayed by applying for the assistance of a special needs teacher. She was therefore astonished to be told that the situation called for a more comprehensive, understanding, substantial, and reconstructing intervention. She virtually exhibited her daughter as if she were a *china* doll: slender, frail with delicate features, and so well groomed that no detail was left to chance, but there was, however, neither any contact nor communication between them. Mrs W does not think twice about entrusting me with her child for individual sessions, wishing rather to leave the building altogether.

Jin Fan then straightaway latches onto me with hollow and at the same time rich chatter, stories about concrete losses and things she misses (e.g., her toys and pencil case) and endowed with a logic that follows an enigmatic line of thought. It is as if the girl has ceaselessly been devoting her mental ability to structure continuity where lacerations have occurred, and explanations where the brutality of facts and abandonments have prevented links from being formed.

The Grinbergs speak of *adjourned mourning* as a possible outcome of the effects of such traumatic events and they specifically qualify emigrations as a cumulative trauma. In this family, however, mourning appears to be frozen, split off rather than adjourned and we also do not know whether a working-out process may be devised: the anxiety generated by the encounter with the other (an intrapsychic, intersubjective, and intercultural stranger) has so far not enabled introjective and working-through processes to be activated and a space to host the other to be opened.

Conclusions

As described in the short clinical case examples, a transcultural psychoanalytical approach always requires plural meetings and inclusive therapeutic relationships which should involve and indeed welcome every member of the family who has been caught up in the problems of the work-through processes needed in order to deal with the trauma of migration. The complexity of the trauma is to be attributed to the interlacement of spatial interruption, abruptly dividing members of the same family, the same country, and the same culture, with temporal interruption, disrupting the development of the identity processes of individuals, families, and nations: moreover, these ruptures have reverberations on the traumatic impact on the host group. Working with families enables the overlapping of losses experienced by families and of the suffering expressed by younger family members to be given meaning and to be properly articulated.

I defined these therapeutic relationships as being multi-ethnic owing to their involving a dimension of cultural otherness, which becomes part and parcel of the therapy that is focused on working-out and acknowledging the other and his traumatic potential. In this light even the presence of an interpreter may stretch to beyond his formal role of translator to become a "transformer", a "bridge" between one culture and another. The therapeutic encounter with the stranger and incomprehensible other, which is frequently felt to be threatening, at all times requires individual and group work of analysis of countertransference and specifically of cultural countertransference: in fact there are always implicit cultural elements, more often than not conflicting, on which the relationship between family and therapist is founded. Also our temporality, both subjective and objective, should be adjusted to meet the demands made by these multiform meetings in order to be successful at various interpretative levels and to comprehend profoundly dissimilar life-routes in a new, meaningful terrain which may be shared by all. The main goal may be claimed to be to create a mutual adoption, in the same way as Mohammed's grandparents had adopted the two girls from their country of adoption.

I have attempted in this chapter to demonstrate how transcultural clinical work, above all with families, may forcefully mobilise and indeed amplify the traumatic aspect inherent in the encounter with the other, which lies at the very heart of psychoanalysis. Even if we may never be able to completely understand this "other", we can nevertheless include it to form a part of our inner world (and consequently our outer world). Accordingly, it is only by approaching the other (which in psychoanalysis is transference) that we may experience ourselves, namely our unconscious. This is a notion recalling Freud's paper on the uncanny, where emphasis is laid on how the *Heimlich* eventually coincides with the *Unheimlich* and where Freud refers to the very borders separating the ego and the others and to their threatening indefinability.

Notes

1. The unconscious is not a mystery, but invented knowledge deriving from a new relationship with the other, which is why perhaps a Freudian unconscious does not exist without Freudian treatment: the invention of a new relationship with the other via the word is exactly what arouses an unconscious field. Moreover, the Freudian concept of repression expresses otherness, or rather the heterogeneity of the unconscious with respect to the conscious. More specifically, the fact that the unconscious is irrevocably the otherness is bolstered by Freud's insistence on postulating primary repression, whose function would specifically be to construct this heterogeneity. Transmission via words of the other ensures that the unconscious is a knowledge and the interpretation is an act. The second topic radicalises the unconscious within us through the death drive's irreducibility, thereby preventing us from attributing a "thing" consistency to the idea of the unconscious (Lacôte, 1998).

2. Masud Khan (1974) wrote a paper about the role of special friendships in the invention of theories or concepts about the world, citing the examples of Montaigne, Rousseau, and Freud. With regard to the last, when editing the correspondence between Freud and Fliess, Anna Freud, Marie Bonaparte, and Ernst Kris, who entitled their work "The Origins of Psychoanalysis" (1954), he established once and for all that this relationship was the channel that made it possible for Freud to exploit his genius and potential to the full. Only by way of this

relationship, characterised as a transference relationship, was Freud able to achieve self-analysis and come up with his method of analysis, founded on creating the possibility for the subject to see himself from the other's point of view. Khan goes on to underline the pivotal role of a specific human object-relationship in achieving self-experience, whereas straightforward mental apprehension leads towards ethics or metaphysics: through his relationship with Fliess, Freud fulfilled the heroic task of recognising the importance of love and hate in self-experience.

3. In *New Introductory Lectures on Psycho-Analysis* (1933a), Freud highlights a point which appears to open the door to the study of inter- and trans-generational transmission. Since parents, failing to recall the problems of their own childhood, identify with their own parents, the child's superego will not take his parents as its model, but rather his parents' superego. In this way, through the superego, the past continues to be handed down and kept alive from one generation to the next, while it is only gradually influenced by the novelties of the present: the fabric of the child's personality is composed of these heterogeneous images which one day may become invaders in the guise of what A. De Mijolla called *The Ego's Visitors* (1986). Moro as well maintains that identity presupposes the notion of otherness (2000).

4. The subject inevitably benefits from a specific theory about social principles which always include enunciations on the origin of this model and consequently its goal. In other words, the subject takes advantage of certitude about origin as well as predictability of development. The "discourse" of the social group gives the subject a solid basis about origins, highly crucial in ensuring that the father and mother do not constitute the exclusive guarantors of knowledge. Access to historicity is essential for both the identifying process and for allowing the ego to reach the threshold of autonomy which is required in order to function. This is impossible when the mother or father or indeed both parents refuse to subscribe to this contract, owing to a serious fault in their psychic structure (a psychotic nucleus). Something equally important happens when the contract is broken by social reality: when the subject encounters a collusion between the historical reality of his infancy and a phantasmatic construction of his perception of the world, so that relativising and giving meaning to the phantasm becomes unfeasible (Aulagnier, 1975).

5. *Metasocial warrantors* are large structures for the organisation and adjustment of social and cultural life; they have a function of guaranteeing stability in social groups: among them are myths and ideologies, beliefs and religions, authority and hierarchy.

Metapsychic warrantors are structures and processes of the psychic environment which allow the individual psyche to be founded and structured: they hold the organising principles of psychic life by means of basic interdictions and intersubjective contracts (for example, narcissistic contract and renouncement of direct fulfilment of drive goals). The metapsychic functions of these basic alliances can be detected when they are in crisis or are failing.

6. See also the concept of cultural *metissage* (Moro), where the acculturation of immigrants meets the transformation of the hosts.

7. The phantasy of the reversal of generations is sustained by a transference onto the child of the parents' relationship with their same-gender parent, in a combination of both hostile and loving features. Jones underlines the deepest reason explaining the grandchild's usual identification with his grandparents: both are in equal measure feared by the father, who is apprehensive of retaliation on their part resulting from his guilty wishes towards them.

8. Devereux's methodological set-up takes as its starting point Einstein's view that we may observe only events which happen to the observer, meaning we may only learn of what happens to or within the experimental apparatus where the observer is the major component. Therefore it is not through studying the subject, but rather the observer that the very essence of the situation may be accessed. At the end of the day, researching data is always the same as analysing oneself and that, inevitably, causes anguish. All thought systems are rooted in the unconscious, and act as defences against anxiety and disorientation. What are considered to be disturbances resulting from the observer's own activity constitute, if put to correct use, the cornerstones of a behavioural science rather than an annoying inconvenience, as they are usually considered, which should be got rid of as quickly as possible. A scientific discipline of behaviour should accept and indeed exploit the observer's subjectivity and his influence on the course of the observed event, in the same way that observation affects (and disturbs) the behaviour of an electron (Devereux, 1967).

References

Aulagnier, P. (1975). *The Violence of Interpretation. From Pictogram to Statement*. Hove, UK: Brunner-Routledge, 2001.

Balsamo, M. (2005). Homo homini lupus. *Psiche*, 2: 47–55.

Bonaparte, M., Kris, E., & Freud, A. (1954). *The Origins of Psychoanalysis. Letters to Wilhelm Fliess, Drafts and Notes: 1887–1904*. New York: Basic.

Bria, P., & Lombardi, R. (2008). The logic of turmoil: some epistemological and clinical considerations on emotional experience and the infinite. *International Journal of Psychoanalysis*, 4: 709–726.

De Micco, V. (2008). *Crescere sulla Frontiera. Percorsi dell'Identità in Bambini Immigrati tra Psicoanalisi e Antropologia*. In: XIV Congresso SPI Giornate Italiane "Cambiamento e identità", Rome, May 23–25.

De Mijolla, A. (1986). *Les Visiteurs du Moi*. Paris: Les belles lettres.

Devereux, G. (1967). *From Anxiety to Method in the Behavioral Sciences*. The Hague, Netherlands: Mouton.

Freud, S. (1915e). The unconscious. *S. E.*, 14: 159–215. London: Hogarth.

Freud, S. (1919h). The uncanny. *S. E.*, 17: 217–256. London: Hogarth.

Freud, S. (1921c). *Group Psychology and the Analysis of the Ego. S. E.*, 18: 65–144. London: Hogarth.

Freud, S. (1933a). *New Introductory Lectures on Psycho-Analysis. S. E.*, 22: 1–182. London: Hogarth.

Freud, S. (1950a [1887–1902]). A project for a scientific psychology. *S. E.*, 1: 281–391. London: Hogarth.

Grinberg, L., & Grinberg, R. (1989). *Psychoanalytic Perspectives on Migration and Exile*. New Haven, CT: Yale University Press.

Grossman, D. (2008). *To the End of the Land*. London: Vintage.

Jones, E. (1950). *Papers on Psycho-Analysis*. Baltimore, MD: Williams and Wilkins.

Kaës, R. (2005). Il disagio del mondo moderno e la sofferenza del nostro tempo. Saggio sui garanti metapsichici. *Psiche*, 2: 57–65.

Khan, M. M. R. (1974). *The Privacy of the Self. Papers on Psychoanalytical Theory and Technique*. London: Hogarth.

Lacôte, C. (1998). *L'inconscient*. Paris: Flammarion.

Matte Blanco, I. (1988). *Thinking, Feeling and Being*. London: Routledge.

Moro, M. R. (2000). *Enfants d'ici venu d'ailleurs. Naitre et grandir en France*. Paris: La Découverte et Syros.

Schelling, F. W. J. (1842). *Historical-critical Introduction to the Philosophy of Mythology*. New York: Suny Series in Contemporary Continental Philosophy, 2007.

Winnicott, D. W. (1971). *Playing and Reality*. London: Tavistock.

CHAPTER SIXTEEN

Old and new couple secrets: how to deal with them?

Giorgio Rigamonti and Simona Taccani

Family and couples secrets: definitions and functions

Racamier (1995) points out that he who is able to find the definition of a secret is clever and shrewd. As an object of knowledge or ignorance, a secret seems to lay itself open while sneaking away, it connects and disconnects at the same time, it is told or concealed, it enriches us or makes us sterile: indeed a secret has not got a singular nature.

From an etymological viewpoint, the word secret stems from the Latin word *secretum*, the past participle of the verb *secernier*, which means to separate and which consists of the separating prefix *se* and of the root *cernere*, which means to divide. In this way the word secret doubly contains the meaning of separation, as it suggests a double separation.[1]

There is also an interesting, not only etymological connection with the word and the concept of seduction, from the Latin word *seduction*, deriving from *seducere*, which also consists of the separating prefix *se*, meaning away and *ducere*, meaning to lead.

The sense of a secret implies a relational field as it is both intrasubjective and intersubjective. At an intrapsychic level it plays a vital role as it protects and helps the mind evolve, as an instrument that establishes and protects the individual's identity.

Castoriadis-Aulagnier (1976) and Lèvy-Soussan (2006) have dealt with the fruitfulness of this.

What defines a family's or a couple's secret is a necessary series of essential conditions that enable a person to avoid the risk of simplifying, like the idea that a secret must be something not to be told, which is obviously in itself not enough to generate one. Tisseron (2002) identifies and puts together three conditions that contribute to generating a *family secret*: it is something not spoken about at home and which opposes communication, but it is also something one is not allowed to know, which seems to distress those who know about it. A family's or couple's secret has painful psychic implications for the children, such as the feeling or the perception that they usually have that a family secret does exist, whose contents they are not allowed to know, but which causes perceptions, representations, and fantasies concerning its purpose of and the reasons for it.

In this regard, the psychoanalyst and writer Grimbert (2004), in his novel *A Secret*, describes a fantasised scenery he built up in his childhood, in particular a fictitious brother, something which actually turned out to be the presentiment of a family secret.

Another feature of a family secret that we can easily notice is that it organises itself and develops as a result of psychic traumas experienced by a previous generation who—being unable to mention and symbolise them, to share them through words or emotions, mental pictures or representations—handed down to the following generations the signs of a secret, such as attitudes, gestures, and facial expressions, confusing, puzzling emotions that cannot be explained.

Racamier (1995) goes further and remarks that the object-secret is protected by spreading traps, through low-rank secrets connected to it and recruited by chance which, in the end, are open secrets. Deception is tempting, and it is such only to conceal a well-guarded secret; each secret conceals another one and the secret in the foreground is just a bait offered to take one's mind off the secret hidden deep down in one's own or the family's psyche. This way there is always another secret ahead of the secret of incest, and behind it there is always the secret of a loss: the grief, never faced and never-ceasing at a never-ending death. This way deception never stops pestering the souls. Who of us has never been tempted to sift through secrets that incessantly let us catch sight of more? This match is lost from its beginning!

What are the functions of family secrets?

In Racamier's opinion (1995):

1. *Functions of preservation* in the sense of keeping the concealment of facts safe, preserving the idealisation of an object which has been lost, which has never been worked through, of preserving from any wound the vulnerable narcissism of the first ones behind the secret.
2. *Functions of chaining* as the secret is an irreplaceable link, a tie among the family members, a kind of shield protecting them from the outer world.
3. *A function of survival.* In this case, the function of the secret is that of being a fetish, the fetish is the reappearance of a bereavement that has not been worked through and which the fetish itself might have substituted. The menace of its disappearance is a threat of death. The door is double-locked: the family members who have so strongly wanted to escape death's mourning end up being threatened by death through the possible loss of their fetish, which has stood as insurance for life. We may consider this fetish-secret the *pacemaker* of the family, if not even their artificial heart.

What effects do these same secrets cause?

Still in Racamier's opinion, they cause effects of confusion, as they disrupt the primary and the play of secondary processes, but also bring-fantasising, dreaming, and escaping affections to a stop; they cause a paralysis as regards the primal thought which is not only the knowledge of our biological or phantasmal origins, but the knowledge of our originators' origin as well: in the final analysis they cause the mind's devitalisation, a paralysis, and a dispersal of ideas.

From a social viewpoint, nowadays a secret is publicly considered as antidemocratic and is perceived as harmful because it sets a limit to common knowledge, and the right to know is a synonym for relational inefficiency: this is the reason why it is banned.

From a psychic viewpoint, Lévy-Soussan (2006) underlines the positive function of an individual secret as an *organising secret*, we might say as something being able to hide, to keep something secret.

Actually a secret must be understood as an instrument of psychic development, as being able to create an illusion, which allows one to relate oneself to reality in the hope of changing and transforming it.

According to Freud, a child's first lieis his first secret: it reveals a capacity for individualisation and for parting as well as his/her ability to part from his/her parents' thought.

We have to confront one of the paradoxes of thought, as it is first necessary to keep one's thoughts in order to discover them and to develop one's Self as well as the meaning of the outer world: only later can the child open up and lay his/her thoughts bare.

There's a link between secrecy and privacy: the function of a secret is to protect one's innermost part as well as all that is unconscious.

Lévy Soussan (2006) depicts as a *child's first secret* (which the child shares with his mother) *the secret of the reality of the world*, a secret also uncovered by Winnicott in a paradoxical formulation of his, according to which each child creates the world pre-existing him/herself.

Especially at first it is necessary for this secret to be kept, so that the reality of the world is not revealed in a premature, ruthless way.

The second secret in a child's life is *the secret of separation*, the thought of his being separated, a useful tool—in the future—for his survival, but also a discovery and a source of pleasure when thinking about it. According to Lévy-Soussan, it is in this space and time of the mind that we can find one of the secret origins of love: the evidence of the experience of the first separation.

According to Lévy-Soussan, in a case of incest, when the Oedipus complex cannot be worked through at a symbolic or phantasmal level, incest attacks the foundations of illusion: the sources of thought, the origins of one's being. In other words the Self. There is a meaningful link between the secret of one's being and that of one's innermost feelings. A daughter who has suffered from incest, Lévi-Soussan remarks, has been deprived of her secret and of her innermost feelings: she is hollow and vulnerable.

Restoring this space of the mind—which is a secret, intimate space—may take a long time.

The very concept of family has lost its meaning: everything is possible, roles and differences have become lost, a daughter is no longer a daughter but a wife, a father is no longer a father but the husband of them all. Concerning incest, Lévy-Soussan remarks that in a true family secret it is the disappearance of the space of a secret which characterises its functioning, meaning that it is a secret which organises every psychism.

The last secret for a child is *the secret of the desire that originated his/her birth, something* questioned after by every child all over the world.

In Lévy-Soussan's opinion, this secret—not to be mistaken for the morbid secret regarding the origins—hides another one: the one concerning the fact that no individual child was ever desired, by her/ his parents wanted just a child, a wish that has nothing to do with the desire of having him/her in and as a person, who is unique in him/ herself.

Tisseron (2002) states that, although this happens not so often, a family secret is not necessarily connected with family events one has to be ashamed of, or that one feels guilty about.

The generation which co-creates a family's or a couple's secret develops a two-sided movement which wavers between a partial spur to symbolise, communicate, and give life and space to the secret event, and a tendency to expel the secret from their minds, to bury it in a kind of tomb or crypt (Abraham & Torok, 1978) and to forget it.

These inward oscillations may cause in the person who is keeping a a secret as many oscillations in their mood and behaviour, due to other people's words or allusions that call to mind, activate, and hit the hidden secret, but which prove inexplicable for the family, above all for the children.

In a family keeping a secret the children are driven to ask themselves several questions and to feel somehow guilty, but they also have to face the risk and the tendency, once they will have become parents, to behave in the same way as their own parents.

In particular, children may wonder whether they themselves can be the cause of the suffering they perceive in their parents, which makes them feel guilty and responsible.

Another question children ask themselves concerns the possibility that their parents may have done something shameful and culpable, so they do not talk about it.

It is also possible that they call into question their perceptions and fantasies concerning their parents' secrets, in this way thinking they have made a mistake.

The new generation originating from a family founded on a secret shows a tendency to develop, in turn, its own secrets, or pseudo-secrets, also defined as *open secrets*, as these are defence secrets, that would stand for the children's identification with their parents, both in justifying them for founding their couple and family on a secret and—in some cases—as if to take revenge for the secrets met with in their family.

In any way, starting from these new secrets of the new family generation, we must take into account that, somewhere back in time, we can trace a hidden secret belonging to a previous family generation.

A secret may hide another, is what Tisseron tells us (2002) who has best remarked upon how family secrets cause different symptoms in each generation, usually the second or third one following the couple or family who were the bearers of the secret.

Especially if unspeakable events originated the secret in a family based on them, for the second generation, that is the children, those their content, but it is their presence and existence that are felt and foreseen.

In relation to this, a clinical case is meaningful and important, which we are not going to relate in details, but in which it was possible to observe a recurring key sentence, often used in the family's daily life, mostly mentioned by the second generation of children, worded as follows: "… and don't let it out."

The second generation may get symptoms and disorders like learning difficulties, maybe without severe personality disorders.

For the third generation the event that originated the secret in the ancestors' family becomes unthinkable. Third generation children perceive certain feelings, actions, and distortions that have a family origin as weird, and are unable to recognise and perceive them as traces and consequences of a family secret.

Besides learning difficulties, the disorders characterizing this generation are as severe as psychotic disorders and severe mental retardation, as well as antisocial behaviour and drug addiction.

After the third generation, couple or family secrets tend to fade away, but they also leave room for new secrets fostered by the new generations …

A hypothesis: typology of couples and secrets

For a psychodynamic diagnosis of the structure of personality, we know and use Bergeret's (1974) criteria, which are basically centered on four factors:

1. the nature of the hidden anxiety
2. the modality of object relations
3. the main defence mechanisms
4. the modalities of the habitual expression of the symptom.

And we know Otto Kernberg's (1984) criteria, which mostly concern the level of identity integration, the defensive actions normally used, and the capacity for analysing reality.

For a couple's typology we can distinguish different ways of functioning:

- fusional-symbiotic
- defensive
- depraved.

Additionally, Eiguer (1998) helps us to identify a structural couple diagnosis:

- normal or neurotic
- anaclitic or depressive
- narcissistic
- depraved.

As regards family secrets, Tisseron (1999, 2002) shows us a first difference between *secrets* and *false secrets* or open secrets, whereas Racamier (1995) has left us with a rich distinction between *libidinal secrets* (or open secrets) and *antilibidinal secrets* (or closed secrets), or secrets of incestualitè (incestuousness), but—up to now—no one has gone so far as to state clearly a complete typology of family or couple secrets.

Above all, we do not know if and to what extent a direct connection between a couple's specific psychic functioning and a specific couple or family secret can be assumed.

From this point of view, just like Bergeret's and Kernberg's criteria used for an individual structural diagnosis, a couple's or family's secret is a psychic concept we can consider as a further element at our disposal when defining a couple's specific functioning and structure.

In order to enlarge and organise a classification of couple/family secrets, besides distinguishing between true and false secrets as well as normal and pathological ones, it is also useful to provide space for the ideas of libidinal and antilibidinal secrets as defined by Racamier.

In a very intriguing way, he wrote that *libidinal secrets* deal with sex, try to tell us about pleasure, are interested in the origins and contribute to the primal thought; and that cookery and bedroom secrets are the secrets of pleasure and again that libidinal secrets act as links among family psyches. It is through them that knowledge and connivance, messages and fantasies are passed on; they establish links among themselves, and it is just in this—rather than in their subject-matter—that their libidinal property lies, and finally that this way libidinal secrets stand surely for our personal psychic intimacy—which English people charmingly call privacy. It is thanks to them that an intimacy which is not hostile to that of other people is safeguarded. In them we can find the ambiguous and yet so precious property of being both individual and collective, of both being kept and handed on (Racamier, 1995).

In contrast, *antilibidinal secrets* are closed and obstructive, as they break off the links between generations, they enclose the space for thinking, they hinder thought and foster the untold.

Racamier (ibid.) warns us that these are secrets of incest. Their main function is hiding the origins, working in this way for narcissistic seduction and its full version: as the thread connecting us to our origins has been cut, narcissistic seduction plays the lord and master.

Another main characteristic of these secrets is being really paradoxical and constraining, as they—besides being rooted in denial—have got a strong power of constraint.

Still Racamier (ibid.) points out how all that is cryptic, or told/untold in libidinal secrets is the outcome of a double affirmation. But, like all that is strong paradoxical and contra-ambiguous, what is shown or hidden in secrets of incest is the outcome of a double denial: these secrets aren't any less utterable than they are discreet.

Anti-libidinal secrets have two possible starting points. They stem from:

1. a shameful or criminal death, which has not been worked through, or
2. a transgression, incest being the main one, closely followed by sexual harassment.

In these circumstances, when thinking, imagining, associating ideas and looking for the truth is not allowed, the object-secret becomes encrypted. It can no longer be touched upon.

In particular, in Racamier's opinion (ibid.), it is prohibition that organises the untold in secrets of incest. If knowing is not allowed, not knowing is equally forbidden: such is the twofold constraint of what is incestuous. We have already seen this double constraint at work in incest proper: let us not forget that incest prevents one from seeking pleasure as well as from refusing it. The objects of incest cannot but enlarge this principle, applying it to the exchange as well as to knowledge.

Going back to the first hypothesis, that is, the possibility of a direct connection between a given couple relationship and a specific kind of secret, here it is fundamental to detect and try to establish a kind of typology of couple and family secrets. This is actually a task wonderfully begun by Racamier and by Tisseron, and later resumed by other authors, amongst whom we will mention Taccani (2005) and Drigo, Monari, and Taccani (2005).

On this behalf, after resuming the useful distinctions between libidinal and antilibidinal secrets formulated by Racamier—which can be considered to be evolutionary and anti-evolutionary as well—and after extending them thanks for further contributions, we have shaped a typology of family secrets.

Rather than distinguish between libidinal and antilibidinal secrets as before, we would rather differentiate and name couple and family secrets again: let us explain about *productive secrets*, having a positive, evolutionary characteristic, and *toxic secrets*, which have a dysfunctional, pernicious tone: both of them are listed in the typology that follows.

Typology of couple and family secrets

Productive secrets:

- *secrets regarding one's origins*
- *secrets regarding sex* (couple intimacies, adultery, homosexuality)
- *secrets regarding death* (traumatic death, a partner's death and the other one's survival)
- *intragenerational secrets regarding the couple's relationship* (modality of the couple's meeting, modality and reasons for the couple's parting).

Toxic secrets:

- *secrets of incestualité* (incestuousness)
- *secrets of incest*
- *secrets regarding death* (shameful, criminal)
- *secrets regarding one's origins* (heterological artificial insemination, adoption, pathological hereditary defects, the secret regarding sterility, the secret of the biological non-couple couple, the secret regarding a biological mother's refusal or rejection of her child
- *pseudo-secrets* or *open secrets*.

At this point, taking into account of the couple's typology suggested by Eiguer (1998), it becomes natural to assume that a neurotic couple comes into existence and develops through libidinal secrets, whereas an anaclitic as well as a psychotic couple keeps mainly antilibidinal secrets, and likewise a depraved couple can make use of antilibidinal secrets in order to maintain a blocking of thought and of the partners' differentiation.

In this perspective, the first basic hypothesis can be outlined this way:

Neurotic couple	Anaclitic couple	Psychotic couple	Depraved couple
Productive secrets	Toxic secrets	Toxic secrets	Toxic secrets
Normal secrets	Secrets of incestualitè (incestuousness)	Secrets of incestualitè (incestuousness)	Secrets of incestualitè (incestuousness)
Regarding one's origins	Secrets of incest	Secrets of incest	Secrets of incest
Regarding sex	Pathological secrets	Pathological secrets	Pathological secrets
	Regarding one's origins	Regarding origins	Regarding one's origins
Regarding death	Regarding death	Regarding death	Regarding death
Regarding couples Relationship	Open secrets	Open secrets	Open secrets

Observing and disclosing a secret

As for couple and family secrets, we know that a therapist must take great care at the observation and detection of the presence of a secret, and most of all for its effects and functions in the environment of the couple's or family relationships.

The content of the secret is not so important, as its disclosure neither modifies nor nullifies the effects of the secret itself or the failure to work through a bereavement which originates the secret—as Racamier (1995) reminds us—nor does it affect the psychic area at the root of an antilibidinal secret based on denial, projection, and splitting, on a thought's interdiction and on symbiotical relationship.

With the same view, Taccani (2005) and her colleagues confirm how naïve and oversimplifying it is to believe that disclosing the secret is enough to stop its evil influence: what has originated the pathology is not so much the hidden content of the secret as the acquisition of a modality of non-thought, the identification with a family mental apparatus characterised by modalities of ejection, expulsion, splitting, and denial, and a kind of ties without individual space and differentiation. Similar examples concern incest and intrafamiliar abuse, in which two people are bound to secrecy by violence or fear, but there is a third person who does not see and stops on the edge of a secret, giving space to it.

Regarding the clinical observation of family and couple secrets, therapists are confronted with partners who spontaneously disclose a secret—sometimes coming straight to the point during the first sessions—in this way entrusting the therapist with it.

This modality of disclosure answers to a number of needs and implies some positive effects for a patient who keeps a secret, like a need for relief and release from an inner paralysis of thought, but also a need for communication, a need to break a psychic and relational barrier, and maybe a need to re-establish different, less tightly closed communications with the family circle.

Concerning this point, Tisseron (1999) thinks that those who keep a family secret had better disclose it than keep it, just because of the ensuing relief and communicative effects, while he however admits that these effects do not wipe out the suffering and the disorders the secret has caused, which is why he also recommends a certain caution when being confronted with the choice regarding the release of a secret. Above all, he warns us against the consequences of brutally disclosing a secret, which usually happens when the secret is not disclosed by a protagonist but by someone outside the family: there is a short circuiting of thought, together with a feeling and fear of going mad for those before whom the secret has been kept so far.

So, as therapists, we perceive the necessity of proceeding with the utmost caution when we approach a couple's or family secret as well as with regards to the meaning and advantages of disclosing it. In Tisseron's opinion (ibid.) a secret is like the unconscious. As regards the place where we thought we found the secret, it always seems to be elsewhere. It follows that the uncertainty connected with a family secret can never be removed.

Still, Tisseron thinks that the only certainty the therapists confronted with a family secret is their ability to express their perception regarding the secret in general, that is, being able to say one day someone hid something to spark off a voicing of experiences and the questions regarding the secret itself as well as of bereavement and depression it hides.

Defontaine (1996) in turn tells us how the disclosure of a family secret and the ensuing therapeutic work on the one hand has set in motion his patient's significant energies supporting a psychic evolution and change but, on the other hand, has created the danger of a paralysing anguish and has also caused an interruption of the analysis.

In particular, the secret—disclosed in the context of a *lapsus* of the patient—partly concerns the death of an overdose, or the suspected suicide, of a twinbrother who was a drugaddict, at the bottom of which lies an expelled family bereavement with which the parents have entrusted the patient and which she has been unable to work through completely. But this first family problem was hiding another one, a secret of incest regarding an incestuous twin relationship between the patient and her brother.

Defontaine finds a paradoxical nature in family secrets and in working with secrets; in particular the disclosing of a family secret implies paradoxical effects for the patients as well as the danger of the interruption of an analysis, because the therapeutic work represents an inner menace, the danger of destroying the inner family organisation, as in the clinical case described and investigated by the French psychoanalyst, who finishes by saying that in order to be herself, the patient has to get rid of her internal objects that are parasites on her ego but, just because she is herself, she is in danger of undoing her self because her ego contains her internal objects; the paradox lies in the very disclosure of the secret (Defontaine, 1996).

Working through bereavement and dealing with secrets

Concerning bereavement, Racamier (1992) has developed and presented the concept of *primary bereavement*, meant as a psychic process thanks to which the ego gives up the complete possession of the object, and works through the bereavement of an absolute, narcissistic union.

This primary bereavement allows those who work through it to reach a *relative immunity,* which means a relative strenght to cope with future bereavements.

Racamier (ibid.) says that going through the primary bereavement allows one to believe either in the object and in oneself and to invest in both of them, and it also enables the subject to have enough confidence in the world and in life, in the object and in him/herself.

This way a bereavement becomes feasible if, on a previous occasion, it was possible to go through the primary bereavement mentioned above, and if the individual makes use of several psychic instruments of the ego such as defence mechanisms, a capability to cope, a mental and practical collection of memories, and the capability of putting on hold and to make new investments.

As therapists, in clinical practice we can see that the ego is not always able to go through a bereavement and will instead develop a depression. In these cases, what Racamier has defined as *expelled bereavement or depression* occurs, which falls onto the family circle.

In the clinical practice we can also see how a lot of people, unable to cope with bereavement, carry out anti-bereavement defences, such as denial and splitting.

This way the bereavement, denied and split off, is distorted and frozen in one's psyche; once it is no longer fantasised about, it forms an amalgam, a psychic inner object that will mostly be spelled out whithin the family circle, through transfer modalities like dilemma and paradox.

Racamier points out that, where this process of expulsion of the bereavement is in force, in which there is also an attack at one's origins and thought, two realities develop: the *secret* and *incest.*

Racamier (1995) has wondered a lot about how to treat secrets of incestualitè (incestuousness): is it necessary to purge the patient's mind of them as if they were distressing memories? Or take them out as if they were obstructive tumours? He found that these are useless temptations, because any secret we sift through is immediately replaced by another one as secrets cluster together and constitute a register which its holders consider an insurance of survival.

In the therapeutic process, whatever the settings, it is essential to stick to the well-known rule of not attacking secrets directly; a rule which, by the way, must not reduce us to impotence. Actually we have two important resources, which are interpretative (ibid.): they are *the illusion of everlastingness*, a powerful resource which works for secrets, and *the prohibition to know and to tell*.

Racamier recommends showing the reason why the secret is forbidden to those who hold a family secret and are afraid of knowing and telling, but also telling them that this prohibition goes back to a long time ago and gets lost in the dim and distant past.

But all this is not enough: you have to perform two tasks, both with the patient and with the family:

- *to treat the sores* connected with the secret itself, which are full of shame and bereavements
- *to re-establish the texture of the origins*.

When viewing the original family and the antecedents in a historical perspective, it is necessary to tie a thread again that had broken off: whether this historicisation is not completely faithful or whether it is a mixture of truth and legend is of little consequence. For this point, the works of Vittorio Cigoli and his colleagues' works are of great significance (2006; Cigoli & Tamanza, 2009).

It is through this first approach to the resistance connected to secrets—and having such therapeutic targets as working through bereavement and the shame connected with secrets and their historicisation—that it is sometimes possible to move from the field of anti-libidinal, anti-evolutionary, and closed secrets to that of libidinal, evolutionary, and open ones.

In particular, Racamier, confronted with patients who are incest victims and whom he defines as "incested"—after working through, in transference, the anxiety and depression deriving from the incests suffered, the forced secrets, from being discredited—dwells upon the importance of a therapeutic intervention aiming at a narcissistic restoration and rebirth, by offering a qualifying shell, by highlighting the person's cleverness and worth to them, by recognizing the *genuineness* of his/her experience. Only then will this person be able to return to life being his true self (Racamier, 1995): it is with this basic confidence and hope that Racamier cheers us up when we are confronted with the difficult therapy of secrets.

In turn Caillot confirms that, when working on family secrets, the secret must be restrained together with its emotional and paradoxical effects.

Inside an individual psychoanalytic treatment, the incested person's push to free themselves from the secret's paradoxical grasp is generally stronger and more favourable.

Inside a family psychoanalytic treatment, where a secret of incestualitè (incestuousness) or of incest does exist, that secret is very difficult to be worked through because the family is an anti-oedipal one, in which separation and differentiation, generation gaps, differences in sex and role and among individual needs cannot be tolerated.

In Caillot's opinion (1996), the core of the job is turning incestuous behaviour or a behaviour of incestualitè into anti-oedipal fantasies which means a move towards anti-oedipal "ben temperati" fantasies, in which there is a recognition of the other one and an evolutionary separation can be tolerated, favouring the development of an oedipal area.

Clinical cases: preliminary remarks

The clinical observation of couples has enabled us to highlight how the couple's relational background seems to be a favourite domain to develop *secrets between the members of a couple* but also *couple secrets*, both intragenerational and transgenerational.

Because of a gradient in the effect of their function, we might distinguish between productive and toxic secrets, meaning that they can help or poison the psychic development of the couple and of the following generations.

Starting from the typology of a couple, it comes naturally to us to think that it is feasible to study a *typology of secrets* in depth, first masterfully structured first by Racamier in 1992, to be exploited as a factor in defining the different ways in which a couple functions.

Some questions seem especially relevant to us: can a given kind of couple secret be considered a specific factor for a given kind of couple?

Can we consider a couple secret as a kind of defence of the couple itself?

Is there a correspondence between the importance of the function of a couple secret and the effect it has on the way the couple functions?

As regards possible couple secrets, their investigation is not only fruitful from a diagnostic viewpoint as an analysis of the couple's structure, but also as regards the detection of its transference and countertransference implications, which is significant, significant in this way when a therapeutic treatment—*a custom-made treatment*—needs to be defined for each couple.

From this perspective further questions arise: in what clinical contexts do we, as therapists and guarantors, witness the birth and existence of a couple's secret?

How to treat it and look after it?

What's the point of disclosing a couple's secret, and what dangers does it involve?

As to this last question, several authors, among them S. Taccani, warn us that disclosing the secrets will effect the couple's getting trapped even further, rather than an improvement in the couple's functioning.

In fact, therapists may be dazzled and fascinated by a couple's secret, but they also risk getting lost in a maze.

We are going to present three clinical cases of couples in support and as an evidence of the clinical theories regarding secrets and of the doubts arising from them.

The second clinical case in particular is based on a secret regarding the origins and belongs to an existing clinical case record that we define as *couples' new secrets* which can be seen in the context of the recent evolution of procreative medicine.

In this couple the woman has had an artificial insemination, which is a more and more common clinical event today, just like the transplantation of fertilised egg cells.

Procreative medicine represents a prospective clinical context in which the couple's new secrets are based and develop; secrets regarding insemination which the partners decide to keep maintaining the secret of insemination, as a *secret regarding the origins* (and an intergenerational secret), with their own offspring, their parents, and the whole family and social circle.

The next clinical cases of couples represent an opportunity to discover the complexity involved when facing the origin of a couple's secrets, their functions, and their relational nature, and live some of the aforegoing questions open for the years to come.

Clinical cases: a secret of incest

In this married couple, which can partially be defined as an *anaclitic couple*, the husband is married for the second time (from his first marriage he has two daughters with whom he has been unable to keep a good rapport because he has been hindered by his former wife). His current wife went through a traumatic childhood and adolescence.

In particular, after being looked after for some years by her grandmother, whose loss she hasn't fully mourned yet, she lived in a religious boarding school together with her three sisters, since her parents had migrated abroad.

From thirteen to twenty years of age she was forced to submit to sexual abuse from her father.

She says she is certain that her sisters also went through the same traumatic experiences, but it is a taboo subject.

When she was fifteen, her mother attempted suicide by swallowing drugs after an induced abortion.

When she was twenty, unable to decide whether to report her father to the police, the patient ran away from home, after organizing her escape (she had previously found a job and had rented a flat in a far-off town). After arriving at her destination, she rang her mother up to ask her to "take care of my sisters, I will look after myself".

Confronted with this inacceptable escape, her father prevented her from returning to her home as well as from keeping in touch with her mother and sisters ("I met my mother and my sisters secretly ... it was the happiest period").

This escape set in motion family quarrels as well as led to the sisters' disclosing their secret regarding the incest they had suffered from, and a subsequent quarrel between mother and father ("My mother wanted to separate from him, but then nothing happened").

Sexual abuse has not been talked about in the original family ever since: the female partner of the couple we are dealing with has not revealed her family secret either to her relatives or to her husband, as she has been parlayzed by fears and fantasies of being abandoned by the latter.

She looks up to him as an ideal husband, she sees him as a quiet, sympathetic person and from him she gets a child, this way having her dream—to marry and to have children of her own—come true.

It is the wife who starts the therapy, after developing anorexia associated with bulimia, an uncontrollable urge for gorging herself with food followed by vomiting and physical as well as psychic exhaustion, together with a severe depression with suicidal danger and a partial identity of suffering of a stain that cannot be removed: all this happening while there is a hidden clash with her employer and her husband is changing jobs (from a day to a night job).

Since the first therapeutic sessions, the patient has been spontaneously disclosing her family secret, as if to leave it with the therapist, since she has no tools to handle it, afraid of speaking of it to her husband, before whom she feels ashamed and has fantasies of being abandoned.

But it is not for this reason that she objects to sharing her secret through the therapist's function of conjunction and mediation in the couple during some couple interviews.

On the one hand the revelation of her secret has relieved the patient by eliminating her fantasies of abandonment and shame before her husband, who has proved empathetic, further reinforcing the couple attachment in this way; on the other—at least at the beginning—it has not reduced the anorexia symptoms nor has it loosened the couple's anaclitic relationship.

It has been possible to observe a tendency for a pause in the patient's bulimic behaviour, chiefly when her anaclitic needs are satisfied, that is when also her husband is also present during his free time, for example at weekends or during the holidays. Concerning this difficulty in governing her affection, at first the wife is ambivalent, as she recognises only in part this psychic and relational functioning of hers only partially and rather tends to a predominantly defensive attitude of denial, collusively backed by her husband.

During the individual therapeutic process, the patient achieves a partial working through of her father's past sexual abuses, of her real parental imago (uncritical and united in their denial and interdiction of thought), managing to carve out a larger niche for individuation and differentiation, and developing—as far as she can—a greater psychic and emotional autonomy.

At first she kept fostering hopes of her parents' (especially her mother's) aknowledgement of her own personal, familiar, and professional realisation, whereas later she has gradually freed herself from these compensatory needs as well as from her needs for a family indemnity.

Regarding her profession, she has liberated herself from a regressive, child is hattitude of complaining about her employer's moral and financial lack of acknowledgement, asking for—and getting—a rise in salary after ten years of loyal work, and—above all—she has moved on and has found a new job. Bacause of this she is now in a position to experience genuine appreciation of and praise for her abilities and her way of working from her superiors, in addition getting a further increase in her wages.

As regards her married life, it remains by and large idealised but, at first, also very painfully—mostly as regards her sex life, which was the scenery of traumatic incest traces of the past—the patient has also been able to gradually find a new life as a couple.

In her inner world, the patient has had meaningful dreams:

- as a child, together with her mother and father, she goes to the psychologist who invites her father to give her a biscuit, but the patient cries her eyes out so the psychologist explains that the mother herself must understand that the daughter refuses her father …
- she dreams that her father rapes her again …
- she has a dream in which she tells her mother about her father's sexual abuses, but the mother pretends not to hear and does not answer her
- finally a recurring dream in which she is unable to find the car she had previously parked …

Nowadays the patient seems no longer to be developing herself based on a wounded identity, as in the past, made of suffering from a stain that cannot be removed, and for which she alone carries the responsibility.

Transference and countertransference

At first the patient—but also the couple, during some therapeutic sessions—got in touch with the therapist showing her need for help in keeping depressive experiences in check, above all showing a particular desperation as well as the need to tell what was on her mind, that is to unload upon the therapist the traumatic burden of her past, of her suffering which grew stronger during every session.

The transference was partly also based both on salvable expectations and trust in the therapist and—as highlighted in the first dream—on persecutory anxieties caused by the father and projected onto the therapist.

On the other hand, the initial countertransference was mainly based on feelings of pain and on reparatory feelings, but also on feelings of uncertainty, impotence, and fear as regards a certain depressive, pernicious atmosphere.

While both the patient and the couple were growing more free and autonomous, a countertransference developed, based on feelings of respect and affection towards the patient, but also of confidence in the shared therapeutic work.

Typology of the couple and its secret

This couple seems to present the characteristics of an *anaclitic couple*. *Regarding the secret* we find *a family secret having an evil origin*, in particular a *secret of incest*.

In this couple, we might say that, disclosing the family secret in the second generation without disclosing it inside the original family that was the depository of the secret, has enabled the daughter, a member of the second generation, to partially free herself from an antilibidinal, anti-evolutionary condition and to consolidate the couple's relationship, with partial excursions into the libidinal, evolutionary field.

Working through bereavement and dealing with the secret

In a therapeutic perspective and in light of the theoretical and clinical contributions examined so far, some considerations and remarks come naturally.

In particular, in this first clinical case concerning a secret of incest, one can see how the patient—during the individual psychotherapy—has been quite able to approach and work through her childhood and adolescence ruined by incest, as well as to face her depression.

In this sense, revealing the secret to her husband during some couple sessions has enabled the patient to feel relieved and to free herself from a secret that lay heavy upon her, causing anxiety and the fear of being abandoned by him, a secret which shut her out and estranged her from a husband-and-wife relationship. We may also assume that disclosing the secret to her husband has also helped the patient's further progress in the working through of her pathological original family as well as her being able to consolidate a major mutual investment in the husband-and-wife relationship.

Thus, through an individual therapeutic approach in combination with some couple sessions, the patient has partially freed herself from her original family, confining her experiences and sufferings to the past.

It is possible, indeed to assume that her evil, antilibidinal incest secret has transformed and weakened to make room for a fruitful, evolutionary, and libidinal field.

Clinical cases: the secret of the origins in a couple that is separating

The couple we are now going to deal with develops from the ashes of each partner's disappointment.

He divorced his first wife, who bore him a child with whom he says he has experienced a formal, distant relationship, without investing in his affective relationship, his parental role or his responsibilities.

In contrast to this, she suffered a great deal because of a relationship with a schoolmate opposed by her mother.

At the beginning the couple is getting over an infidelity of the man, because the he—unbeknown to his partner—has resumed a triangular relational reality.

Actually he seems that he has not completely parted with his former wife, and has been experiencing recurring separations and reunions with her for some years.

After a while he reveals to his new partner his skeleton in the cupboard and the couple goes through this crisis by means of acting out, that is, through the couple's non-choice/choice of getting married.

At first the married couple experienced an anaclitic relationship of mutual understanding and support, in which the wife had conflictual feelings of separation from her original family, mostly feeding on the relationship with her husband.

Later on they decide to have a baby, resorting to in vitro fertilization because, in the past, the husband had undergone a vasectomy.

After a first failure of the in vitro fertilization, the wife develops an oncological illness, which she goes through and interprets as caused by the hormone treatment necessary for the fertilization, without any other search for a meaning, even a psychic meaning, in the context of her life.

In particular, there hasn't been any intermediary space of time to think over this cancer and to assume that, even if partially, it could be a somatic answer in the context of a partial bereavement not worked through (this being the husband's secret relationship with the former partner) which was at the heart of her marriage plan.

She is successfully treated with surgery.

Against the gynaecologist's opinion, the couple gives up further attempts of in vitro fertilisation and, acting out once more, agrees on a pregnancy based on heterologous fertilization that is artificial insemination with thw sperm of another man.

This choice is felt by the wife to be a sacrifice and a love token from her husband, but also as a confirmation of the strength of their marriage tie. As for the husband, we assume that his choice not to father a child may be a prohibition to his own generational identity, as he is jammed by the couple's collusive secret.

When a daughter was born from the artificial fertilization, the parents decided not to reveal the secret regarding the fertilization, either to their daughter or their original families.

Some years later, during a second session due to a marriage crisis, the wife entrusted her therapist with the secret.

This new conjugal clash had developed from a change in the balance of the relationship between the partners, and came to light through the wife's investment in social and professional commitments barely tolerated by the husband.

The husband started having persecutory and interpretative doubts, as well as fits of anger and jealousy, going so far as to watch his wife's movements and to shadow her.

Little by little the conjugal relationship became incurable, in spite of the couple'sinitial anxiety over the prospect of separation, especially the husband's.

Eventually the husband left home and the partners started to live separately: the husband experienced quite a lot of difficulties—something which he denied—in accepting and working through this separation.

Both, first the wife and then—as if in response to it—the husband have established new love relationships, something that antibereavement functions would easily presage.

At first the partners—during some couple sessions centered on their parental role and on their daughter's origin—proved adequately collaborative as a parental couple, even if only on and off. Indeed they proved united and determined to keep their couple secret regarding their daughter's genetic origin (heterologous fertilisation), without calling into question their choice or its psychic implications for the daughter.

At first this daughter born of a secret—confronted with her parents' separation as requested by her mother—showed understandable distress. She had some trouble sleeping in her own bed, as if to protect and look after her sad, anxious mother.

But, what is more important, for a long time she refused to go and sleep in the paternal house, which may be interpreted as a trace of the secret kept by her parents, as well as her capability to perceive her father's shady relational atmosphere towards her.

Even their daughter's refusal didn't shake the parents' decision regarding their couple secret, because it created no willingness to think over or to wonder about their daughter's sufferings and doubts.

The father has also moved into another flat where, for his daughter, there is no room but a small area in the living room, a non-space the daughter tries to adjust to, but she suffers and she may have further questions that she takes great care not to ask.

Transference and countertransference

We might define the couple's transference as a conflict transference as it offers further room for conjugal conflict. An incurable couple conflict—based on a mutual acting up and, especially regarding one partner, on the denial of his shared responsibility as well as his persecutory misinterpretations and defenses—proves to be founded also in the couple's transference.

In one of the partners, whom we may think of as having a psychotic core, the prevailing transference is constituted of a severe strain with projective, persecutory experiences towards the therapist, with a clear acting out, for instance when interrupting—at its very start—a session centered on the parental couple, similar to the persecutory attitude assumed by the same partner in the couple relationship.

The countertransference which followed was characterised by feelings of impotence, fear, and uneasiness: the patient was unable to think freely or with pleasure and curiosity because a condition of alarm was prevalent.

Relief prevailed on the one hand when the couple came to a judicial separation, after violent conflicts had been revived during the interviews with the counselors, as well as on the other hand a deep concern for the daughter of this couple in separation, on whose future life quite a lot of psychic suffering will lie heavily.

Typology of the couple and its secret

Just like the previous couple discussed, this one also seems to show the prevailing characteristics of an anaclitic couple: in this case one partner, who exploits such massive defenses as projection and the denial of reality, also reveals psychotic features.

We can notice an intragenerational couple secret, which can be characterised as evil and antilibidinal, and which is a secret of the origins regarding the daughter's birth through artificial heterologous fertilization.

As therapists, we should wonder what the functions of this secret are and what will be its consequences, which will fall upon the daughter to bear, in other words on the second generation.

A possible function of this couple's secret may be to enable husband and wife—on their way to separation, but also after getting divorced—to preserve, as far as possible, a parental relationship, which might otherwise be in danger of breaking up, as the separation of the couple might turn into a separation of the parents and, above all, into a transgenerational separation between the father and his daughter.

This way a repetition could be triggered off in the father's history, that is, his incapacity to steadily keep his fatherly role and responsibility steadily.

All this leads us, as therapists, into the temptation of gathering the meaning of this paternal functioning, by means of a historicization of the partner's original family, and perhaps of finding out further family secrets but—following Racamier's saying—let us not get into a dead end: which of us has never been tempted to sift through the heap of secrets that keep letting us see some more? This match is lost from its beginning!

Working through bereavement and dealing with the secret

In this second clinical case—characterised by a secret of the origins, that is, the birth of a daughter through artificial heterologous fertilization—introducing couple sessions with a prevailing observation of the parental couple, in order to try to make room for thinking about the meaning of this couple's secret and its consequences, which will lie heavily on the daughter, has enabled us to see how strong and stubborn the secret over their daughter's origin is.

It comes naturally to us to assume that this evil secret, in this couple that is getting separated, has got an important function in keeping—as much as possible—a tie as a parental couple and one of filiation between father and daughter, which otherwise may run the risk of breaking.

For the daughter, in contrast, there is a prospective evidence of a secret between her parents, to her detriment.

An antilibidinal, anti-evolutionary secret persists and prevails in this couple, which—at least in this period of their life—cannot be transformed.

As a conclusion to this couple's clinical case, in which it is possible to highlight a secret that can be defined as a new couple secret regarding the origins (heterologous fertilization), we think it useful to mention another clinical case, which is a way mirrors it.

In this case the female partner of the couple had undergone a heterologous egg fertilization, experiencing a pregnancy full of maternal feelings but also full of unease regarding this heterologous origin, which the couple has kept secret both from the family circle and from the child she was expecting at the time.

The partners' intention was to tell their son about his origins, but they were uncertain and baffled concerning the when and how, and reached a dead end regarding the know-how of their couple secret (even in this case regarding their son's origins) which had defensive functions and which could be defined as a new couple secret.

In this clinical context, the therapist—following Racamier's advice not to attack secrets directly—has respected the partners' choice to temporarily keep their couple secret, gradually working through, with one of the partners, the bereavements and the narcissistic defenses involved.

Clinical cases: an open secret

Suddenly and unexpectedly in this couple a secret breaks out from the husband, who finds himself obliged to reveal it when charged with sexual harassment to the detriment of a young, psychically handicapped adult.

In retrospective, after the birth of their children, husband and wife had had no sexual intercourse for years, in a kind of collusion and conspiracy of silence, without breathing a word about their fantasies, as they were afraid of hurting and distressing each other: the wife tried to compensate for her grief by finding new opportunities for social work and in religious faith, whereas the husband withdrew into silence and secrecy, as he was becoming aware of a latent homosexuality, which he had not acted out for a long time.

The husband's family history is incomplete: he was left motherless soon after being born and the cause of his mother's death is unknown. At the same time, he has never met his father, who seems to have been addicted to drinking. When he was a baby, he was looked after in a cradle, then he grew up in two religious boarding schools, until he met his wife-to-be and her family, by whom he felt warmly welcomed, we might say nearly adopted.

This couple's secret—the husband's latent homosexuality—may be considered as a false secret, a so-called open secret, which actually hides a further, more burdensome one, started in and constituted by the husband's original family.

We might outline and define this family secret as a secret of the origins, which involves an untold story concerning his siblings, about whose existence the patient found out only when he was an adult.

Through initial individual sessions, alternated with couple sessions, husband and wife have been able to broach their own shock as a couple, caused by the above-mentioned charge against the husband.

What is more important, the partners have consolidated their tie by acknowledging and sharing past reciprocal responsibilities and collusions based on silence and on the untold, experiencing mutual feelings of shame and guilt—mostly felt by the husband—and, at first, on the wife's part, also of anger and then of sorrow and joint responsibility.

Joining couple sessions has favoured the birth of a space for conjugal evolution and enabled each partner to partially work through the loss of the couple's own Self.

This change has turned into a consolidation of their tie as a couple, recreating their care for mutual needs, except for sexual intimacies.

In particular, the couple has invested its future in a new, shared, professional project, this way building up a new, possible couple identity.

Transference and countertransference

As for this couple, we have been able to notice a transference consisting of feelings of shame and guilt, especially on the part of the husband, who—at first-transferred past experiences of moral blame on to the therapist, so that the therapist was perceived as a judge.

Later a transference developed, full of the hope of receiving help and relief from the therapist, perceived as a depository and point of reference in the change of the family's distress and suffering.

At first the countertransference was permeated by a feeling of danger, with fantasies of self-destruction acting out on the husband's part, but also of sadness and pain for the him and, above all, for the relatives.

Surprisingly, in the end a countertransference has occurred, which can be defined as a feeling of satisfaction for the couple's improvement, made possible by the husband's acting out of guilt and responsibility but also of tolerance and sharing on the wife's part: both husband and wife have been the authors of the couple's progress and growth.

Typology of the couple and its secret

This couple seems to belong to a typology having a mainly psychotic functioning. The married couple have turned their initial antilibidinal nature into a partially libidinal, evolutionary one.

The intragenerational couple secret, which could be better describe as the husband's untold story regarding his homosexual tendencies, looks rather like a false secret.

This *open secret* hails back to a secret of the origins started by the previous generation, that is the parents and their family circle, together with a possible collusion from the patient's reception centers during his childhood and adolescence.

Working through bereavement and dealing with the secret

In this third clinical case, concerning an open secret protecting a secret of the origins, individual sessions with the patient together with some couple sessions have acted as a background for transformation, a space where to face, together with the patient, the bereavement of his original family, and a subsequent depression at the age of development.

It has been possible to give a meaning to his frail sexual identity and to the couple's secret, as they were intertwined with and originating in a previous family secret of the origins.

From an antilibidinal, anti-thought, and anti-fantasy register, on which the open secret and the previous secret of the origins were based, this married couple—also thanks to their positive prognostic factor concerning the absence of evil toxic elements—has changed. Eventually they proceeded towards an evolutionary, libidinal process of transformation in which it is not the law of acting out which is in force, but the law of words, of thought, of emotional needs and mutual appreciation, of the necessity of a space for the couple's relationship and its revitalization.

Conclusions

The clinical observation of the couple has enabled us to explore and study the dimension of couple secrets in depth and, most of all, to highlight a new clinical truth concerning those couples who turn to procreative medicine.

Starting from old couple secrets (of the origins, of incestualitè, or incestuousness, etc.) up to the new couple secrets (of the origins, concomitant with procedures of heterologous fertilization), it seems quite obvious but nevertheless fundamental advice to notice their complexity especially in regards to the first contacts and the necessary support we, as therapists, have to give. From this perspective, the know-how concerning both old and new secrets seems to us to be still undergoing a process of definition and completion.

From a diagnostic viewpoint, some questions (and their in-depth analyses) have seemed useful to us: can a couple's secret be specific to a given kind of couple?

Can we think of a couple's secret as constituting a defense of that couple?

Is there a relationship between the severity of a couple's secret and the severity of the couple's malfunctioning?

Contrastingly, for a therapeutic approach, other questions seem relevant: in what clinical context can a couple's secret be noticed?

How can it be treated and handled ?

What's the sense in disclosing a couple's secret, and what risks does this involve?

If, in the individual (and familiar) clinic of psychoses, the therapeutic target detects a family secret and—as far as possible—working through it, in a couple's clinical context our experience has shown how an approach based on a *varying therapeutic position* is necessary when dealing with a couple's secret, especially in regards to new couple secrets.

In confirmation of this, let us remember Racamier's basic rule, which tells us to be very careful when dealing with secrets, which we had better not attack and reveal directly.

In particular, it is not always possible and realistic—at least in a short time—to make a couple's secret mentionable and utterable or possible to elaborate, as we have shown in the second clinical couple case and only touched upon in the subsequent one, both of them concerning a secret of the origins (heterologous fertilization).

In the second clinical case it was useful, as suggested by the therapist, to respect a toxic secret that was the couple's defense, having the function of keeping their parental tie and, above all, of keeping a tie between father and daughter which could otherwise be in danger of falling apart or getting stuck. We believe that, an unveiling of this "new secret couple", we would turn into a "disclosure wild" with this couple that is partly anaclitic and partly psychotic, and which is opposed to disclosing their secret, with persecutory strength and frailty. This separated married couple, which is also a conflicting parental couple, has not allowed a necessary, adequate therapeutic alliance nor does it have adequate capabilities to elaborate and restrain themselves when confronted with their daughter's possible working through of her own origins, and the risk of her getting a depression while still at a developing age, maybe even with psychotic symptoms.

Note

1. Nachin Claude *"Working day about secret"*, Quatrieme Groupe, Organisation Psychanalytique de Langue Française, Lyon (1.11.2003). Unpublished. [translated for this edition].

References

Abraham, N., & Torok, M. (1978). *The Shell and the Kernel: Renewals of Psychoanalysis*. Chicago, IL: University of Chicago Press, 1994.

Bergeret, J. (1974). *La Personalité Normale et Pathologique*. Paris: Bordas.

Caillot, J. -P. (1996). Notes sur la technique du travail avec les secrets de famille. *Groupal*, 2: 165–169.

Castoriadis-Aulagnier, P. (1976). Le droit au secret: condition pour pouvoir penser. *Nouvelle Revue de Psychanalyse, 14*: 141–157.

Cigoli, V. (2006). *L'albero della Discendenza. Clinica dei Corpi Familiari*. Milan, Italy: Franco Angeli.

Cigoli, V., & Tamanza, G. (2009). *L'Intervista Clinica Generazionale*. Milan, Italy: Cortina Raffaello.

Defontaine, J. (1996). Paradoxalité du dévoilement du secret. *Groupal, 2*: 149–164.

Drigo, M. L., Monari, C., & Taccani, S. (2005). Coppie, famiglie e segreti transgenerazionali. In: A. M. Nicolò & G. Trapanese (Eds.), *Quale Psicoanalisi per la Famiglia?* (pp. 246–252). Milan, Italy: Franco Angeli.

Eiguer, A. (1998). *Clinique Psychanalytique du Couple*. Paris: Dunod.

Grimbert, P. (2004). *Un Secret*. Paris: Éditions Grasset et Fasquelle.

Kernberg, O. F. (1984). *Severe Personality Disorders*. New Haven, CT: Yale University Press, 1993.

Lévy-Soussan, P. (2006). *Eloge du Secret*. Paris: Hachette Littératures.

Racamier, P. -C. (1992). *Le Génie des Origines: Psychanalyse et Psychoses*. Paris: Payot.

Racamier, P. -C. (1995). *Inceste et Incestuel*. Paris: Collège de psychanalyse groupale et familiale.

Taccani, S. (2005). Riflessioni sulla trasmissione intergenerazionale e trans generazionale. In: A. M. Nicolò & G. Trapanese (Eds.), *Quale Psicoanalisi per la Famiglia?* (pp. 211–216). Milan, Italy: Franco Angeli.

Tisseron, S. (1999). *Nos Secrets de Famille*. Paris: Éditions Ramsay.

Tisseron, S. (2002). Les ricochets du secret. *Le Coq Heron, 169*: 29–35.

CHAPTER SEVENTEEN

Family myths* and pathological links

Anna Maria Nicolò

Ariela and Beatrice

Beatrice was forty when she was referred to me by an analyst who had held a consultation with her for her adoptive daughter. Her mother's

---

*Anthropologists are the scientists interested in myths. In the late 1950s their research was based on the concept that a myth cannot be understood outside the role it plays inside social communities. For Malinowski (1926), myths establish the foundations of social organisation and represent the charter on which a community is established. According to anthropologists, myths maintain traditions in a society where the past is more important than the present and represent models where the present cannot be but repetition. They also play their function when strong tensions emerge. But it was Ferreira (1963) who first defined family myths from a cognitive purview. Ferreira argues that a family myth is a set of integrated beliefs shared by the whole family concerning its members and their mutual relationships. These beliefs are not denied by the members involved, not even if the existence of the myth requires distortions of reality. A myth, then, differs from the image that a family as a group wants to show to strangers, but, according to Ferreira, is rather a part of the internal image of the group that all members contribute to and try to preserve. The roles and attributions of members in their mutual interactions, although fake and illusory, are accepted by all without anyone daring to challenge or question them. So a myth explains the individual behaviours of family members just as it hides their motives.

279

family had fled from the East to Italy for political reasons when Beatrice was five. Serious financial problems had characterised the patient's otherwise happy youth in a family where all members spoke other languages in addition to their own, as part of a refined upbringing. Beatrice and her family remember that period as a myth-fantasy of an aristocratic and princely family, provided with fabulous riches acquired suddenly after they had moved to that Eastern country, but lost just as suddenly—and this is the actual truth—due to political persecution. They remember how afraid their mother was of getting lost on the steamer on which they crossed the sea to reach Italy, a totally unknown country, although it was the country of origin of the family.

Beatrice's father was a rather manic man with grandiose fantasies aimed at creating an allegedly noble past that contrasted with his occupation in trade. Beatrice had been brought up with somewhat eccentric habits and with contradictory views on the role of women, who on one side were expected to be self-sufficient and well organised, while on the other were demeaned in favour of males, in particular her brother, later affected by serious depression and dying in a mysterious way that hinted at suicide.

After various vicissitudes Beatrice married in late adolescence because she was pregnant, but her parents forced her to abort. This awfully painful early experience was useful in helping her to separate from her contradictory and frustrating family and led her to be "adopted"—in some aspects—by her very young husband's family, in particular by his mother, who performed a structuring function for her.

A few years later she left this adolescent relationship and after a period of autonomy she started the fundamental romantic relationship of her life.

Giovanni, her second husband, lived in the East for professional reasons and was a very well educated person, hailing from an aristocratic family. Having married him, she joined him abroad where the couple decided to adopt a child. Adoption soon became an element of conflict in their marriage, as quite a few problems emerged that had been masked by the heroic investment of the first years.

Giovanni wanted to adopt a preadolescent boy who seemed to have some handicap. Beatrice insisted on a very beautiful little girl who seemed less deprived and inhibited than the other available children. Luckily she got the upper hand.

From this event on, Giovanni's depressive symptoms emerged with greater clarity. They were also evidence of Beatrice's unconscious choice of partner. By choosing that husband, Beatrice had materialised the grandiose aristocratic fantasy that was the basis of her family's history and at the same time continued the relational model and the manic reparation that had characterised her relationships with her ailing father and brother.

A long part of her analysis was dedicated to the elaboration of her mourning for not having been able to conceive a child and to understanding the reasons that led to her adopting a little girl. She could clearly see her anger at having felt that her femininity had been denied by her parents: denied by her father despite her efforts at becoming the efficient son that her brother had never managed to be, denied by her mother whose rejection and jealousy became clearer and clearer, despite Beatrice's moving efforts at being accepted.

In a dream in the second year of treatment, she is in a foreign country and finds an oddly duck-shaped Easter egg and thinks of giving it to her mother. She has only 50,000 lire and she buys the egg although it costs 35,000. She associates thirty-five with the age she was when she adopted Ariela and the duck with her mother who had always been somewhat thick-headed (like a hen, we say in Italian) and had never understood.

To want to give a daughter to her mother, but not being able to do it and thus being obliged to adopt one was one of her main torments.

In addition to her obvious anxiety at having abducted her daughter from her biological parents, Beatrice held a fantasy that Ariela in truth had noble origins. We know how frequent this fantasy is in adopting parents. In this case, however, the fantasy had an organised and articulated character, given the fact that mystery surrounded the girl's date and place of birth. It seemed that Ariela had been found crying in a market place wearing elegant clothes. Ariela's adoptive parents attributed her habits to a previous grand upbringing.

These fantasies, however, colluded with the fantasies Ariela brought into treatment. In fact she had started treatment because she found it very difficult to learn Italian. She continued speaking the "aristocratic" language of her home country, as she did when she happened to be abroad and in her grandmother's family.

Beatrice talked at length about the actual evidence that she thought proved Ariela's princely origins and was upset when she told me that Ariela herself held and cultivated this fantasy.

The girl spent a lot of time drawing matryoshka-like dolls, one inside the other.

In both the mother's and the daughter's sessions it emerged that giving up their original language, considered aristocratic and unusual in Italy, corresponded to giving up their fantasies of a grandiose self and with it the possibility of accepting their real identity, experienced as trivial or commonplace.

The issue of a double identity, one hiding the other, characterised Ariela, who considered herself alternatively as an unreachable princess or as a very poor child who would end up marrying a prince, thus replicating the original myth of her adoptive mother's family.

Comment

I think that this case provides material for reflection on various aspects, but I want to dwell only on one, the myth.

Emigration and the arrival in a new world can influence identity and imply experiences similar to birth that can be catastrophic or depressive, depending on what we choose to privilege between the sense of persistence and continuity and the sense of change from previous experiences. For this reason in these families a mythical organisation has a defensive function, in that it represents a bridge in continuity with the past. A myth is different from a narrative because of its typical features:

1. it is handed down from one generation to the next
2. it is shared by all family members
3. it pertains to issues that contributed to the creation of family identity and therefore of each member's identity
4. despite containing an intact core of reality at its origin, it implies an elaboration often based on mechanisms such as the idealisation of a person, or it plays a superegoic function with each member building his own version of the myth.

A myth therefore contributes to the organisation of the family's fantasy life and represents the memory of an event and of the relationships that allowed it and characterised it.

The most relevant aspect of this case, however, is the reflection it prompts on the link between a transgenerational family myth and an individual myth-fantasy. In this case, the myth of family origins coincides with and affects Ariela's myth of her own origin.

We could probably better define Ariela's fantasies as her "family romance", assuming that both myth and family romance played a protective function for the family and for her. In fact they allowed the processing of the traumatic events that marked the origin of family life and of Ariela's history.

In this case we can clearly see the positive function of a myth as a precursor to elaboration, as I will discuss later, but also the two aspects of the same myth that can be read both ways: on one side we see how easy it is to acquire and to lose wealth and on the other that one cannot accept reality unless it is princely or aristocratic. Beyond this there is only poverty and disaster.

Even when the family myth is shattered, just because it is shattered, it keeps its value and meaning in time. The myth thus becomes the source of a paradox: whoever shatters a myth and seems not to obey it, is also the first one to believe in it and maintain it. The very breach becomes an integral part of the myth.

The function of myths

If we analyse the function of myths in a family, we realise that it is more complex than what has been described by Malinowski and Ferreira. A myth does not only tell a story, but speaks through its narrative. The narrative material that forms the myth is the tool through which a myth communicates. Thus, as Lévi-Strauss (1962) said, it is rather a semiotic object, like a language where "a certain significant material (the narrative) has the function of conveying a certain meaning". For this reason, a myth links different levels of reality and cannot be read only at the anthropological, psychoanalytical, or sociological level. All these levels are present. A myth tells us how reality is made, thought, and perceived.

It also links different levels of reality and its great importance derives from its ability to be a true code between the levels. While a myth seems to describe reality, it also teaches and prescribes[1] how reality should be read (Nicolò, 1987, 1997); it is therefore both a way to convey knowledge of an event and of rules, and a code of behaviour. In this way a narrative or iconic system is turned into a prescriptive system that invests the level of acting (a self-fulfilling prophecy).

In Ariela's myth we can imagine a collective construction. For generations all family members supply their share and, in organising the myth, establish the continuity of culture and the identity of the family, passing on a possibly traumatogenic functioning in pathological situations.

If I had to close the discussion of this aspect here, I would define myth as "a multidimensional structure, a code between levels of reality that starts as an unconscious group fantasy, but in time and with further generations takes up a defensive function and, in pathological situations, a prescriptive function that organises knowledge and prescribes behaviours" (Nicolò, 1987).

As in Ariela's case, a person must confront the myth in order to be born as an individual, to differentiate, and to find personal meanings autonomous from it, as the myth represents a construction of meanings shared by the whole family.

But a myth is not always a looming curse. If we boldly compare this with what Bion (1961, 1965) says about public myths considered as a reservoir from which symbols can be tapped, as a primitive form of preconception, we realise that it is only the meeting of the myth carried on by the family with that specific member, his elaboration skills, and his experience that will produce a specific effect. To borrow Bion's words, myth is a precursor of our knowledge that meeting up with reality gives rise to conception. Its effects do not only depend on the family's functioning but also on each member's personality.

Mythopoietic activity as precursor of knowledge

But what kind of elaboration does myth allow us to make?

Even if a group and a family have a greater capacity for elaborating traumas because they have easier access to the coexistence of more primitive and more evolved levels,[2] this functioning might encounter obstacles. I think that a myth can be a tool for this activity but does not allow a full elaboration, being in itself an obstacle.

To the extent that a family builds a myth starting from a real life event or from a traumatic experience, it is also creating a metaphor with which it tries to master, contain, and represent the powerful emotions characterising that event. I argue, then, that a myth is an effort at elaborating an experience and a trauma and is grafted in the family group when a complete elaboration fails. Myth is an elaboration underway. If the elaboration had been full, a complete digestion, there would be repression, forgetfulness. But, as this is a difficult function, we then use the group as a tool for elaboration and for passing on what we could not elaborate through and across generations.

Enza Pulino Fiderio, quoting Barthes, argues that a myth depletes, distorts, and suspends the sense of an event. We could say that historical (geographic, environmental, temporal) data is cancelled. What is left in its place is a plot, a network of links, "a system of values that becomes a system of facts" (2001, p. 82).

Yet that event could be so disrupting that it completely overwhelms the subject's or the group's ability to contain it. A first containment effort is represented by the myth.

But in a group holes can form in elaboration and can be passed on from one generation to the other. What Granjon (2000)[3] calls "rough objects, containers of negative".

So a myth is a source of identifications, it works through, builds, and rebuilds an experience, a traumatic event and in this way transfigures it, deferring it to further elaborations and further impacts with other experiences.

Let us take another example:

Angela and Filippo had separated years earlier, but never divorced. When therapy started Filippo was living with another woman while Angela lived with their four children: the eldest was a girl, then came Riccardo, the patient for whom treatment was requested.[4]

In a session about one year into treatment, while trying to highlight the conflicting relationships of this family, I stressed how difficult it was for the mother to overcome, even briefly, her depressed, sacrificing attitude as a woman who was ready to give up anything for her family. I said that her attitude reminded me of that of a war widow.

My words made the other family members burst out laughing and the children told me a story that was rarely mentioned at home.

Their maternal grandmother, who had died many years ago, was in reality a war widow. She came from a noble family and had married a handsome and brave young man against her parents' will. He was a very well-known top-rank officer and died in a plane crash after having killed many enemies. The marriage had lasted only a few months during which Angela had been conceived. So, when she was born, she was already an orphan.

All her early life had passed in mourning of this father and when she was a child there was always an empty place set for him at the table.

She had married a handsome and elegant man, but had soon got rid of him because he did not correspond to the over-idealised model of her father. He had complied with his wife's devaluation by progressively losing his working skills.

Riccardo, the son, was a very clever young man. He would have liked to be an artist, but was never satisfied with his work.

The mythical construction of this family, as it appeared in the sessions, could be summarised as follows: in order to be valued and considered, men must be extraordinary heroes, like the grandfather. All other men are passive, impotent, or ill.

The mother held idealised expectations for Riccardo, the first male offspring: what he did had to be extraordinary, superior, but in reality this never happened.

The father was the opposite: he theorised his failure as father, husband, and professional. He kept saying that nothing could be expected of him because, even if he had wanted to give, he was unable to.

Even Ginevra with her marriage had looked for an extraordinary man.

The family's attitude was dismissive, omnipotent, and haughty. This omnipotence made everything useless and unreal. In this environment Riccardo's protest had turned into an omnipotent destructiveness. It was difficult for him to have forms of dependence that were not extraordinary in positive and negative terms. One of his conflicts depended on his family, because in that family one existed only as a hero, but the only possible hero was the grandfather.

Two years after the end of sessions, Angela called me to inform me of something she considered important. She said that she had succeeded in moving her father's corpse from the burial ground of heroes, where it had been since the end of the war, to a small graveyard in their native village, thus giving a ritualistic ending also to her father's myth. I do not know if in doing this the family realised the implications of this removal for their past, but the apparent spontaneity and unexpectedness of the situation seemed to me the best answer to a long process of elaboration that had been completed.

If we go back to the clinical example of a family myth originating with the grandfather, a reckless airman who heroically fought in World War I, bombing enemy positions and landing back in his homeland on the last drop of fuel, we can explore what mechanisms are at work.

In my opinion they are:

a. construction-reconstruction. Each family member in later generations shares in the reconstruction of the grandfather's story and the heroic episode; each member has his own version and thus constructs the myth, every time adding new aspects that do not belong in the original event
b. idealisation of a figure that becomes mythical and is seen as an object for structuring identifications
c. projection of each family member because each member puts aspects of his projection in the myth
d. and, obviously, the most important of all: condensation. We see in fact that one or more characters in the myth, in general the central character, condense different aspects of various figures of that story or experience.

However, the most relevant aspect in the clinical evaluation of myths does not concern their conscious narrative but rather the dimensions that are conveyed unconsciously. Returning to our bold airman, if on one side the myth could convey the identifying definition "the men in this family are heroes and boldly despise dangers", it could also unconsciously convey its apparent opposite: "the men in this family are reckless and bold up to the point of meeting death".

When the family organisation is flexible enough and the individual personality is strong and provided with elaboration skills, the prescriptive aspect of myth is overshadowed and only some aspects are highlighted at the expense of others.

Pathological myths and alienating identifications

We could then state that all families have their own myth. In some families it can play a structuring function, but can be disproved or elaborated or changed by any member. When this happens, each member can find his own personal route. In the families where this is not possible, because their functioning is based on control, and the ego of each member is fragile, a family myth becomes the only safety net. Acting in the unconscious dimension, rather than in one known to all, it ends up becoming a tyrannical law that prevents any trespassing. In this sense it plays an important function in the most difficult moments and becomes a defensive tool with which the group can face catastrophic change anxieties.

We should then distinguish the situations where myths have a pathological meaning and those where a myth can be mitigated or disproved or trespassed upon by each member.

In the families where the ego of each member is fragile, a family myth plays the function of a substitute ego and cannot be easily changed. In fact it counters fragmentation and the loss of continuity, by maintaining the traditions of a social group and providing a model where the present can only be a repetition of the past.

I do not think it is useful to distinguish between various types of family myths (heroism, seduction, filiation, etc.) as many authors do (Nagy, Stierlin, Byng Hall, Eiguer). It is more useful to understand the features of dysfunctional myths. A first criterion could be rigidity and timelessness or, at the opposite, a flexibility that allows for regression and reintegration. Another criterion is how much a myth is secret and sequestered from family life. In some situations I think that the myth's defensive organisation corresponds to that defensive construction that Steiner (2004) calls "retreat". Seriously ill adolescents use these fantastic retreats, which can be masturbatory or delusional. In adolescence this fantastic production, when it is not excessive and does not sequester the mind, can be useful for growth or as a defence from imbalances.

I will close this brief discussion of myths by mentioning the relation between myth and identification.

From the clinical example above it appears clear enough that a myth is a source of identification both for the individual member and for the family and also provides group identity.

But we should also look at another aspect, that is, myths as a source of alienating and abusing identifications, situations where the subject builds part of his identity on a mythical character that cannot be easily changed because it does not belong to the present and has lost its real features, having been transfigured by the projections of all family members.

These identifications become alienating because they alienate the subject from himself, aggressively enslave him to an alien identity, and more and more invade his true and spontaneous personality. As Badaracco (2000) noticed, they are pathological and pathogenetic, in that they exert a constant action. But they are very dangerous and not easy to address because they do not concern only one member but all the other members tied to the one we are working with. If we use the example of the heroic grandfather, a son will identify with such an ancestor in order to try to replicate his deeds or, on the contrary will feel overwhelmed and unable to stand up to him. But a parent can also be enmeshed, possibly hoping that his son can replicate the deeds of a grandiose ancestor, thus adding the burden of his own expectations on the son.

Relieving oneself from these identifications and/or transforming them can then become a goal not only for the son, but also for his parent(s) and all the other family members.

But, as Freud taught us, one cannot defeat an enemy in effigy and myths are the transformation of a system of values and—I would add—of rules and relationships into a system of facts, in an articulated form. So in the analytic scenario we need to change this emotional form of the myth (as Pulino Fiderio, 2001 says), turning it into a meaning that can be elaborated, represented, and then forgotten.

To enact a myth can be the best way to give back time to an atemporal element in the here and now in order to deconstruct it, starting from its unreal dimensions, rebuild it with its historical dimensions, and extract it from the family's unconscious to make each member aware of it. In the sessions the therapist must play the function of reconstruction-construction of the myth through the narrative of all family members present. Most of all he will have to highlight how the myth acts in the here and now and determines identity, challenging what each member knows and reconstructs, putting them in touch and in opposition with the aspect of our personality that wants to escape it and decode it.

In this sense Angela's story is very interesting because it ends with a ritual—a burial—and shows that a family does not only need myths but also rites, but this aspect we can leave for a later discussion.

Notes

1. It works in a prescriptive way because it organises knowledge and attributes to it an order that is symbolic and therefore transcends individuals. It conveys the sense, the meaning of relations in organised, historicised, and narrative form and therefore passes on how reality is coded and conceptualised.

2. A family plays this elaboration function in various ways and Meltzer provides us with quite a few examples in his *Child, Family and Community: A Psychoanalytical Model of the Learning Process* (Meltzer & Harris, 1983).

3. In this paper Evelyn Granjon argues that the functions of family myths correspond to the functions of the same fantasy group that she calls "family psychic apparatus" as suggested by Anzieu and Ruffiot. According to Granjon, these main functions are: 1) close-knitting the group, because the myth shapes family ties contributing to defining expectations and prohibitions, and I would add also roles and attributions of the various family members; 2) signifying-interpreting, a source of identifications; 3) conveying the group's unconscious as it enrols the family in a filiation and a history; and 4) adjustment and transformation.

4. Separation had never really taken place and the father kept his furniture and clothes at his former home and periodically went to retrieve them. Between the parents there still was a confused and warm relationship and conflicts on money issues. Angela too had a relationship with another man. The eldest daughter, Ginevra had left very early. At eighteen she had married an older man, a romantic wanderer always searching for something extraordinary to do. Riccardo made large use of light drugs, had quit school, and was supported by his mother.

   The myth of the heroic grandfather, dead at a young age, had influenced not only Angela (Riccardo's mother) but the whole family, including the children. For the mother this myth was not only an unfinished mourning that influenced her choice of a partner, but was also an ever-present male role model, to whom all referred, mostly unconsciously. It maintained a grandiose male ideal that death prevented from being downsized. Faced with this myth, any real life figure was blotted out.

References

Bion, W. R. (1961). *Experiences in Groups and Other Papers*. London: Tavistock.

Bion, W. R. (1965). *Transformations*. London: Heinemann.

Ferreira, A. J. (1963). Family Myth and Homeostasis. *Archives of General Psychiatry, 9*(5): 457–463.

Garcia Badaracco, J. (2000). *Psicoanálisis Familiar: los Otros en Nosotros y el Descubrimiento del sí Mismo.* Buenos Aires: Paidos.

Granjon, E. (2000). Mythopoïése et souffrance familiale. *Le divan familial,* 4: 13–23.

Lévi-Strauss, C. (1962). *La Pensée Sauvage.* Paris: Plon.

Malinowski, B. (1926). *Myth in Primitive Psychology.* New York: W. W. Norton.

Meltzer, D., & Harris, M. (1983). *Child, Family and Community: A Psychoanalytical Model of the Learning Process.* Paris: Organisation for Economic Co-operation and Development.

Nicolò, A. M. (1987). La relation thérapeutique en thérapie familiale. In: A. Ackermans & M. Andolfi (Eds.), *La création du système thérapeutique.* Paris: ESF.

Nicolò, A. M. (1988). La famiglia come matrice del pensiero. *Terapia Familiare,* 28: 5–16.

Nicolò, A. M. (1997). L'importanza diagnostica delle interazioni nella valutazione della famiglia e delle sue difese trans personali. *Interazioni,* 10(2): 53–66.

Nicolò, A. M. (1999). La dimension transgénérationnelle entre le mythe et le secret. In: B. Prieur (Ed.), *Les héritages familiaux.* Paris: ESF.

Pulino Fiderio, E. (2001). Risposta all'Intervista/Dibattito: C'era una volta … la Famiglia. *Interazioni, 15*(1): 82–87.

Steiner, J. (2004). *Psychic Retreats: Pathological Organizations in Psychotic, Neurotic and Borderline Patients.* London: Routledge.

INDEX

Abdel
  doudou 45–46, 52
  maternal grandfather of 50
  relationship with mother 44–45
  separation from mother 49
  spaciogram 45–48
Abend, S. M. 139
Abraham, A. 57, 205
Abraham, N. 253
adjourned mourning 243
adoptive families 97–107
  clinical experience 97–98
  clinical vignettes 101–105
  destabilising and distressing
    experiences 100
  function of "psychic incubator"
    101
  fusion relationship in 101
  intersubjectivisation 100
  parents experience difficulty 98
  parental function 98

puberty challenges 101
sense of foreignness 99
therapy to adopted child 98–99
threat to identity 101
traumatic experiences 99–100
affiliation 238
AFT (analytic familial therapy)
  135
aggression 159
Alexander, F. 129
Allen, E. S. 220
alliances
  defensive 13
  offensive 14
  slide of 13
  structuring 14
Amato, R. 219
anaclitic couple 258, 264, 266,
  268–269, 272, 277
anamorphosis, genealogical
  psychical 200–203, 206, 214, 216

antilibidinal secrets 255–259,
    268–269, 272–273, 275
anti-spanking law 133
anxiety
    death 78–79
    primitive 88
Anzieu, D. 43–44, 76, 146, 202
applied psychoanalysis 4
A Project for a Scientific Psychology
    (Freud) 235
Aral Sea 196
Aramburu, I. 220
Armant, C. 222
Artoni Schlesinger, C. 98–100
A Secret (Grimbert) 250
Atkins, D. C. 220
Aulagnier, P. 239, 246
Avron, O. 178

Badaracco, G. 69–70
Baldassarre, L. 110
Balint, E. 109
Balint, M. 173
Balsamo, M. 234
Baltrusaïtis, J. 202
Baranès, J. J. 70
Baucom, D. H. 220
Beebe, B. 71
"behavioural howl" 175
Benghozi, P. 41–43, 45–46, 48–50,
    52, 54–56, 58–61, 202–206, 209,
    213–225, 228
benign infidelity 223, 229
bereavement
    as hidden secret 251, 258,
        260
    expelled 261
    primary 260–261
    working through 262, 268–269,
        272–273, 275–276
Berenstein, I. 69, 76, 192
Bergeret, J. 254–255

big history 41
    collective 49–50
biological rock 178
Bion, W. R. 43, 58, 75, 94, 100, 201,
    214, 284
Bleger, J. 43, 74, 200
Blow, A. J. 220
Bocquet, F. 144
Bonaparte, M. 245
Bollas, C. 124
Boubli, M. 44, 202
boxing, fraternal 140, 146
Bria, P. 240
Britton, R. 70
Bydlowski, M. 214

Cabré, V. 220
Caillot, J. -P. 148, 262–263
Camilla
    developments in case history of
        68–69
    dreams 67–68
    once-a-week treatment of 66–67
    opinion of family therapist 69–70
    spontaneous interpretation 66
Carau, Bachisio 162
Carel, A. 100
Carratelli, T. J. 122
Caspian Sea 196
Castoriadis-Aulagnier, P. 250
Catania, J. A. 220
catastrophe 204–206
catastrophic birth 242, 282
Catholic family 211
chain (einer Kette) 12
changes/invariables 130–131
Chatav, Y. 220
cheat the void 206–210
child-king 132
child's first secret 252
Choi, K. 220
choice-non-choice 142, 146

chrysalis families 203
Cigoli, V. 262
Civilization and Its Discontents
    (Freud) 13, 187
Coles, P. 140
community identity, kaleidoscopic
    support for 59–60
community of rights 13
Conrath, Y. 139–140, 144, 146,
    148–149
container
    boundaries and interfaces
        between territories of 49
    of intimate 55–56
    transference onto setting as 42–44
couch-oriented psychoanalysis 4
countertransference 58, 267–268
couple secret 263
    defined 249
    functions 249
couple's new secrets 264, 276
couple's paradoxical oscillation 161
Cournut, J. 135
Crise, Rupture et Dépassement
    (Anzieu) 43
crisis 204–206
cupola of the link 28, 31, 33, 37
cure-type supporters 172
cure-type treatment 174
custom-made treatment 264

David, C. 146
Davins, M. 220
daydream(s) 54, 210, 214–215
    Abdel 46–47
    group 48
de Brusset, B. 182
de Butler, A. 139–140, 144, 146,
    148–149
Decherf, G. 148
deconstruction 42
    dream 52–53

narrative 53–54
    therapeutic 60
defence mechanisms 73–75
Defontaine, J. 260
De Micco, V. 240
De Mijolla, A. 245
Derrida, J. 42
developmental psychology
    parents relationship in 70–72
    pre-reflexive unconscious 71–72
    relational patterns 71
Devereux, G. 242, 247
Díaz, R. 219
Dicks, H. V. 168, 220–224, 229
Dicks's theories on dyad 220
Diego, psychotherapy of 102–104
Dolcini, M. M. 220
Dolto, F. 203
Dolto-Tolitch, C. 203
double existence 179
Drass, E. 220
dream deconstruction 52–53
Drigo, M. L. 257

Ehrenberg, A. 129
Eiguer, A. 69, 124, 140, 145, 189, 255,
    258
emotional infidelity 220
Enriquez, M. 70
erotic desire 159
Es 175

Faimberg, H. 70
false secrets 255
family identity
    kaleidoscopic support for 59–60
    wounded 50–52
"family-making" 200
family myths
    comment 282
    function of myths 283–284
    mythopoietic activity 284

pathological myths and
  alienating identifications
  287–288
family's capacity, for psychical
  representation 42
family secrets
  functions of 251
family spaciogram 45–46
Feldman, M. 94
Ferenczi, S. 103, 194, 196
Ferreira, A. J. 279, 283
Ferro, A. 81
fiddler on the roof 211
Fidelio, Enza Pulino 285
figural representation, new capacity
  for 60
filial link 49
  harki community 55
Fiorini, G. 123
Fisher, J. V. 79
flea market home 210
Fonagy, P. 93
Font, J. 222
forgetfulness 42–43
Forste, R. 220
founding myths 55
fraternal link
  configurations of fraternal incest
    191–192
  eroticism and sexuality 192–196
  functions of group 188–191
  necessarily incestuous 188
  presentation 187–188
fraternisation 139
Freud, A. 69, 73–74, 81, 234–235,
  245–246
Freud, S. 132, 157, 160, 166, 172,
  174, 178–179, 187, 190 193, 216,
  233–234, 244–245
Freymann, J. -R. 148
frightened couple 85–94
  aggression and violence 86, 91

agoraphobic–claustrophobic
  dilemma 90, 92
capacity for mentalisation 93–94
core complex 90, 92
difficulties of working with 90–91
emotional reaction 88
fear and anxiety 87–88, 92–93
object relationship 90–92
passivity and 89
psychological self and 93
sadomasochistic atmosphere and
  89
sex and 87
unconscious marital fit, structure
  of 90
unstable relationship 87
Fromm, E. 129
Furtos, J. 216

Gabriela-style reactions 225
Gaddini, E. 112, 152
Garcia Badaracco, J. 69–70
Gear, M. C. 69
genealogical family fresco 53–54
genogram 47–48, 52–53, 213, 215
geno-spaciogram 47–48, 53
Giannakoulas, A. 168
Giovanni's depressive symptoms 281
Girard, R. 178
Glass, S. P. 220
Glasser, M. 86, 90–92, 158
Glocer Fiorini, L. 123
Gomel, S. 151
Gordon, K. 220
Gordon, K. C. 220
Granjon, E. 285, 290
Green, A. 111, 122, 137, 147, 151, 195
Greenacre, P. 166
Grimbert, P. 250
Grinberg, L. 241–243
Grinberg, R. 241
Grossman, D. 233, 239

group dreaming 48–49
group emotionality 178
group imaginings 45–46
group-objects 184
group psyche 5
group psychic object 183
Group Psychology and the Analysis of the Ego (Freud) 4, 187, 235
Guillaumin, J. 43, 152
guzzling down 22

Haag, G. 44, 202
harki community 49–52, 55, 61
    being a child of 49–50
    filial link 55
    transmission of murmurs 56
Harris, H. 73
Harris, M. 290
Hartmann, H. 129
Hartnett, K. 220
Héritier, F. 188
horizontal axis 149, 151
Horney, K. 129
hypothesis
    bereavement and dealing with secrets 260
    observing and disclosing secret 258
    typology of couple and family secrets 254, 257–258

identification 73
    alliances 18
    child's 99
    complexity of 101
    introjective 22, 29, 147
    masochistic 80
    mutual projective 76, 106
    primary 30
    projective 73
identity 182
    chrysalis 203

wounded family 50–52
Imparato, G. 139
incest 13, 18, 25, 44, 52, 56, 61, 129, 135, 150, 180, 199, 208, 250, 252, 267
    fraternal 187–188, 191–192, 195–198
    secrets of 255–265, 268–269, 276
incestuous society 215
incorporation 22, 36
in crisis 204–206
individual identity, kaleidoscopic support for 59–60
individual unconscious 72
infidelity 219–220, 222, 229–230
    benign 223–224
    case study 225–229
    combined 220
    emotional 220
    incitement to 224
    malignant 223–225
    marital 222
    psychoanalytic perspective 220–225
    sexual 220, 222
ingrainment 76
Instincts and Their Vicissitudes (Freud) 28
interactive folly 81
interpersonal defence 74, 75
interpretative hypothesis 149–152
intersubjectivity 6, 16, 21
intersubjectivisation 100
intimate
    territories of containers for 79
    topical collapse of 54–56
intrafamilial transmission 56
intragenerational couple secret 272, 275
intrapsychic and relational meeting 242
intrusive projections 79

Jacobson, E. 76
Jacques, E. 43
Jaffe, J. 71
Jaitin, R. 139, 142, 149, 190–193, 197
Jones, E. 241, 247

Kaës, R. 42, 57, 70–71, 74, 77, 101,
    139–140, 145–147, 149, 150–152,
    189, 194, 201, 239
kaleidoscope metaphor 60
Kancyper, L. 139–140, 143–144
Kaspi, R. 43
Kernberg, O. F. 109, 158–159,
    221–222, 254–255
Khan, M. M. R. 157, 160–161, 166,
    245–246
Klein, M. 110, 187
Kris, E. 245

Lacan, J. 143, 150, 187, 193
Lachman, F. M. 71
Lacôte, C. 234, 236, 245
Laplanche, J. 150
Lassegue, J. 44, 202
Lavalle, G. 44, 202
Lawrence, J. 221
Leblanc, G. J. 220
Legrand, B. 139–140, 144, 146,
    148–149
Lemaire, J. 97, 139–140, 144, 146,
    148–149, 171
Lévi-Strauss, C. 283
Lévy-Soussan, P. 250–252
libidinal secrets 255
Liendo, E. C. 69
link (ein Glied) 12
linking 8
    Alliances and Shared Spaces 16
    logical dimension 9
    psychical space of linking 8
    psychical work 9–11
    unconscious alliances 11

links 75–80, 183
    case history 77–78
    cluster of 77
    comment 78–80
    filial 49, 55
    horizontalisation of 152
    pathology 82
    primitive 82
    psychoanalytical family therapy
        and 44–45
    specificity of 81
Litovsky de Eiguer, D. 69
little histories 41
    singular 49–50
Lombardi, R. 240
Losso, R. 69
Luzzatto, L. 100

maddening object 70
malignant infidelity 224
Malinowski, B. 279, 283
Matte Blanco, I. 239
Matus, S. 152
Melissa, psychotherapy of
    104–105
Meltzer, D. 73, 79, 158, 290
mental functioning 102
mesh-palimpsest 53–54
metasocial warrantors 246–247
migratory experiences 238
mirages 35
Missenard, A. 43
Mitchell, J. 140, 147
modern couples, model for
    the ancestor as model 142
    the B couple 140–145
    Morley's hypothesis 147
Monari, C. 257
Morel, B. A. 69
Morin, E. 202
Morley, E. 139, 147, 150
Moro, M. R. 237–238, 242, 246–247

mother's greed 151
multi-ethnic therapeutic setting
    236–238
mutual exploitation 159
myths, founding 55

narcissism 12, 17, 25, 43, 59, 69, 99,
    149, 178–179, 183, 235, 251
narcissistic contracts, secondary 12
narrative figurability 214
neo-container
    in psychoanalytical family
        therapy 41–61
    mesh-palimpsest 53–54
    mythical narrative 53–54
neo-imaginings 48–49
    interpretations break into 57–58
Neri, C. 101
New Introductory Lectures on Psycho-
    Analysis (Freud) 246
Nicolò, A. M. 71, 75, 98, 122, 139, 158,
    221, 283–284
No Exit (Sartre) 79
non-conscious space 175
Non-Self-envelope of Self 183
Norsa, D. 110, 122, 158

obsessive ideations 67–68
Oedipus complex 130
    and, transformation 132–134
    from group to family 134
one body psychology 173
open secrets 250, 253, 255, 257–258
operating internal models (OIM) 27
organising secret 251
Ortman, D. 219
Othello-style reactions 225
oud 211

Pallier, L. 101
parental couple, of origin 111–112
parent–child relations 50

parent–child transmission 56
Pasche, F. 137
Pérez-Testor, C. 220–222
Perrot, J. 69
persecutory 67–68
perverse 158
    comments 168
    crisis 163–166
    defined 158
    functioning of couples 158
    link in the couple 160
    main issues 166–168
    Meltzer comments 158
    peculiar quality of relationship
        161–162
    rituals 162
    use 161–162
Petacchi, G. 101
Pichon-Rivière, E. 75
Pontalis, J. -B. 148
pre-reflexive unconscious
    71–72
Previti, D. 219
private history 54–56
processes of subjectivisation and
    mastery 173
processes of transformation and
    mediation 18
process of foreclosure 37
projective identification 73
psyche, the three pillars 7
psychic phenomena 176
psychical anamorphosis 201
psychical reality
    concept and applications 4–5
    spaces of 7
    transversal dimension of 5
psychical representation, family's
    capacity for 42
psychoanalysis 5, 179, 234
psychoanalytical family therapy
    asking for therapy 44–45

family's capacity for psychical
    representation 42
family spaciogram 45–46
group imaginings 45–46
illustration of 42
indication of 42
meta-setting for elaboration
    60–61
neo-container in 41–61
new capacity for figural
    representation 60
problem of links during 44–45
transference in 58–59
psychoanalytical theory of linking,
    proposition for 6
psychodramatist 172
psychotherapy's contribution
    conceptual aspect, first 174–175
    conceptual aspect, second
        175–182
    conceptual aspect, third 182–184
public history 54–56
Puget, J. 57, 69, 76
Pulino Fiderio 285, 289

Racamier, P. -C. 76, 81, 249–251,
    255–258, 260–263, 272–273
reconstructed families,
    transformations in 109–124
    couple relationship 110
    first clinical case 112–117
    overview 109–111
    parental couple of origin
        111–112
    second clinical case 117–122
    sexuality in psychoanalysis 111
    use of analyst in transference
        115–117
reflexive identification
    29–30
relative immunity 261
Rey, H. 90, 92

Richard, F. 100, 103, 106
Rivera, S. 219
Robert, P. 42
Romero, A. 219
Rosenfeld, H. 86
Rosolato, G. 143
Roussillon, R. 151
Rufflot, A. 69, 71
Ruszczynski, S. 86

sadism 91
sadistic violence 91
Salamero, M. 220
Sami-Ali, M. 220
Schelling, F. W. J. 235
Schlesinger, A. 98–101
seduction 31
self-consciousness 181
self-image 181
self-preservative violence 91
self-world 182
sexuality 111
Shackelford, T. K. 220
shared unconscious 69–70
sloughing of containers 200
small death 180
Snyder, D. K. 220
Soavi, G. C. 101
Sommantico, M. 139–140, 146, 149,
    152
spaciogram 209
    Abdel's 46–48
    confusion 211–212
    differentiation of spaces 212
    family 45–46
speechless voice 176
Steiner, J. 288
Stern, D. 71
Stoller, R. 85
strange signifiers 177
subjectivity 27
symbolic parenting 98

syntactic forms
    attributive 23
    passive 23
    reflexive 23

Taccani, S. 249, 257, 259, 264
Tagliacozzo, R. 101
Tamanza, G. 262
Tanfer, K. 220
Target, M. 93
Teruel, G. 221
The Dissolution of the Oedipus Complex
    (Freud) 132
The Ego's Visitors (De Mijolla) 246
theory of collusion 221
The Psychoanalysis of the
    Psychoanalytic Setting (Bleger) 200
The Uncanny (Freud) 235
The Skin Ego (Anzieu) 203
Tisseron, S. 44, 202, 257, 259, 264
toilet-ego 183
topical collapse, of intimate 54–56
Torok, M. 57, 205, 253
Totem and Taboo (Freud) 4, 187
To the End of the Land (Grossman) 233
toxic secrets 257
trans-containing, topical approach
    to 59–60
transference 58–59, 267–268
    onto setting as container 42–44
transference–countertransference
    dynamics 148
transgenerational links 32–35
transitional object 46, 157, 223–224,
    229
transitional space 157, 173, 183–184,
    242
transitional time 242
transmission of murmurs 56
transpersonal defence 73, 75

Trapanese, G. 140, 148–149
traumatic organisation of links 81
treason 44
    and identity hatred 50–52
typology of secrets 254–255, 257–258,
    263, 268
    of the couple and 268, 272, 275

un–avowable 205
unconscious 234
    denial 205
    individual 72
    intergenerational transmission
        of 70
    peculiar relationship and 79
    pre-reflexive 71–72
    primary 178
    shared 69–70
unconscious alliance 77
    clinical issue 16–18
    epistemological issue 15–16
    functions 14–15
    metapsychical guarantor 14–15
    types of 12
Unheimlich 235

Vallino, D. 107
vínculo 75

Wainrib, S. 100, 103, 106
Whisman, M. 220
Willi, J. 168, 222
Winnicott, D. W. 46, 55, 59, 97, 100,
    106, 110, 112, 117, 123, 151, 173,
    179, 215, 239
wounded family identities 50–52
Wright, T. L. 220

zapping 131
Zavattini, G. C. 122, 168